Autodesk CFD 2018
Black Book

By
Gaurav Verma
Samar
(CADCAMCAE Works)

ISBN # 978-1-988722-32-0

NOTICE TO THE READER

DEDICATION

To teachers, who make it possible to disseminate knowledge
to enlighten the young and curious minds
of our future generations

To students, who are the future of the world

THANKS

To my friends and colleagues

To my family for their love and support

Training and Consultant Services

At CADCAMCAE WORKS, we provide effective and affordable one to one online training on various software packages in Computer Aided Design(CAD), Computer Aided Manufacturing(CAM), Computer Aided Engineering (CAE), and Computer programming languages(C/C++, Java, .NET, Android, Javascript, HTML and so on). The training is delivered through remote access to your system and voice chat via Internet at any time, any place, and at required pace to individuals, groups, students of colleges/universities, and CAD/CAM/CAE training centers. The main features of this program are:

Training as per your need

Highly experienced Engineers and Technician conduct the classes on the software applications used in the industries. The methodology adopted to teach the software is totally practical based, so that the learner can adapt to the design and development industries in almost no time. The efforts are to make the training process cost effective and time saving while you have the comfort of your time and place, thereby relieving you from the hassles of traveling to training centers or rearranging your time table.

Software Packages on which we provide basic and advanced training are:

CAD/CAM/CAE: CATIA, Creo Parametric, Creo Direct, SolidWorks, Autodesk Inventor, Solid Edge, UG NX, AutoCAD, AutoCAD LT, EdgeCAM, MasterCAM, SolidCAM, DelCAM, BOBCAM, UG NX Manufacturing, UG Mold Wizard, UG Progressive Die, UG Die Design, SolidWorks Mold, Creo Manufacturing, Creo Expert Machinist, NX Nastran, Hypermesh, `SolidWorks Simulation`, Autodesk Simulation Mechanical, Creo Simulate, Gambit, ANSYS and many others.

Computer Programming Languages: C++, VB.NET, HTML, Android, Javascript and so on.

Game Designing: Unity.

Civil Engineering: AutoCAD MEP, Revit Structure, Revit Architecture, AutoCAD Map 3D and so on.

We also provide consultant services for design and development on the above mentioned software packages

For more information you can mail us at:
cadcamcaeworks@gmail.com or info@cadcamcaeworks.com

Table of Contents

Chapter 4 : Solving Analysis

Chapter 5 : Analyzing Results

Chapter 6 : Comparing and Visualization

Chapter 7 : Practical

Chapter 8 : Practical and Practice

Preface

Autodesk® CFD is a software developed by Autodesk Inc. to perform computational dynamic study and thermal simulation on the model. There are various areas where CFD is implemented in Design industry. Some examples of CFD applications are finding: Wind resistance of a car or motorcycle, Pressure drop through a valve, Component temperatures in an electronics enclosure, Comfort of people in a crowded meeting hall, and so on.

The `Autodesk CFD 2018 Black Book`, is the 1st edition of our series on Autodesk CFD. The book is targeted for beginners of Autodesk CFD. This book covers the basic equations and terms of Fluid Dynamics theory. The book covers all the major tools of Flow Simulation modules like Fluid Flow, Thermal Fluid Flow, and Electronic Cooling modules. This book can be used as supplement to Fluid Dynamics course if your subject requires the application of Software for solving CFD problems. Some of the salient features of this book are:

In-Depth explanation of concepts

Every new topic of this book starts with the explanation of the basic concepts. In this way, the user becomes capable of relating the things with real world.

Topics Covered

Every chapter starts with a list of topics being covered in that chapter. In this way, the user can easy find the topic of his/her interest easily.

Instruction through illustration

The instructions to perform any action are provided by maximum number of illustrations so that the user can perform the actions discussed in the book easily and effectively. There are about 300 illustrations that make the learning process effective.

Tutorial point of view

The book explains the concepts through the tutorial to make the understanding of users firm and long lasting. Each chapter of the book has tutorials that are real world projects.

Project

Free projects and exercises are provided to students for practicing.

For Faculty

If you are a faculty member, then you can ask for video tutorials on any of the topic, exercise, tutorial, or concept.

Formatting Conventions Used in the Text

All the key terms like name of button, tool, drop-down etc. are kept bold.

Free Resources

Link to the resources used in this book are provided to the users via email. To get the resources, mail us at ***cadcamcaeworks@gmail.com*** or ***info@cadcamcaeworks.com*** with your contact information. With your contact record with us, you will be provided latest updates and informations regarding various technologies. The format to write us e-mail for resources is as follows:

Subject of E-mail as ***Application for resources of ....Book***.
You can give your information below to get updates on the book.
Name:
Course pursuing/Profession:
Contact Address:
E-mail ID:

For Any query or suggestion

If you have any query or suggestion please let us know by mailing us on ***cadcamcaeworks@gmail.com*** or ***info@cadcamcaeworks.com***. Your valuable constructive suggestions will be incorporated in our books and your name will be addressed in special thanks area of our books.

About Author

Gaurav Verma is a Mechanical Design Engineer with deep knowledge of CAD, CAM and CAE field. He has an experience of more than 10 years on CAD/CAM/CAE packages. He has delivered presentations in Autodesk University Events on AutoCAD Electrical and Autodesk Inventor. He is an active member of Autodesk Knowledge Share Network. He has provided content for Autodesk Design Academy. He is also working as technical consultant for many Indian Government organizations for Skill Development sector. He has authored books on SolidWorks, Mastercam, Creo Parametric, Autodesk Inventor, Autodesk Fusion 360, and many other CAD-CAM-CAE packages. He has developed content for many modular skill courses like Automotive Service Technician, Welding Technician, Lathe Operator, CNC Operator, Telecom Tower Technician, TV Repair Technician, Casting Operator, Maintenance Technician and about 50 more courses. He has his books published in English, Russian and Hindi worldwide.

He has trained many students on mechanical, electrical and civil areas of CAD-CAM-CAE. He has trained students online as well as offline. He has a small workshop of 20 CNC and VMC machines where he tests his CAM skills on different Automotive components. He is providing consultant services to more than 15 companies worldwide. You can contact the author directly at cadcamcaeworks@gmail.com

Introduction to Autodesk CFD 2018

Chapter 1

Topics Covered

The major topics covered in this chapter are:

- *Introduction to Fluid Mechanics*
- *Introduction to CFD*
- *Introduction to Autodesk CFD 2018*
- *Downloading Autodesk CFD 2018*

INTRODUCTION OF FLUID MECHANICS

During the course, you will know various aspects of Autodesk CFD for various practical problems. But, keep in mind that all computer software work on same concept of GIGO which means Garbage In - Garbage Out. So, if you have specified any wrong parameter while defining properties of analysis then you will not get the correct results. This problem demands a good knowledge of Fluid Mechanics so that you are well conversant with the terms of classical fluid mechanics and can relate the results to the theoretical concepts. In this chapter, we will discuss the basics of Fluid Mechanics and we will try to relate them with analysis wherever possible.

BASIC PROPERTIES OF FLUIDS

There are various basic properties required while performing analysis on fluid. These properties are collected by performing experiments in labs. Most of these properties are available in the form of tables in Steam Tables or Design Data books. These properties are explained next.

Mass Density, Weight Density, and Specific Gravity

- Density or Mass Density if the mass of fluid per unit volume. In SI units, mass is given by kg and volume is given by m³. So, mathematically we can say,

$$\text{Density (or Mass Density) } \rho = \frac{Mass\ of\ Fluid}{Volume\ Occupied\ by\ Fluid}\ \text{kg/m}^3$$

- If you are asked for weight density then multiply mass by gravity coefficient. Mathematically it can be expressed as:

$$\text{Weight Density w} = \frac{Mass\ of\ Fluid \times Gravity\ Coefficient}{Volume\ Occupied\ by\ Fluid}\ \text{N/m}^3$$

- Most of the time, fluid density is available as **Specific Gravity**. Specific gravity is the ratio of weight density of fluid to weight density of water in case of liquid. In case of gases, it is the ratio of weight density of fluid to weight density of air. Note that weight density of water is 1000 kg/m³ at 4 °C and weight density of air is 1.225 kg/m³ at 15 °C.

Note that as the temperature of liquid rises, its density is reduced and vice-versa. But as the temperature of gas rises, its density is increased and vice-versa.

Viscosity

Viscosity is the coefficient of friction between different layers of fluid. In other terms, it is the shear stress required to produce unit rate of shear strain in one layer of fluid. Mathematically it can be expressed as:

$$\mu = \frac{\tau}{(\frac{dx}{dy})}\ \text{N.s/m}^2\ \text{or Pa.s}$$

where μ is viscosity, τ is shear stress (or force applied tangentially to the layer of fluid) and (dx/dy) is the shear strain.

As the density of fluid changes with temperature so does the viscosity changes with temperature. the formula for viscosity of fluid at different temperature is given next.

For Liquids, $\mu = \mu_0 \dfrac{1}{1 + \alpha t + \beta t^2}$

For Gases, $\mu = \mu_0 + \alpha t - \beta t^2$

here, μ_0 is viscosity at 0 °C

　　　　α and β are constants for fluid (for water α is 0.03368 and β is 0.000221)
　　　　　　　　(for air α is 5.6×10^{-8} and β is 1.189×10^{-10})

　　　　t is the temperature

PROBLEM ON VISCOSITY

Dynamic viscosity of lubricant oil used between shaft and sleeve is 8 poise. The shaft has a diameter of 0.4 m and rotates at 250 r.p.m. Find out the power lost due to viscosity of fluid if length of sleeve is 100 mm and thickness of oil film is 1.5 mm; refer to below figure.

Oil film 1.5mm
Shaft Dia 0.4 m
Sleeve length 100mm

Solution:

Viscosity μ = 8 poise = 8/10 N.s/m² =0.8 N.s/m²

Tangential velocity of shaft $u = \dfrac{\pi \times D \times N}{60} = \dfrac{\pi \times 0.4 \times 250}{60} = 5.236$ m/s

Using the relation, $\tau = \mu \dfrac{dx}{dy}$

where dx is 5.236
and   dy is 1.5×10^{-3}

$$\tau = 0.8 \times \dfrac{5.236}{1.5 \times 10^{-3}} = 2792.53 \text{ N/m}^2$$

Shear force F = τ x Area

$$F = \tau \times \pi D \times L = 2792.53 \times \pi \times 0.4 \times 100 \times 10^{-3} = 350.92 \text{ N}$$

Torque (T) = Force x Radius = 350.92 x 0.2 = 70.184 N.m

Power = 2 π.N.T/60 = (2 π x 250 x 70.184)/60=1837.41 W Ans.

Now, you may ask how this problem relates with CFD. As discussed earlier, the viscosity changes with temperature and as fluid flows through pipe or comes in contact with rolling shaft, its temperature rises. In such cases, CFD gives the approximate viscosity and temperature of fluids in the system at different locations. This data later can be used to find solution for other engineering problems.

TYPES OF FLUIDS

There are mainly 5 types of fluids:

Ideal Fluids: These fluids are incompressible and have no viscosity which means they flow freely without any resistance. This category of fluid is imaginary and used in some cases of calculations.

Real Fluids: These are the fluids found in real world. These fluids have viscosity values as per their nature and can be compressible in some cases.

Newtonian Fluids: Newtonian fluids are those in which shear stress is directly proportional to shear strain. In a specific temperature range, water, gasoline, alcohol etc. can be Newtonian fluids.

Non-Newtonian Fluids: Those fluids in which shear stress is not directly proportional to shear strain. Most of the time Real Fluids fall in this category.

Ideal Plastic Fluids: Those fluids in which shear stress is more than yield value so say fluid deforms plastically. The shear stress in these fluids is directly proportional to shear strain.

THERMODYNAMIC PROPERTIES OF FLUID

Most of the liquids are not considered as compressible in general applications as their molecules are already bound closely to each other. But, Gas have large gap between their molecules and can be compressed easily relative to liquids. As we pick pressure to compress the gas, other thermodynamic properties also come into play. The relationship between Pressure, Temperature, and specific Volume is given by;

$$P.\forall = RT$$

P = Absolute pressure of a gas in N/m^2
$\forall$ = Specific Volume = $1/\rho$
R = Gas Constant (for Air is 287 J/Kg-K
T = Absolute Temperature
ρ = Density of gas

If the density of gas changes with constant temperature then the process is called Isothermal process and if density changes with no heat transfer then the process is called Adiabatic process.

For Isothermal process, p/ρ = Constant
For Adiabatic process, p/ρ^k = Constant
Here, k is Ratio of specific heat of a gas at constant pressure and constant volume (1.4 for air).

Universal Gas Constant

By Pressure, Temperature, volume equation,

$$p.\forall = nMRT$$

Here,

p = Absolute pressure of a gas in N/m^2
$\forall$ = Specific Volume = $1/\rho$
n = Number of moles in a Volume of gas
M = Mass of gas molecules/ Mass of Hydrogen atom = n x m (m is mass gas in kg)
R = Gas Constant (for Air is 287 J/Kg-K
T = Absolute Temperature

MxR is called Universal Gas constant and is equal to 8314 J/kg-mole K for water.

Compressibility of Gases

Compressibility is reciprocal of bulk modulus of elasticity K, which is defined as ratio of Compressive stress to volumetric strain.

Bulk Modulus = Increase in pressure/ Volumetric strain

K = -(dp/d$\forall$)x$\forall$

Vapour Pressure and Cavitation

When a liquid converts into vapour due to high temperature in a vessel then vapours exert pressure on the walls of vessel. This pressure is called **Vapour pressure**.

When a liquid flows through pipe, sometimes bubbles are formed in the flow. When these bubbles collapse at the adjoining boundaries then they erode the surface of tube due to high pressure burst of bubble. This erosion is in the form of cavities at the surface of tube and the phenomena is called **Cavitation**.

PASCAL'S LAW

Pascal's Law states that pressure at a point in static fluid is same in all directions. In mathematical form $p_x=p_y=p_z$ in case of static fluids.

FLUID DYNAMICS

Up to this point, the rules stated in this chapter were for static fluid that is fluid at rest. Now, we will discuss the rules for flowing fluid.

Bernoulli's Incompressible Fluid Equation

Bernoulli's equation states that the total energy stored in fluid is always same in a closed system. In the language of mathematics,

$$p + \frac{1}{2}\rho V^2 + \rho gh = constant$$

Here, p is pressure
ρ is density
V is velocity of fluid
h is height of fluid
g is gravitational acceleration

Eulerian and Lagrangian Method of Analysis

There are two different points of view in analyzing problems in fluid mechanics. The first view, appropriate to fluid mechanics, is concerned with the field of flow and is called the eulerian method of description. In the eulerian method, we compute the pressure field p(x, y, z, t) of the flow pattern, not the pressure changes p(t) that a particle experiences as it moves through the field.

The second method, which follows an individual particle moving through the flow, is called the lagrangian description. The lagrangian approach, which is more appropriate to solid mechanics, will not be treated in this book. However, certain numerical analyses of sharply bounded fluid flows, such as the motion of isolated fluid droplets, are very conveniently computed in lagrangian coordinates.

Fluid dynamic measurements are also suited to the eulerian system. For example, when a pressure probe is introduced into a laboratory flow, it is fixed at a specific position (x, y, z). Its output thus contributes to the description of the eulerian pressure field p(x, y, z, t). To simulate a lagrangian measurement, the probe would have to move downstream at the fluid particle speeds; this is sometimes done in oceanographic measurements, where flowmeters drift along with the prevailing currents.

Now, we know the two methods of analyzing fluid mechanics problem. But, there are further three approaches for these two methods by which problems are derived to solution. These approaches are:

1. Control Volume
2. Differential
3. Experimental

Control volume analysis, is accurate for any flow distribution but is often based on average or "one dimensional" property values at the boundaries. It always gives useful "engineering" estimates. In principle, the differential equation approach can be applied to any problem. Only a few problems, such as straight pipe flow, yield to exact analytical solutions. But the differential equations can be modeled numerically, and the flourishing field of computational fluid dynamics (CFD) can now be used to give good estimates for almost any geometry. Finally, the dimensional analysis applies to any problem, whether analytical, numerical, or experimental. It is particularly useful to reduce the cost of experimentation.

Since the Differential Equation approach is more concerned to CFD so we will discuss this approach a little deeper.

DIFFERENTIAL APPROACH OF FLUID FLOW ANALYSIS

As discussed earlier, in this approach, the fluid is divided in to very small finite number of elements via a computer process called meshing. Various equations for different properties of a fluid are given next.

Acceleration

Acceleration **a** can be given as:

$$\mathbf{a} = \frac{d\mathbf{V}}{dt} = \mathbf{i}\frac{du}{dt} + \mathbf{j}\frac{dv}{dt} + \mathbf{k}\frac{dw}{dt}$$

Various components of acceleration **a** are:

$$a_x = \frac{du}{dt} = \frac{\partial u}{\partial t} + u\frac{\partial u}{\partial x} + v\frac{\partial u}{\partial y} + w\frac{\partial u}{\partial z} = \frac{\partial u}{\partial t} + (\mathbf{V} \cdot \nabla)u$$

$$a_y = \frac{dv}{dt} = \frac{\partial v}{\partial t} + u\frac{\partial v}{\partial x} + v\frac{\partial v}{\partial y} + w\frac{\partial v}{\partial z} = \frac{\partial v}{\partial t} + (\mathbf{V} \cdot \nabla)v$$

$$a_z = \frac{dw}{dt} = \frac{\partial w}{\partial t} + u\frac{\partial w}{\partial x} + v\frac{\partial w}{\partial y} + w\frac{\partial w}{\partial z} = \frac{\partial w}{\partial t} + (\mathbf{V} \cdot \nabla)w$$

Summing these into a vector, we obtain the total acceleration as

$$a = \frac{dV}{dt} = \frac{\partial V}{\partial t} + \left(u\frac{\partial V}{\partial x} + v\frac{\partial V}{\partial y} + w\frac{\partial V}{\partial z}\right) = \frac{\partial V}{\partial t} + (V.\nabla)V$$

Similarly, you can divide other parameters as vector like Force, Pressure, Temperature, and so on.

INTRODUCTION TO CFD

The CFD stands for Computational Fluid Dynamics. The Autodesk CFD 2018 book is truly for beginners. Absolutely no prior knowledge of CFD is assumed on your part, only your desire to learn something about the subject is considered.

Computational Fluid Dynamics constitutes a new "third approach" in the philosophical study and development of the whole discipline of fluid dynamics. In the seventeenth century, the foundations for experimental fluid dynamics were laid in France and England. The eighteenth and nineteenth centuries saw the gradual development of theoretical fluid dynamics, again primarily in Europe. As a result, throughout most of the twentieth century the study and practice of fluid dynamics involved the use of theory on the one hand and pure experiment on the other hand.

However, to keep things in context, CFD provides a new third approach-but nothing more than that. It nicely and synergistically complements the other two approaches of pure theory and pure experiment, but it will never replace either of these approaches. There will always be a need for theory and experiment. The future advancement of fluid dynamics will rest upon a balance of all three approaches, with computational fluid dynamics helping to interpret and understand the results of theory, experiment and vice-versa; refer to Figure-1.

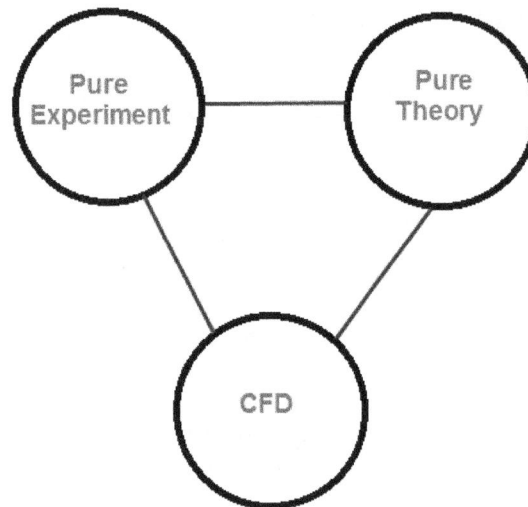

Figure-1. The three dimensions of fluid dynamics

Finally, we note that computational fluid dynamics is commonplace enough today that the composition CFD is universally accepted for the phrase "Computational Fluid Dynamics". We will use this composition throughout the book.

Computational fluid dynamics (CFD) is the use of applied math, physics, and computational software package to examine how a gas or liquid flows, also as how the gas or liquid affects objects as it flows past. Computational fluid dynamics is based on the Navier-Stokes equations. These equations describe how the velocity, pressure, temperature, and density of a moving fluid are related.

Navier-Stokes equation

The Navier-Stokes equations are the elemental partial differentials equations that describe the flow of incompressible fluids. Using the rate of stress and rate of strain, it can be shown that the parts of a viscous force F during a non rotating frame are given by-

$$
\frac{F_i}{V} = \frac{\partial}{\partial x_j}\left[\eta\left(\frac{\partial u_i}{\partial x_j} + \frac{\partial u_j}{\partial x_i}\right) + \lambda\delta_{ij}\nabla\cdot\mathbf{u}\right]
$$

$$
= \frac{\partial}{\partial x_j}\left[\eta\left(\frac{\partial u_i}{\partial x_j} + \frac{\partial u_j}{\partial x_i} - \frac{2}{3}\delta_{ij}\nabla\cdot\mathbf{u}\right) + \mu_B\delta_{ij}\nabla\cdot\mathbf{u}\right],
$$

Where η is the dynamic viscosity, λ is the second viscosity coefficient, δ_{ij} is the Kronecker delta, $\nabla\cdot\mathbf{u}$ is the divergence, μ_B is the bulk viscosity and Einstein summation has been used to sum over j=1,2,and 3.

• **Dynamic Viscosity**

Dynamic viscosity is the force required by a fluid to overcome its own internal molecular friction so the fluid can flow. In other words, dynamic viscosity is defined as the tangential force per unit area required to move the fluid in one horizontal plane with reference to other plane with a unit velocity whereas the fluid's molecules maintain a unit distance apart.

A parameter η is defined as

$$[\text{Shear Stress}] = \eta\,[\text{Strain Rate}]$$

Written explicitly.

$$\sigma = \eta\dot{e} = \eta\frac{1}{l}\frac{dl}{dt} = \eta\frac{u}{l},$$

Where l is the length scale and u is the velocity scale. In cgs η has units of $g\,cm^{-1}\,s^{-1}$. Dynamic viscocity is related to kinematic viscocity ν by

$$\eta = \rho\nu$$

Where ρ is the density.

• **Second Viscosity Coefficient**

For a compressible fluid, i.e. one for which $\nabla.u = 0$, where $\nabla.u$ is the divergence Σ of the velocity field, the stress tensor of the fluid can be written

$$S_{ij} = \eta\left(\frac{\partial u_i}{\partial x_j} + \frac{\partial u_j}{\partial x_i}\right) + \lambda\delta_{ij}\nabla\cdot\mathbf{u},$$

Where δ_{ij} is the Kronecker delta, η is the dynamic viscosity, and λ is the second coefficient of viscosity. λ is analogous to the first Lame constant. For an incompressible fluid, the term involving λ drops out from the equation, so λ can be ignored.

• **Kronecker Delta**

The simplest interpretation of the Kronecker delta is as the discrete version of the delta function defined by

$$\delta_{ij} = \begin{cases} 1 & i = j \\ 0 & i \neq j \end{cases}$$

The Kronecker delta is implemented in the Wolfram language as KroneckerDelta[i, j], as well as in a generalized form KroneckerDelta[i, j, ...] that returns 1 if all arguments are equal and 0 otherwise.
It has the contour integral representation

$$\delta_{mn} = \frac{1}{2\pi i}\oint_\gamma z^{m-n-1}\,dz,$$

Where γ is a contour corresponding to the unit circle and m and n are integers.

In three space, the Kronecker delta satisfies the identities

$$\delta_{ii} = 3$$
$$\delta_{ij}\,\epsilon_{ijk} = 0$$
$$\epsilon_{ipq}\,\epsilon_{jpq} = 2\,\delta_{ij}$$
$$\epsilon_{ijk}\,\epsilon_{pqk} = \delta_{ip}\,\delta_{jq} - \delta_{iq}\,\delta_{jp},$$

where Einstein summation is implicitly assumed. i,j=1,2,3,and ϵ_{ijk} is the permutation symbol.

Technically, the Kronecker delta is a tensor defined by the relationship

$$\delta_i^k\,\frac{\partial x_i'}{\partial x_k}\frac{\partial x_l}{\partial x_j'} = \frac{\partial x_i'}{\partial x_k}\frac{\partial x_k}{\partial x_j'} = \frac{\partial x_i'}{\partial x_j'}.$$

Since, by definition, the coordinates x_i and x_j are independent for i=j,

$$\frac{\partial x_i'}{\partial x_j'} = \delta'^i_j,$$

So

$$\delta'^i_j = \frac{\partial x_i'}{\partial x_k}\frac{\partial x_l}{\partial x_j'}\,\delta_i^k,$$

and δ'^i_j is really a mixed second-rank tensor. It satisfies

$$\delta_{ab}{}^{jk} = \epsilon_{abi}\,\epsilon^{jki}$$
$$= \delta_a^j\,\delta_b^k - \delta_a^k\,\delta_b^j$$
$$\delta_{abjk} = g_{aj}\,g_{bk} - g_{ak}\,g_{bj}$$
$$\epsilon_{aij}\,\epsilon^{bij} = \delta_{ai}{}^{bi}$$
$$= 2\,\delta_a^b.$$

• **Divergence**

The divergence of a vector field **F**, denoted div(**F**) or $\nabla.$**F** (the notation used in this work), is defined by a limit of the surface integral

$$\nabla \cdot \mathbf{F} \equiv \lim_{V \to 0} \frac{\oint_S \mathbf{F} \cdot d\mathbf{a}}{V}$$

Where the surface integral provides the value of **F** integrated over a closed small boundary surface $S = \partial V$ surrounding a volume component V that is taken to size zero using a limiting method. The divergence of vector field is thus a scalar field. If $\nabla.$**F**=0, then the filed is alleged to be a divergence less field. The symbol $\nabla.$ is referred to as nabla or del.

• **Bulk Viscosity**

The Bulk viscosity μ_B of a fluid is defined as

$$\mu_B = \lambda + \tfrac{2}{3}\mu,$$

Where λ is the second viscosity coefficient and μ is the shear viscosity.

• **Reynolds Number**

The Reynolds number for a flow through a pipe is defined as

$$\mathrm{Re} \equiv \frac{\rho \bar{u} d}{h} = \frac{\bar{u} d}{\nu},$$

Where ρ is the density of the fluid, **u** is the velocity scale, d is the pipe diameter and v is the kinematic viscosity of the fluid. Poiseuille (laminar) flow is experimentally found to occur for **Re<30**. At larger
Reynolds numbers flow become turbulent.

• **Density**

A measure of a substance's mass per unit of volume. For a substance with mass **m** and volume **V**,

$$\rho \equiv \frac{m}{V}.$$

For a body weight w_a placed in a fluid of weight w_w,

$$\rho = G_s \rho_w = \frac{w_a}{w_a - w_w}\rho_w,$$

Where G_s is the specific gravity for an ideal gas,

$$\rho = \frac{mP}{kT}.$$

• **Kinematic Viscosity**

A coefficient which describes the diffusion of momentum. Let η be the dynamic viscosity, then

$$\nu \equiv \frac{\eta}{\rho}.$$

The unit of kinematic viscosity is Stoke, equal to $1\ cm^2\,s^{-1}$

$V_{water} = 1.0 \times 10^{-6}\ m^2\ s^{-1} = 0.010\ cm^2\ s^{-1}$

$V_{air} = 1.5 \times 10^{-5}\ m^2\ s^{-1} = 0.15\ cm^2\ s^{-1}$

INTRODUCTION TO AUTODESK CFD 2018

Autodesk CFD 2018 is a powerful tool used to understand the behavior of fluid on a component design (Inside or Outside). The fluid can either be liquid or gas depends on the Designer's choice and real time environment. To understand and calculate the power of various natural and man-made process or operation had been a challenge for the humanity since history. This inspired the greatest scientist to develop the science of fluid dynamics and its equations to harness the power of operations. These equations are very difficult to solve and also consume lots of time. Equations like, Continuity Equation, X- Momentum Equation, Y- Momentum Equation, Z- Momentum Equation, and some equations are stated above. These equations are so complex that even sometimes scientist are unable to solve these equations by hand. Due to the complexity of solving these types of equation by hand, it led to a software revolution that uses computers to solve these types of equations and to predict the behavior of fluid in a real-time situation. With the use of these software, one can easily understand and predict the behavior of fluid on the design of product.

Use of Autodesk CFD 2018

CFD is used in various aspects of a dynamics study. Fluids affect the properties of component, device, or structure through various ways. To predict these affect, we use the CFD based software. CFD is a important part of design process which benefits the areas like risk reduction, energy efficiency, and innovation.

- **Increase Efficiency**

Fluids are all around us and they take energy to move from one place to another. By understanding the effects and forces of fluid dynamics, you can make a design of a particular product that uses less energy of fluid and also improve efficiency.

- **Risk Reduction**

You have heard these problems before, like product failure, vehicle failure, structure failure, computer overheats, structure collapse due to high winds. In these cases, there may be a reason of unfair prediction of structure or parts with respects to the fluids. By running CFD analysis throughout the design process, one can reduce the chances of failure of product by solving many issues before they turn into a problem.

- **Innovation throughout Insight**

The testing of prototype of a model in real situation could be costly and give discrete data. Also this process is time consuming. The CFD analysis in a software gives us a complete view of the flow and effects of fluid on the model structure. This can reduce the risk of failure of a component.

Applications of Autodesk CFD 2018

- Optimization of HVAC designs.
- Validation of diverse design parameters.
- Aerodynamics

- Industrial Fluid Dynamics

- Fluid Structure Interaction
- Heat Transfer
- Hydrodynamics
- Multi-phase Flows

- CFD helps in design verification of systems like, Displacement ventilation system, vestibule smoke system, natural ventilation system.

How does CFD works

CFD software uses computer to solve mathematical equations for the problem. The main component of CFD design cycle are listed below:

- The Designer or Analyst who states the problem to be solved.
- Scientific knowledge of model and methods, expressed mathematically.
- The software which embodies this knowledge and provides detailed instructions in the form of algorithm.
- The computer hardware which perform the actual calculations.
- The analyst who inspects and interprets the simulation results.

Advantages of Autodesk CFD 2018
You can do CFD analysis throughout the design process to enhance the properties of structure to make a good design.

- Good insight into systems that might be difficult to prototype or test through experimentation.
- Ability to foresee design changes and optimize accordingly.
- Predict mass flow rates, pressure drops, mixing rates, heat transfer rates & fluid dynamic forces.

Sometimes, CFD is able to simulate real conditions like:
- Some flow and heat transfer processes cannot be tested, e.g. hypersonic flow.
- CFD provides the ability to theoretically simulate any physical condition
- CFD permits great control over the physical processes and offers the ability to isolate specific phenomena for study.

- CFD permits the analyst to examine a large number of locations in the area of interest, and yields a comprehensive set of flow parameters for examination.

DOWNLOADING AUTODESK CFD 2018

- Connect your PC with the internet connection and then login to **https://www. autodesk.com/education/free-software/cfd** as shown in Figure-2.

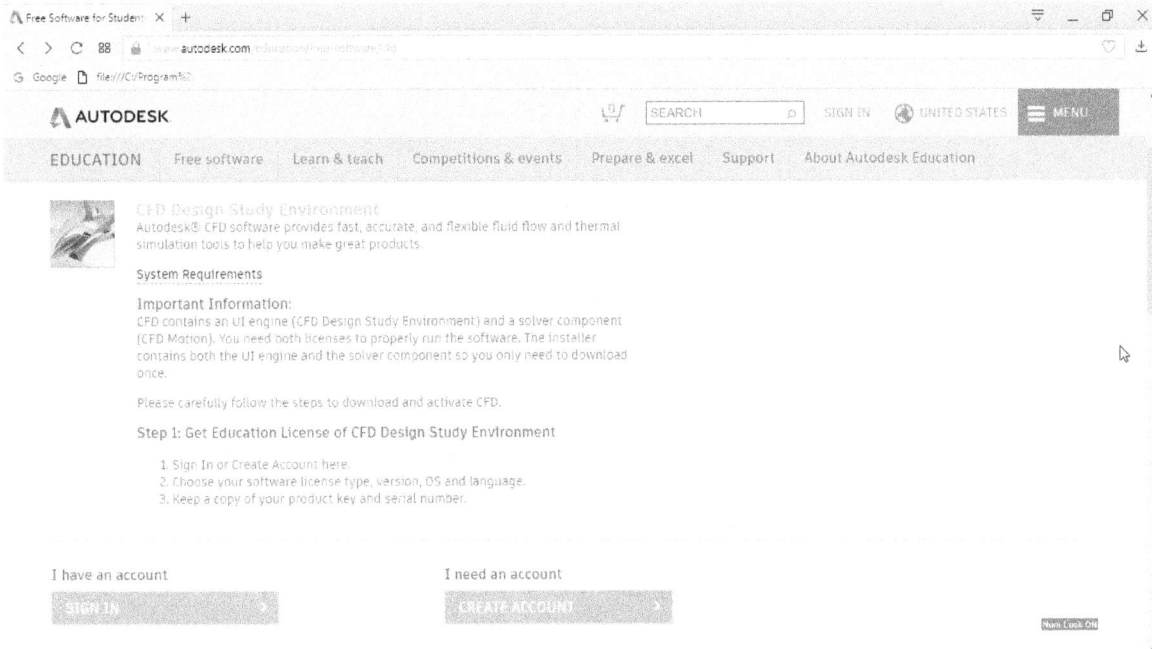

Figure-2. Autodesk.com

- If you have an account of Autodesk, click on the **Sign In** button. If not, click on the **Create Account** button from the displayed web page. The next page will be displayed regarding registration of account.
- On next page, select your Country and Education role. In **Country** drop-down, select your Country and in **Education role** drop-down, you need to select **Student** (There is free subscription for students with license term of 3 years) as shown in Figure-3.

Figure-3. Select country and education role

- After filling the details, click on **NEXT** button. The next page of this website opens. In this page, you need to fill your personal details and then click on **Create Account** as shown in Figure-4.

Create account

First name   Last name

Email

Confirm email

Password

☐ I agree to the A360 Terms of Service, the Education
Special Terms Terms and to the use of my personal
information in accordance with the Autodesk Privacy
Statement (including cross-border transfers as described
in the statement).

CREATE ACCOUNT

ALREADY HAVE AN ACCOUNT? SIGN IN

Figure-4. Creating account

- After creating account, you need to verify your E-mail address by login into your E-mail account. After verifying E-mail address, you need to give your **Education details**.

- After completion of these processes, you need to sign-in into your Autodesk Account and search the **Autodesk CFD (Computational fluid dynamics software)**. The page will be displayed; refer to Figure-5

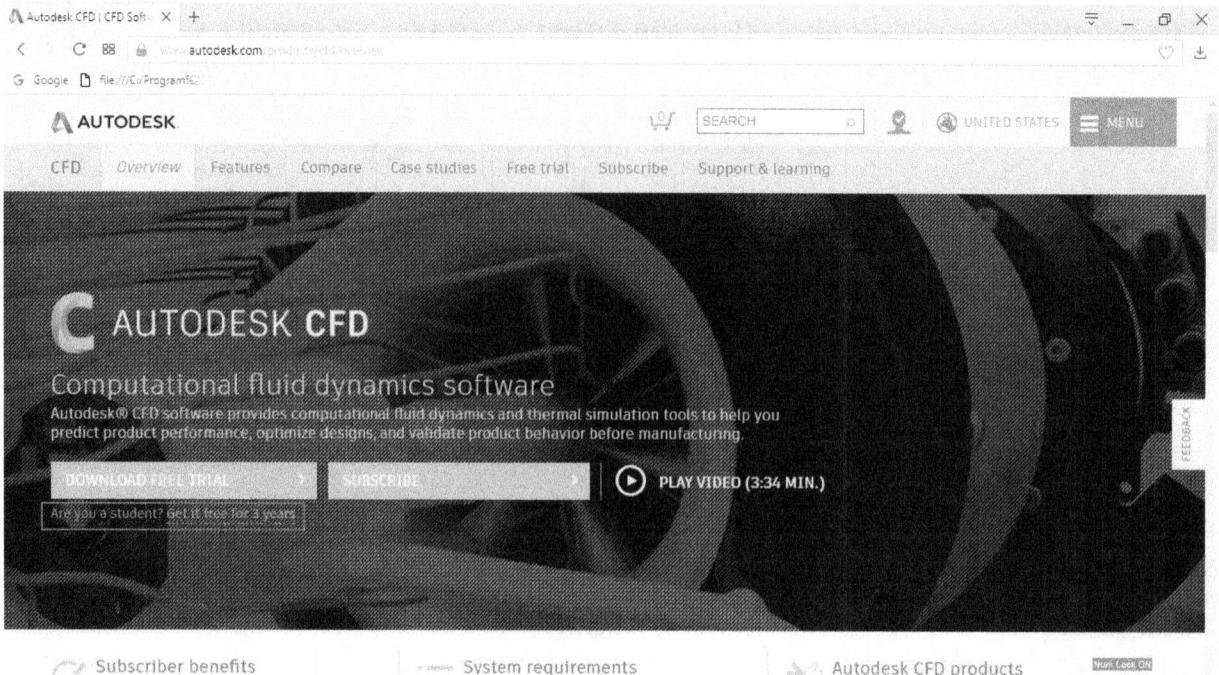

Figure-5. Autodesk CFD webpage

- Click on the **Get it free for 3 years** button which is placed just below the **DOWNLOAD FREE TRIAL** button. This button will let you download a student version of **Autodesk CFD** in which you have access to all tools of CFD software but, you can't use this version commercially.
- On clicking the button, you will be redirected back to CFD page from where we had started the installation process.
- Scroll down on this page, you will see Welcome back, followed by your name or account name; refer to Figure-6.

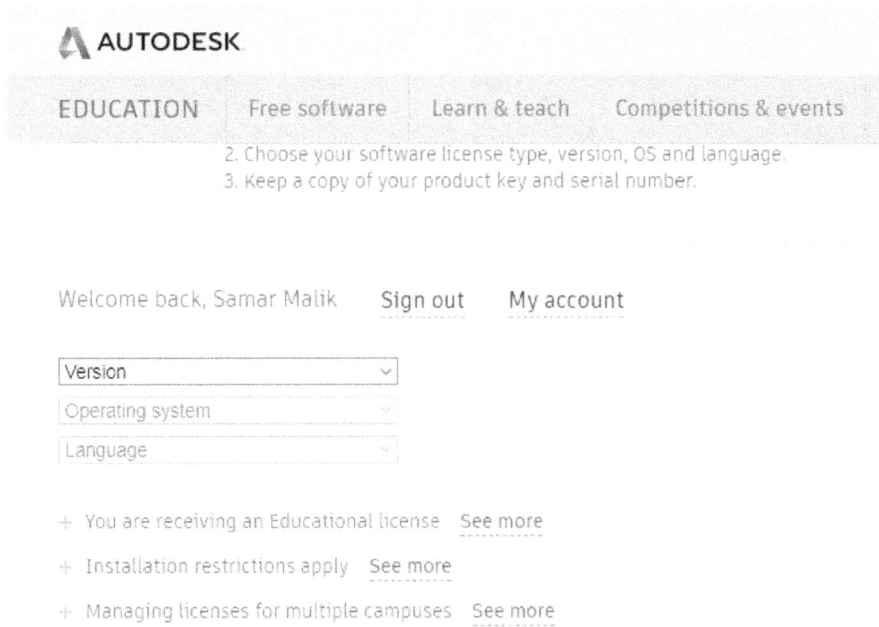

Figure-6. Selection of software version

- Click on the **Version** drop-down from web page and select **CFD Design Study Environment 2018**.
- Click on the **Operating system** drop-down and select **Windows 64-bit**. Here, this software is only works in for 64-bit system. This software could not be operated in 32-bit system because the hardware configuration of 32-bit is not applicable for operating the processes and operation of Autodesk CFD 2018.
- Click on the **Language** drop-down and select the required language. Since, we are studying this software in **English**, so it will be better if you select English.
- On selecting the language, an E-mail will automatically be sent to your E-mail id containing the license key of this software.
- Click on the **Go to this Page** button from Step 2 section of the same web page. A new web page of CFD Motion software will open; refer to Figure-7.

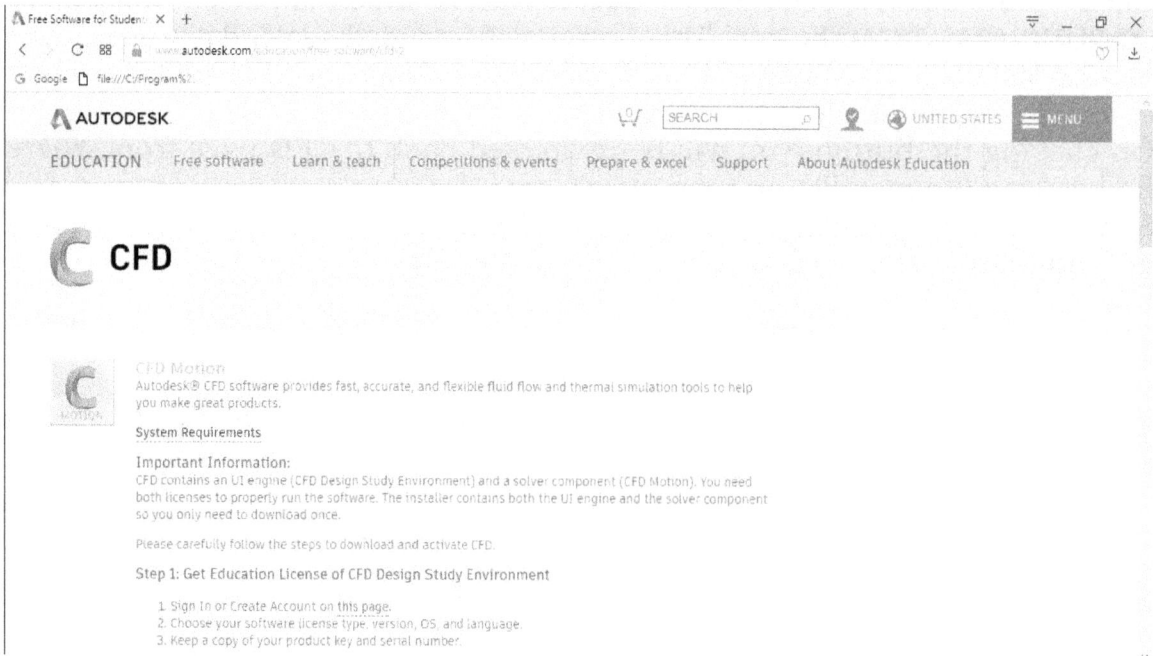

Figure-7. CFD Motion web page

- Scroll down on this page and specify the Version, Operating system, and Language as per your requirement. The **Install Now** button will be activated; refer to Figure-8.

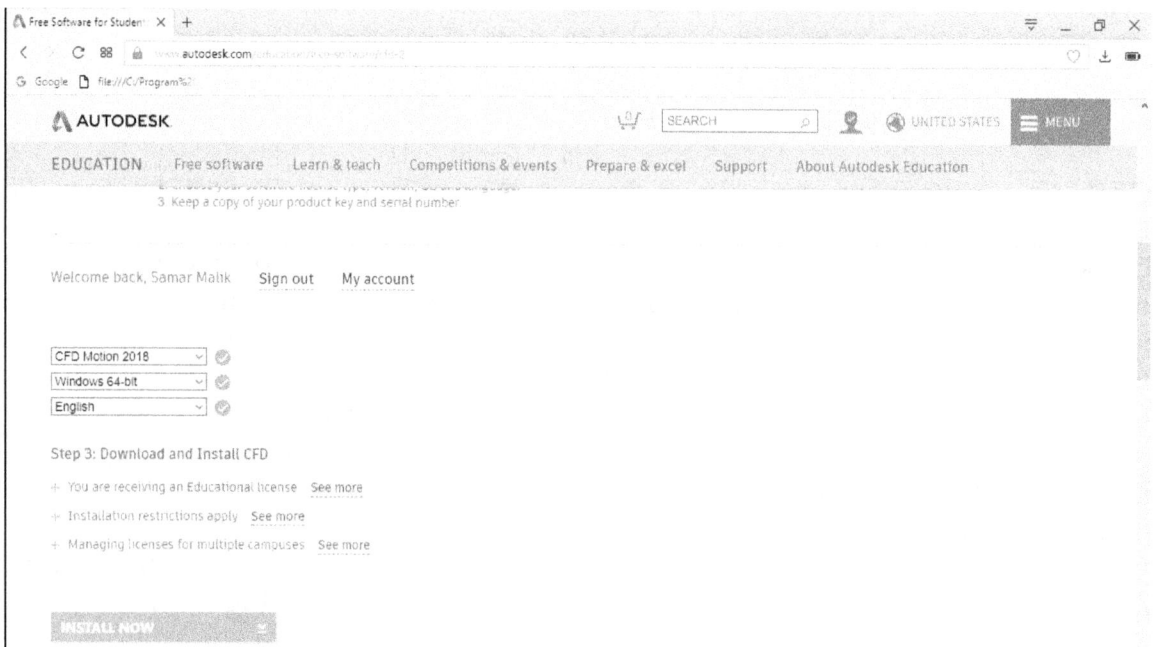

Figure-8. CFD Motion installation

- Click on the **INSTALL NOW** button, the Autodesk LICENSE AND SERVICES AGREEMENT box will be displayed; refer to Figure-9.

Figure-9. Autodesk License and Service Agreement

- After reading the agreement, click on the **I Accept** radio button. The **Install** button will be activated.
- Click on the **Install** button, the **Save As** dialog box will be displayed; refer to Figure-10.

Figure-10. Save As dialog Box

- Select the location to save the setup of Autodesk CFD 2018 and click on the **Save** button. The downloading of setup will be started.
- After downloading, extract the setup of Autodesk CFD 2018 along with Autodesk CFD Motion in a desired location of your PC.

INSTALLING AUTODESK CFD 2018

- To install the Autodesk CFD 2018, go to the folder containing setup file; refer to Figure-11.

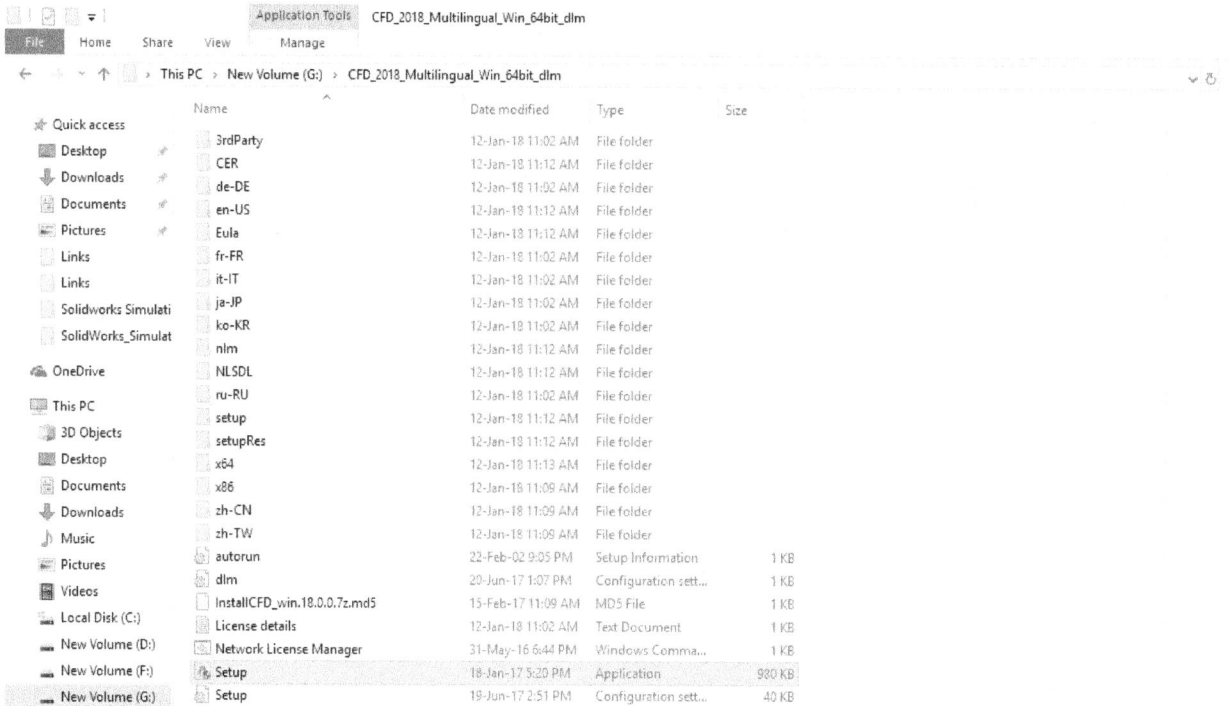

Figure-11. Setup file of Autodesk CFD 2018

- Double-click on the Setup file, the **Autodesk CFD 2018** dialog box will be displayed; refer to Figure-12.

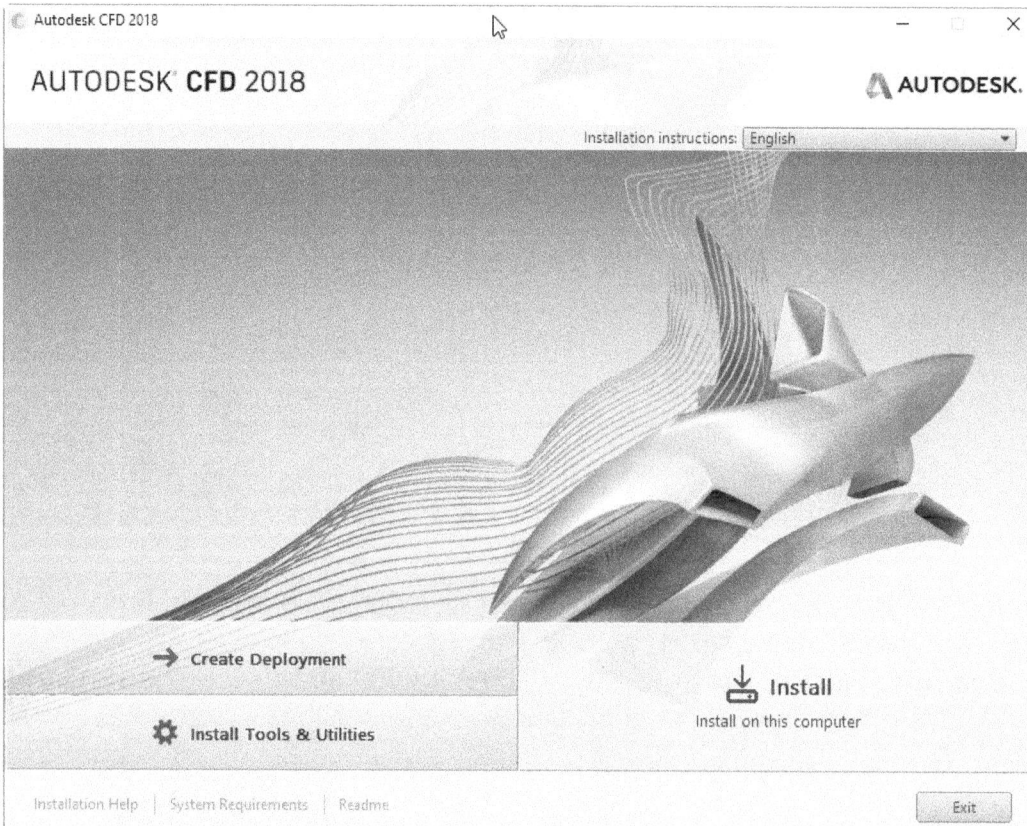

Figure-12. Autodesk CFD 2018 dialog box

- Click on the **Install** button from **Autodesk CFD 2018** dialog box and install the software as per instruction. The software will be installed in couple of minutes.
- After installation, click on the Autodesk CFD 2018 icon from Desktop. The software will be started and options will be displayed to activate the current software. Activate the software by using the license key provided to you via E-mail by Autodesk.

STARTING AUTODESK CFD 2018

- To start **Autodesk CFD 2018** from **Start** menu, click on the **Start** button in the **Taskbar** at the bottom left corner, click on **Autodesk folder,** and select the **CFD 2018** icon; refer to Figure-13. The Autodesk CFD 2018 software welcome window will be displayed; refer to Figure-14.

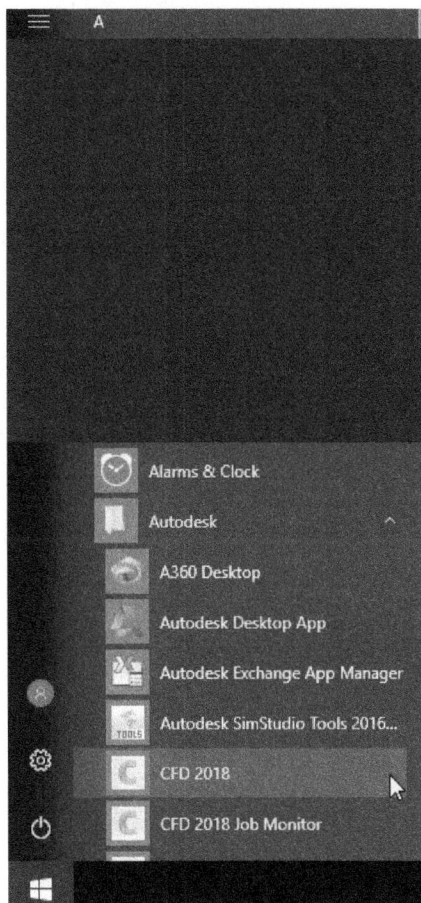

Figure-13. CFD 2018 icon from Start Menu

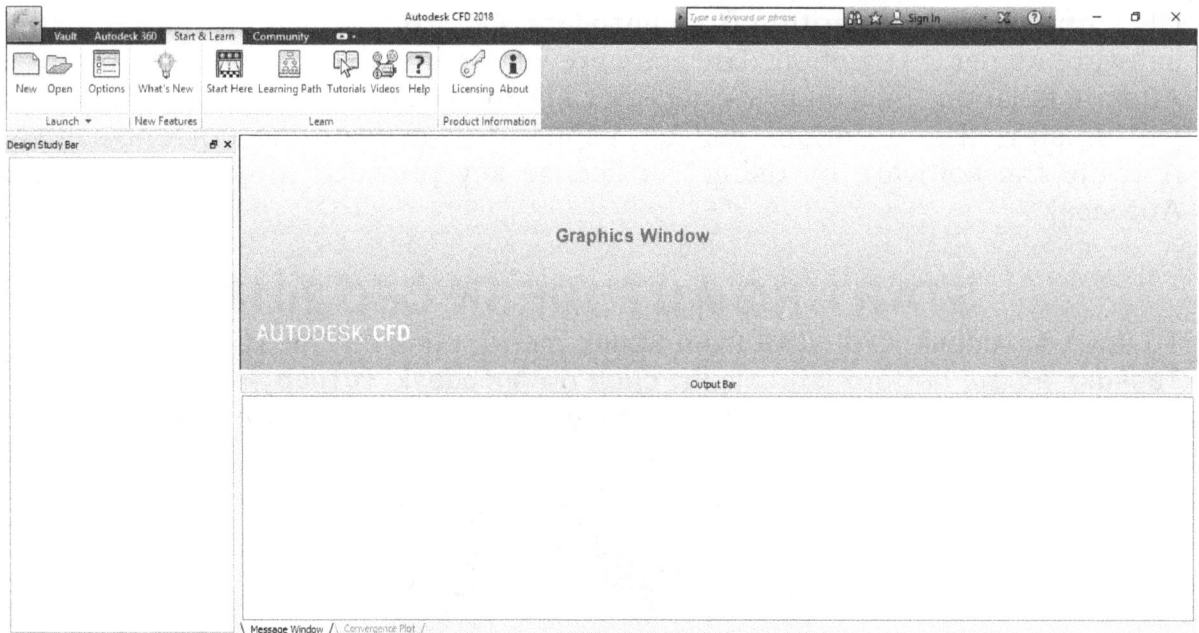

Figure-14. Autodesk CFD 2018 welcome screen

- The **Start & Learn** tab will be displayed in the **Ribbon** with various tools to learn new topics of Autodesk CFD. Various tabs in the Welcome screen are discussed next.

Vault tab

- Click on the **Vault** tab from **Ribbon**. The tools and options related to this tab will be displayed; refer to Figure-15.

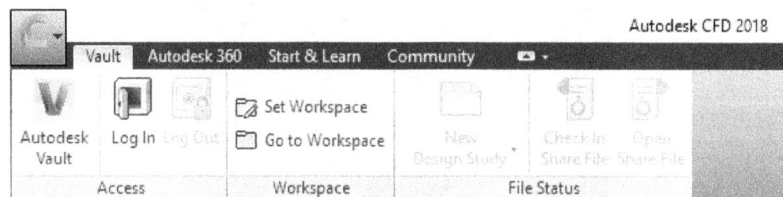

Figure-15. Vault tab

Autodesk Vault

The **Autodesk Vault** tool is used to store and manage Autodesk CFD data in cloud storage safely. Click on the **Autodesk Vault** button from **Ribbon**, the Vault webpage will be displayed from Autodesk Website.

- You can gather some more information about **Autodesk Vault** tool from this webpage about subscription, System requirements, etc.

Log In

The **Log In** tool is used to access your vault account to save or update the data of analysis generated in Autodesk CFD 2018. The procedure to access vault is given next.

- Click on the **Log In** tool from **Access** section of **Vault** tab. The **Log In** box will be displayed; refer to Figure-16.

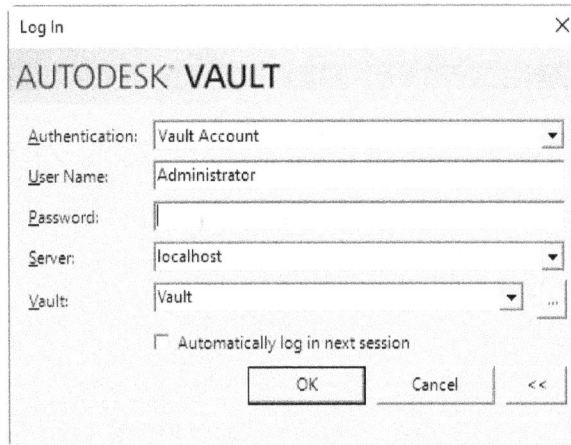

Figure-16. Log In dialog box

- Specify the required information in **Log In** box and click on the **OK** button. You will be logged-in in your account. Now you are able to save or update the current data of CFD in no-time.

Log Out

The **Log Out** tool is used to exit the current activated account. This tool will shut the access to your vault account.

- Click on the **Log Out** tool from **Access** section of **Vault** tab to close the access from vault account.

Set Workspace

The **Set Workspace** tool is used to manage and access the local storage folder where data of your CFD analysis will be stored. The procedure to set workspace is given next.

- Click on the **Set Workspace** tool from **Workspace** panel of **Vault** tab to set the location in your computer for saving your CFD data. The **Set default Vault working Directory** dialog box will be displayed; refer to Figure-17.

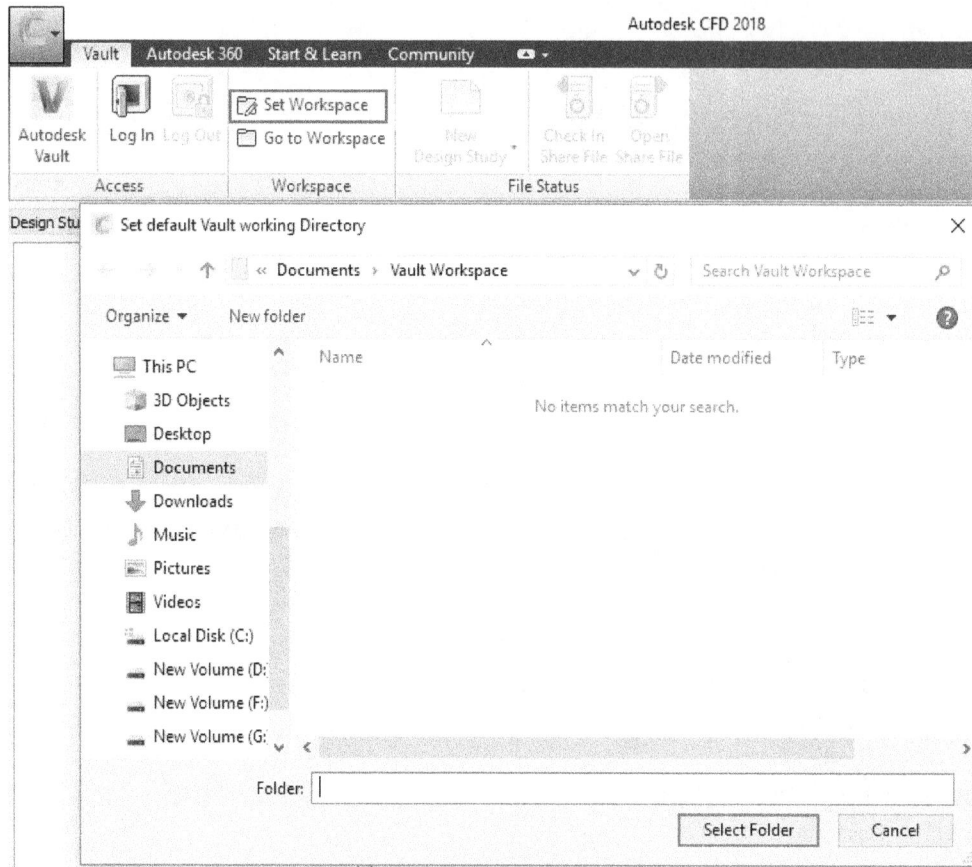

Figure-17. The Set default Vault working Directory dialog box

- Select the desired folder and click on the **Select Folder** button. The selected folder will be specified as saving directory for CFD files.

Go to Workshop

The **Go To Workshop** tool is used to open the storage folder of CFD files.

- Click on **Go To Workshop** tool from **Workspace** section of **Vault** tab, the storage folder will be displayed.

Start & Learn tab

The tools of **Start & Learn** tab are used to explore and learn Autodesk CFD 2018. There are also tools to create or open a analysis of CFD. These tools are discussed next.

New

The **New** tool is used to create a new study file in Autodesk CFD 2018. The procedure to use this tool is discussed next.

- Click on the **New** button from **Launch** section to create a new design study. The **New Design Study** dialog box will be displayed; refer to Figure-18.

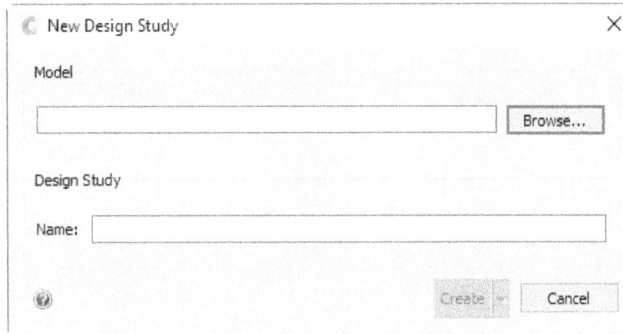

Figure-18. New Design Study dialog box

In Autodesk CFD 2018, you cannot create or design a part file. This software is only for analysis of model or structure as per given condition. To create a part, you will need a CAD software like Autodesk Fusion 360, Autodesk Inventor, SolidWorks, AutoCad, etc. You can check our other books like, AUTODESK FUSION 360 BLACK BOOK, SOLIDWORKS 2018 BLACK BOOK, AUTODESK INVENTOR 2018 BLACK BOOK to learn about these softwares.

- Click on the **Browse** button from **New Design Study** dialog box, the **Create New Design Study** dialog box will be displayed; refer to Figure-19.

Figure-19. Create New Design Study dialog box

- Click on the **File Format selection** drop-down and select the required format for file to be opened; refer to Figure-20.

Figure-20. File Format Selection drop-down

- Select the desired file from **Create New Design Study** dialog box and click on the **Open** button. You will return to **New Design Study** box where you can check the name of your selected file.

- Enter the required name for new design study and click on the **Create** button. The model will be displayed in graphics window along with all options activated; refer to Figure-21.

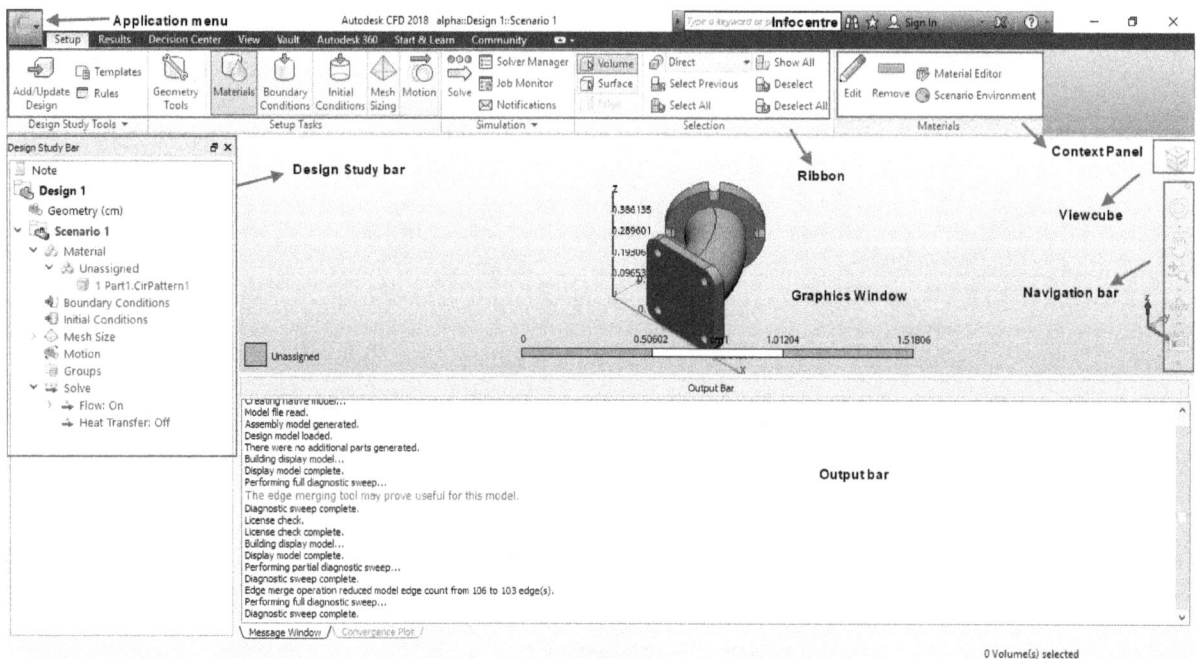

Figure-21. Model interface

Open

The **Open** tool is used to open an existing design study.

- Click on the **Open** button from **Launch** panel to open an existing design study. The **Open** dialog box will be displayed; refer to Figure-22.

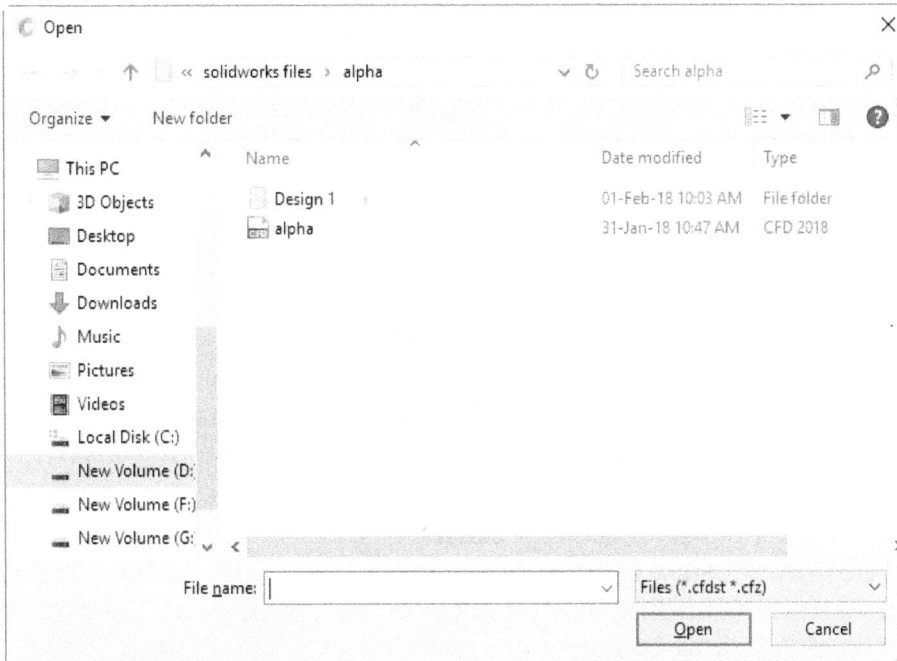

Figure-22. Open dialog box

- Select the design study file which you want to open and click on the **Open** button from **Open** dialog box. The file will open in Autodesk CFD 2018 along with the access of all tools.

Options

The **Options** tool is used to customize the user interface to suit the work habits of designer and working environment.

- Click on the **Options** tool from **Launch** panel to customize the user interface, the **User Interface Preferences** dialog box will be displayed; refer to Figure-23.

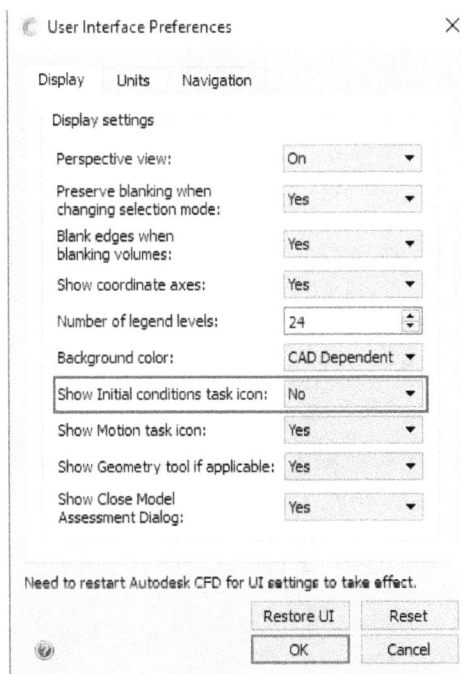

Figure-23. User Interface Preferences dialog-box

- Specify the desired parameters to change the user interface from **Display** tab, **Units** tab, and **Navigation** tab.
- Click on the **Restore UI** button to restore the user interface of Autodesk CFD 2018 to default.
- Click on the **Reset** button to reset the default values of **User Interface Preferences** dialog box.
- After specifying the parameters, click on the **OK** button. The changes to customize the user interface will be saved.

New Features

The **New feature** section is used to check the updates of software provided by Autodesk. Click on the **What's New** tool from the **New Features** panel of **Start & Learn** tab in the **Ribbon**. Latest updates of software will be displayed..

Learn

The tools and button of **Learn** section are used to learn and understand the software. For learning and understanding, Autodesk provided many way like, tutorials, videos, and help file to understand better.

Product Information

The tools of **Product Information** panel provide the information about software version and available license for the installed software.

*** End of Chapter ***

Model Setup in Autodesk CFD

Chapter 2

Topics Covered

The major topics covered in this chapter are:

- *Edge Merge*
- *Void Fill*
- *ViewCube*
- *Navigation bar*
- *Diagnostics*
- *Mesh Refinement Regions*

INTRODUCTION

In the last chapter, we have learned many things about CFD, fluid mechanics, and Autodesk CFD 2018 like a first time user interface which will be useful for upcoming chapters. In this chapter, we will learn about various tools to create a design study, applying material, creating mesh, and running the simulation.

MODEL SETUP IN AUTODESK CFD 2018

To create a design study in Autodesk CFD 2018, you will need a pre-created design model, created with the help of Autodesk CFD 2018 supported software which was discussed in last chapter.

- Open Autodesk CFD 2018 software by double-clicking on icon from Desktop. You can also open the same from Start menu. The welcome window of Autodesk CFD 2018 will be displayed.
- Click on the **New** button of **Launch** panel from **Start & Learn** tab, the **New Design Study** dialog box will be displayed. Select the file which you want to open and click on the **Create** button. The software will start to read file design and status will be displayed in **Output bar.**
- Sometimes, when there is some error with the design or there is a need to improve the quality of model for CFD, the **Geometry Tools** dialog box will be displayed; refer to Figure-1.

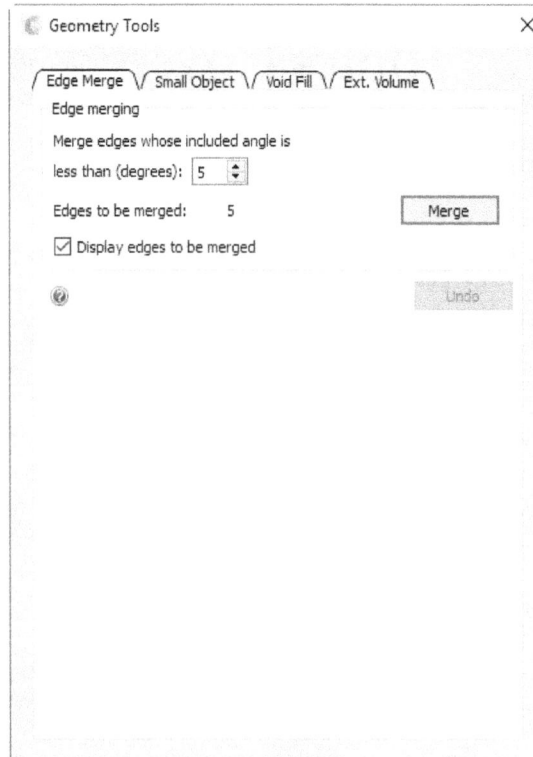

Figure-1. Geometry Tools dialog box

You can also open the **Geometry Tools** dialog box by clicking on the **Geometry Tools** button from **Setup Tasks** panel of **Setup** tab.

Edge Merge

Options in the **Edge Merge** tab are used to unite edges that share a common vertex at an inflection angle less than a specified tolerance. This tool is helpful in generating mesh and reducing computer time because it reduces the number of small edges in a design to make analysis faster; refer to Figure-2.

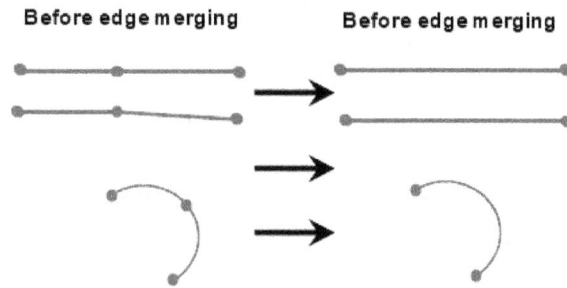

Figure-2. Edge merging

- The **Inclination** angle is determined by value of included tangency angle which has a maximum limit in **Edge Merging** tab of 15 degrees. The edge merging will have no effect on vertex where two or more edges are joining. Also it will have no effect on edges whose angle is greater than the specified angle.
- Click in the edit box from **Edge Merge** tab and enter the desired value in degree to merge the edges whose included angle is less than the specified value. On entering the value, software will automatically calculate the number of edges which are going to merge and the value is displayed in **Edge Merger** tab.
- Select the **Display edges to be merged** check box from **Edge Merge** tab to view the edges to be merged. The edges will be displayed along with the arrows; refer to Figure-3.

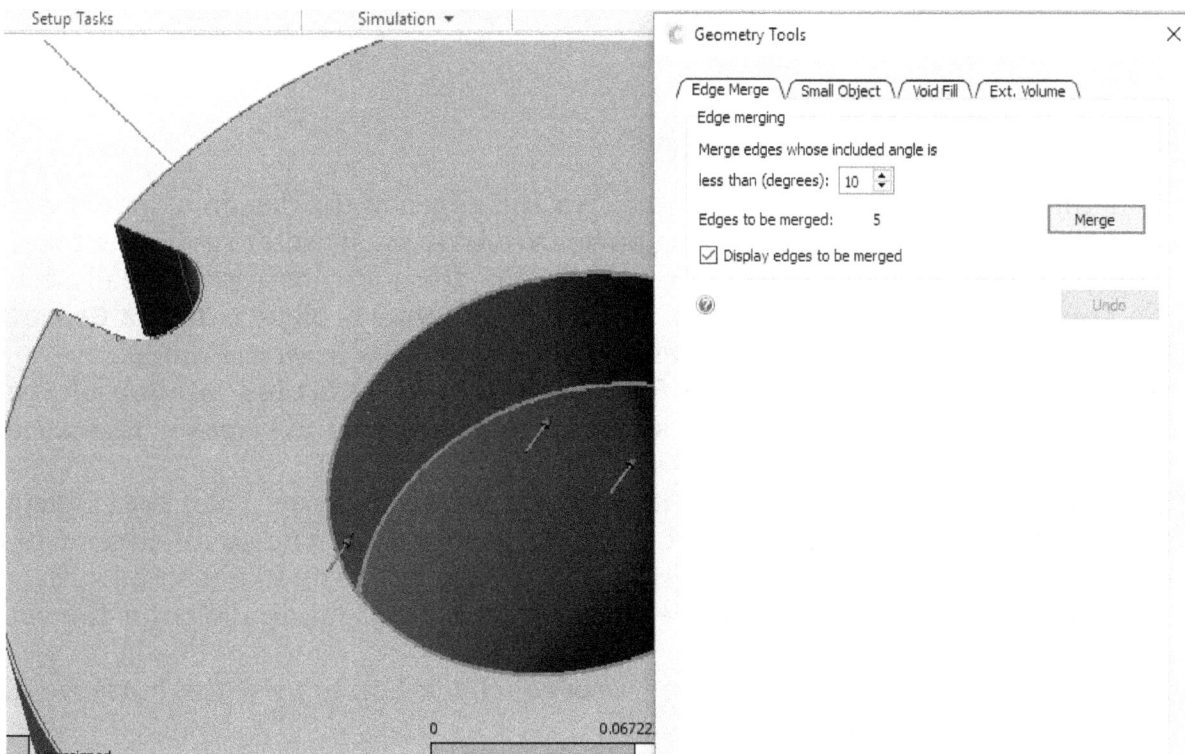

Figure-3. Displaying edges to be merged

- After specifying the parameters, click on the **Merge** button from **Edge Merge** tab. The selected edges will be merged.
- Click on the **Undo** button from **Edge Merge** tab to undo the action of edge merging.

Small Object

The **Small Object** tab is used to remove geometry from model, like surfaces and edges, which are too small to see in a mesh; refer to Figure-4. The process of removing small edges and surfaces from model will decrease the time taken by computer for analysis processing and mesh generation.

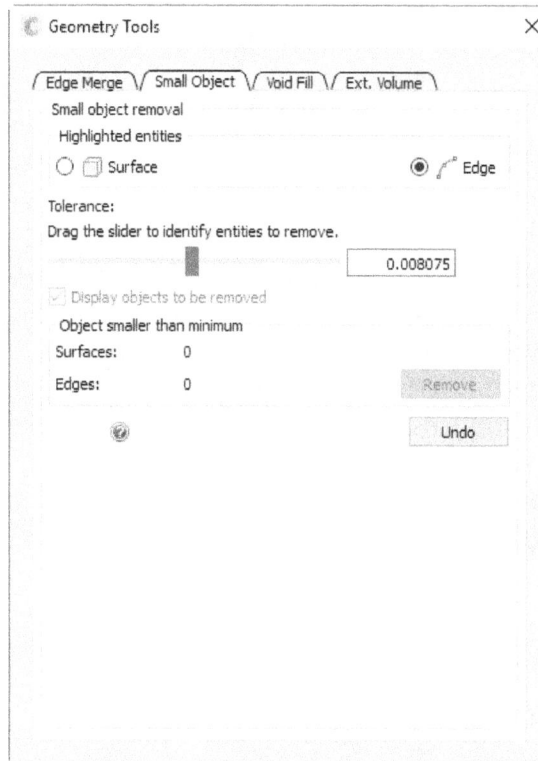

Figure-4. Small Object Tab

- Sometimes, there are some small surfaces and edges in the design of model which consume more time and processing power to create mesh and to generate results. When we open this type of file in Autodesk CFD, the software automatically detect the smaller edges and surface, and displays the **Small Object** tab of **Geometry Tools** dialog box to minimize excess edges or surfaces from the model.
- Select the **Surface** radio button from **Highlighted entities** section of **Small Object** tab to highlight the extra small surface of model to remove. The surface will be highlighted along with the arrows.
- Select the **Edge** radio button from **Highlighted entities** section of **Small Object** tab to highlight the small edges of model to be removed. The small edges will be highlighted along with the arrows generated by software to highlight small surfaces.
- Move the slider to set the tolerance value. You can also manually enter the value in **Tolerance** edit box.
- Select the **Display objects to be removed** check box to view the surfaces and edges which are going to be removed.
- In **Object smaller than minimum** section, the number of surfaces and edges which are going to be removed will be displayed.
- After specifying the parameters, click on the **Remove** button from **Small Object** tab. The small surface and edges will be removed.

Void Fill

Mostly CAD models are consists of solid body and fluid flow inside them or around them, but sometimes there are some openings in the solid body as a part of geometry model where the working fluid enter or leaves. In such case, the geometric model is not suitable for a flow analysis. The, **Void Fill** options are used to create capping surfaces that bound a water-tight internal void on the openings of solid body. The surfaces and volumes that are created, are actual geometries that can have boundary conditions, material, and other CFD parameters. When creating a cap on the opening, always remember to not overlap void fill volume with other volume.

- Select the desired radio button from **Model entity selection** section of **Void Fill** tab.
- The **Edge** radio button is selected by default. You need to select the edge from model to close the opening; refer to Figure-5.

Figure-5. Void Fill tab

- On selection of edge from model, the number of edges will be displayed in Edges selection box.
- After selecting the required edges, click on the **Build surface** button from **Void Fill** tab. The surface will be created based on the selected edge; refer to Figure-6.

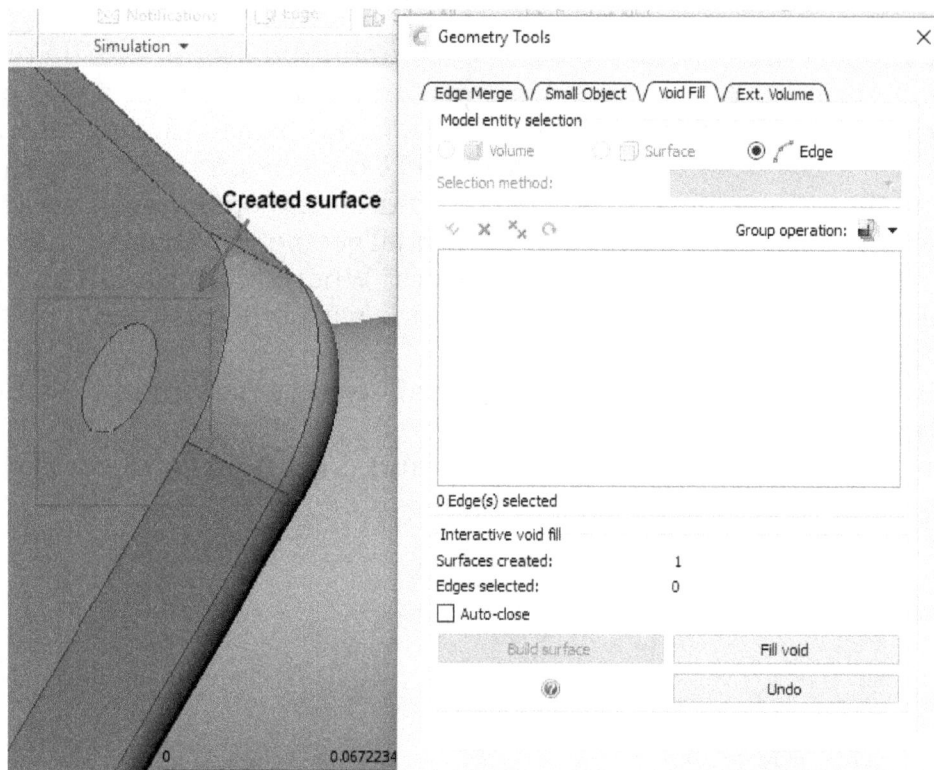

Figure-6. Created surface

- The dialog box will be updated after creating surface. You can see the number of created surfaces next to of **Surface created**. The **Fill Void** button will be activated on creation of surfaces.

- Click on the **Fill Void** button from the **Fill Void** dialog box. If the void fill region is created, a message "There was 1 additional part generated", will be displayed in the **Message** box; refer to Figure-7.

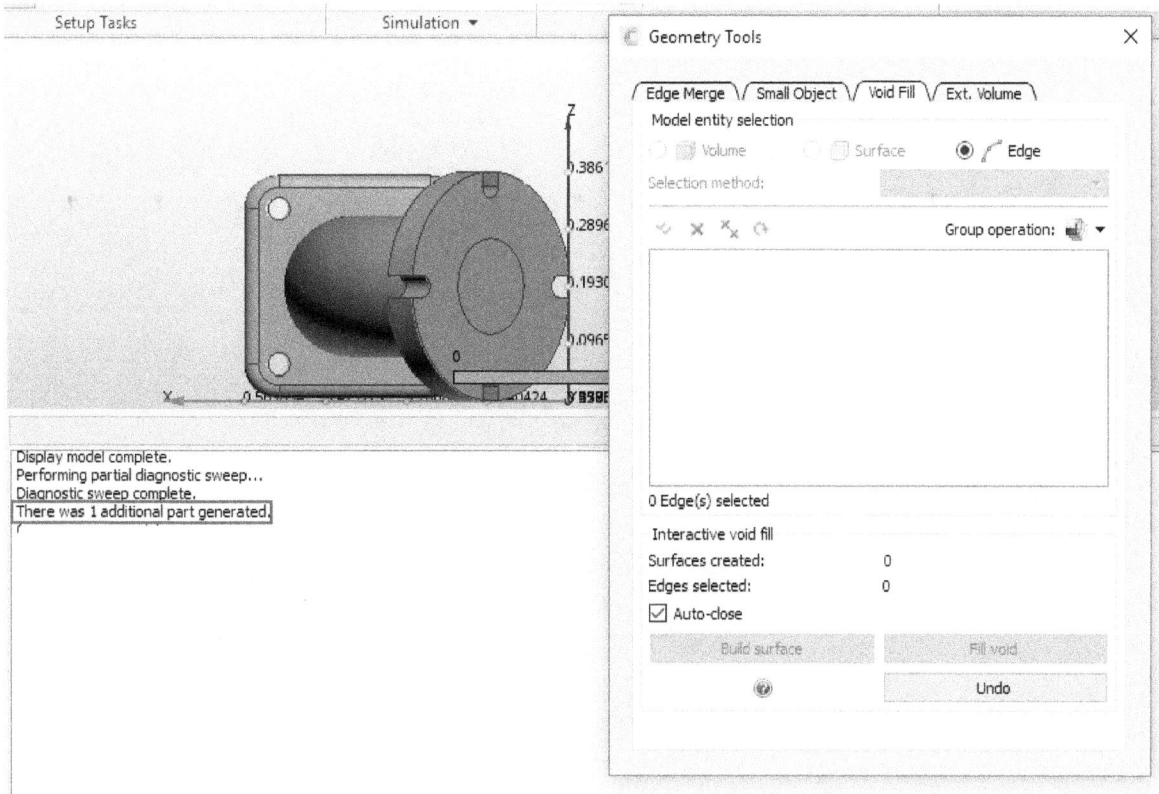

Figure-7. Created Fill Void

Ext. Volume

The options in the Ext. Volume tab are used to define external fluid volume for different analyses like wind analysis on motorcycle, aircraft, and other objects. In most cases, the volume that surround the model is not included as part of model design. For analysis, one needs to add the surrounding in the form of external volume of fluid to the model with the help of **Ext. Volume** tab. It adds the surrounding fluid to the model without adding it to the CAD geometry.

- Click on the **Ext. Volume** tab from **Geometry Tools** dialog box, the preview of external volume will be displayed; refer to Figure-8.

Figure-8. Automatically created external volume

- Always remember while creating a surrounding, whole model should be immersed in the fluid or we can say, the external volume should totally cover the model. To resize the external volume as per requirement, click and hold the left mouse button on a grab handle and drag the mouse to resize the length; refer to Figure-9.

Figure-9. Resize the external volume

- On grabbing the drag handle, the color of arrow will be changed from blue to red. Adjust the length of external volume as required. If you want to specify the length of external volume manually, click on the value of parameter from **Ext. Volume** tab and enter the desired value; refer to Figure-10.

Figure-10. Specifying manually

- If you want to reset the entered parameter for creating an external volume, click on the **Reset** button from **Ext. Volume** tab. The values will be reset to default.
- After specifying the parameters to set up an external volume, click on the **Create** button from **Ext. Volume** tab. The external volume will be created and displayed; refer to Figure-11.

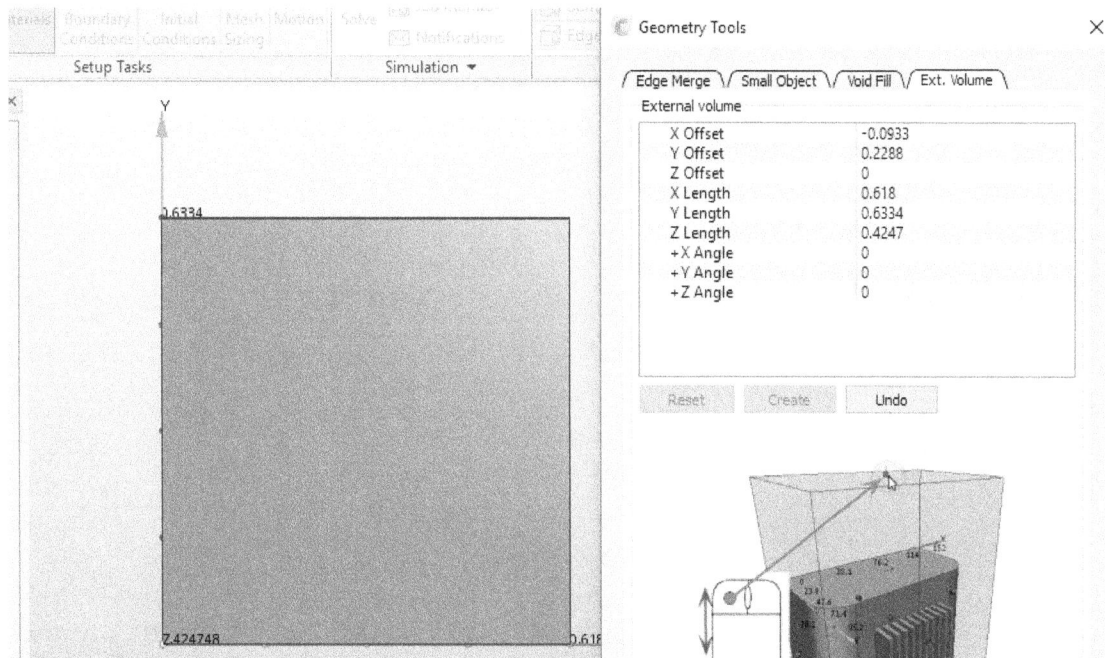

Figure-11. Created external volume

- To undo the process of creating the external volume around the model, click on the **Undo** button from **Ext. Volume** tab. The **Warning** box will be displayed to asking you whether to undo the process or not; refer to Figure-12

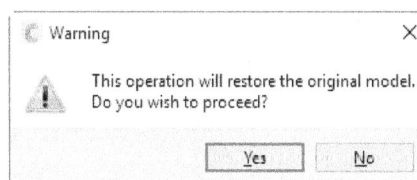

Figure-12. Warning box

- Click on the **Yes** button from **Warning** box. The created external volume will be deleted and model will be returned to its initial position.

NAVIGATION

The **Navigation bar** is a user interface element where you can access the model through different aspects; refer to Figure-13. There are two types of navigation tools, i.e. Unified navigation tools and product-specific tools. The Unified navigation tools are those tools that can be found in almost all Autodesk software. The Product-specific tools are those tools which are software specific. The tools of **Navigation bar** are discussed next.

Figure-13. Naviga-tion bar

ViewCube

ViewCube is used to display orientation of model and reorient the model; refer to Figure-14.

Figure-14. View Cube

- Names of the views are displayed on the faces of **ViewCube**. To orient the model in a particular view, click on the respective view name. The model will be displayed as per clicked view.
- Click on the **Home** button from **ViewCube** to quickly move to the Isometric view.

Full Navigation Wheel

Full Navigation Wheel, also known as wheels, are menus that provides 2D and 3D navigation command from a single source. These menus are known as tracking menus, which means they follow your cursor. **Full Navigation wheel** consists of many navigation command into a single interface. The procedure to use this is discussed next.

- Click on the **Full Navigation Wheel** button from **Navigation bar**. The **Navigation Wheel** will be attached to the cursor; refer to Figure-15.

Figure-15. Navigation wheel

- Click and hold the left mouse button on **ZOOM** button from **Navigation Wheel** and move the cursor upward and downward to Zoom-in and Zoom-out respectively.
- Click and hold the left mouse button on **ORBIT** button from **Navigation Wheel** and move the cursor as per requirement to move the model.
- Click and hold the left mouse button on **PAN** button from **Navigation Wheel** and move the cursor as required to move the model.
- Click and hold the left mouse button on **REWIND** button from **Navigation Wheel** and move the mouse towards left or right to rewind the last action. On selecting **Rewind** button, an array of pictures will be displayed from which you can select the desired previous state of model.

Figure-16. Rewind tool

- Click and hold the left mouse button on **CENTER** button from **Navigation Wheel** and select a point on the graphics window and release the left mouse button. The model moves so that the selected point is at the centre of screen.
- Click and hold the left mouse button on **UP/DOWN** button from **Navigation Wheel** and move the cursor towards up or down to adjust the height of current viewpoint

along the Z-axis of the model. On clicking this button, a slider to navigate from up to down will be displayed; refer to Figure-17.

Figure-17. UP DOWN slider

- Click and hold the left mouse button on **Look** button from **Navigation Wheel** and move the cursor to rotate the current view vertically and horizontally. While rotating, your line of sight rotates about the current eye position like turning your head.
- Click again on the **Navigation Wheel** button from **Navigation bar** to deactivate the **Navigation Wheel**.
- Click on the **Mini Full Navigation Wheel** button from Navigation Wheel drop-down of **Navigation bar** to activate the mini navigation wheel. The wheel will be attached with the cursor; refer to Figure-18. This wheel works like the **Full Navigation Wheel** which was discussed earlier.

Figure-18. Mini Navigaton Wheel

- Move the cursor in desired section of the **Mini Navigation Wheel** to activate the respective tool. Click and drag the cursor to perform the selected operation.
- Click on the down arrow below the **Navigation wheel** tool from **Navigation bar**. The menu will be displayed; refer to Figure-19.

Figure-19. Navigation Wheel drop-down

View Object Wheel

- Click on the **Basic View Object Wheel** button from the drop-down to activate the **View Object Wheel**. The **View Object Wheel** is used to view individual objects or features in model; refer to Figure-20.

Figure-20. View Object Wheel

- The buttons of **View Object Wheel** are same as discussed in **Full Navigation Wheel** section.
- Click on the **Mini View Object Wheel** button from **Navigation Wheel** drop-down of **Navigation bar** to activate the mini object wheel. The wheel will attached with the cursor; refer to Figure-21.

Figure-21. Mini Object Wheel

- The working of this wheel is same as discussed earlier.

Tour Building Wheel

- Click on the **Basic Tour Building Wheel** from **Navigation Wheel** drop-down of **Navigation bar** to activate the **Tour Building Wheel.** The wheel will be attached to the cursor; refer to Figure-22. The **Tour Building Wheel** is used to move through model like building, assembly line, ship, or oil rig.

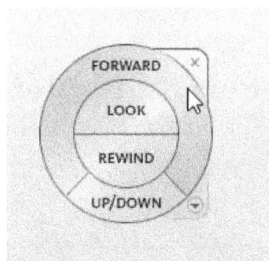

Figure-22. Tour Building Wheel

- Click and hold **Forward** button from **Tour Building Wheel** to adjust the distance between the current point of view and defined pivot point of the model. Move the cursor forward and backward to zoom in and out through the model respectively.

- You can also activate the **View Object Wheel** and **Tour Building Wheel** from Navigation Wheel drop-down of **Navigation Wheel**; refer to Figure-23.

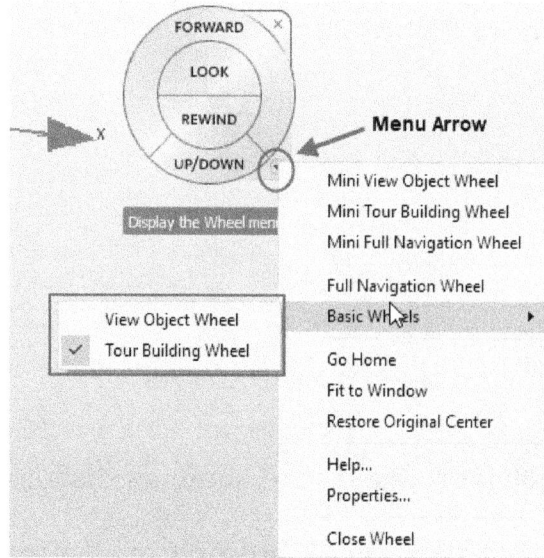

Figure-23. Menu arrow of navigation wheel1

- Click on the **Mini Tour Building Wheel** button from **Navigation Wheel** drop-down of **Navigation bar** to activate the mini tour building wheel. The wheel will be attached with the cursor; refer to Figure-24.

Figure-24. Mini Tour building wheel

- The working of this wheel was discussed earlier.

2D Wheel

The **2D Wheel** provides the basic navigation command for 2D navigation. This wheel is useful when you don't have a mouse with scroll wheel. The procedure to activate this wheel is discussed next.

- Click on the **2D Wheel** button from **Navigation Wheel** drop-down of **Navigation bar** to activate the 2D Wheel. The wheel will be attached to the cursor; refer to Figure-25.

Figure-25. 2D Wheel

- The tools of 2D navigation wheel were discussed earlier.

Zoom

The **Zoom** tool is used to increase or decrease the magnification of current view of model.

- Click on the **Zoom** button from **Navigation bar**. The tool will be activated and a magnifier will be displayed in place of your mouse cursor.
- To zoom in and zoom out, roll up and roll down the middle mouse button.
- To deactivate the **Zoom** tool, click again on the **Zoom** button from **Navigation bar**. You can also press left click of mouse anywhere on the graphics window to do the same work.
- Click on the **Zoom (Fit All)** button from **Navigation Wheel** drop-down of **Zoom** button, so that entire model is visible; refer to Figure-26.

Figure-26. Zoom menu arrow

- Click on the **Zoom (Displayed)** button from **Navigation Wheel** drop-down of **Zoom** button to zoom the displayed view or visible parts of model to the screen.
- Click on the **Zoom (Window)** button from **Navigation Wheel** drop-down of **Zoom** button to zoom selected region. You need to select a region of model to zoom with the help of box selection; refer to Figure-27.

Figure-27. Zoom window selection

Orbit

The **Orbit** tool is used to change the orientation of a model. The procedure to use this tool is discussed next.

- Click on the **Orbit** button from **Navigation bar**. The tool will be activated and cursor will change to orbit shape.
- Press and hold the left mouse key and move the cursor to change the orientation of model; refer to Figure-28. When you have reached at desired orientation, leave the left mouse button.

Figure-28. Changing orientation

- Click on the **Orbit (Constrained)** tool from arrow menu of **Orbit** button to rotate about a single axis. This tool is equivalent to moving the eye position about the model in latitude and longitude.

Look At

The **Look At** tool is used to focus on a specific face. The procedure to use this is discussed next.

- Click on the **Look At** tool from **Navigation bar**. The tool will be activated and the cursor will be modified accordingly.
- Click on the particular face from the model; the face will be displayed parallel to the screen; refer to Figure-29.

Figure-29. Using Look At tool

Center

The **Center** tool is used to change the center of rotation by clicking a point on the model. The model will moves towards the selected point to make the selected point as center of screen.

- Click on the **Center** tool from **Navigation bar**. The tool will be activated and the cursor will be modified accordingly.
- Click on the graphics window to select a center point. The model will move as per selected point.

Customize Menu

The default position of **Navigation bar** is at the top right side of the Graphics window. The **Customize menu** of **Navigation bar** is used to change the position of **Navigation bar**. The procedure to use **Customize menu** is discussed next.

- Click on the small arrow on the lower right corner of the **Navigation bar**. The menu will be displayed; refer to Figure-30.

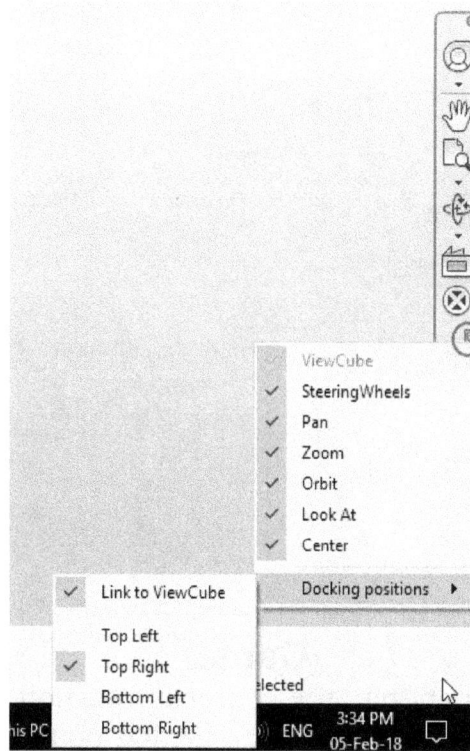

Figure-30. Customize menu

- The ticks in front of tools in menu show the availability on **Navigation bar**. Click on the specific tool to add/remove the tool from **Navigation bar**.
- Select the **Link to ViewCube** button from **Docking positions** cascading menu to tie the position of **ViewCube** and **Navigation bar** together. By default, this tool is activated.
- If you want to change the position of **ViewCube**, disable the **Link to ViewCube** button and move the **Navigation bar** manually by using drag and drop at the top edge **Navigation** bar.
- Click on the **Top Left**, **Top Right**, **Bottom Left**, **Bottom Right** button from **Docking positions** cascading menu to move the **ViewCube** and **Navigation bar** together towards top left, top right, bottom left, and bottom right respectively.

Context Toolbar

The **Context Toolbar** provide convenient access to frequently-used functions specific to the current task. The procedure is discussed next.

- Left-click of the mouse on the Graphics Window, the **Context Toolbar** will be displayed; refer to Figure-31.

Figure-31. Context Toolbar

- Left-click on the **Edit** button of **Context Toolbar** is used to assign or modify the last setting.

- Left-click on the **Remove** button of **Context Toolbar** is used to deselect the last command.
- Left-click on the **Show All** button of **Context Toolbar** is used to show all hidden entities.
- Left-click on the **Hide** button of **Context Toolbar** is used to hide the selected entity.

Meshing Context Toolbar

The **Meshing Context Toolbar** is used to control and define mesh. The procedure to use this is discussed next.

- To use the **Meshing Context Toolbar**, you will need to select the model from Graphics window with the help of left-click of mouse. The **Meshing Context Toolbar** will be displayed along with the changed color; refer to Figure-32.

Figure-32. Meshing Context Toolbar

- The **Define the mesh automatically** button is used to apply sizing of mesh automatically. Click on this button, the mesh will be generated automatically on the model.
- You can also use this tool from **Automatic Sizing** section of **Setup** tab after selecting the **Mesh Sizing** tool from the **Setup Tasks** panel in the **Ribbon**; refer to Figure-33.

Figure-33. Automatic Sizing section

Mesh Refinement Region

- The **Locally control the mesh** button is used to construct refinement regions of mesh. Click on this button, the **Mesh Refinement Regions** dialog box will be displayed; refer to Figure-34. You can also use this tool by clicking on **Regions** button from **Automatic Sizing** section of **Setup** tab.

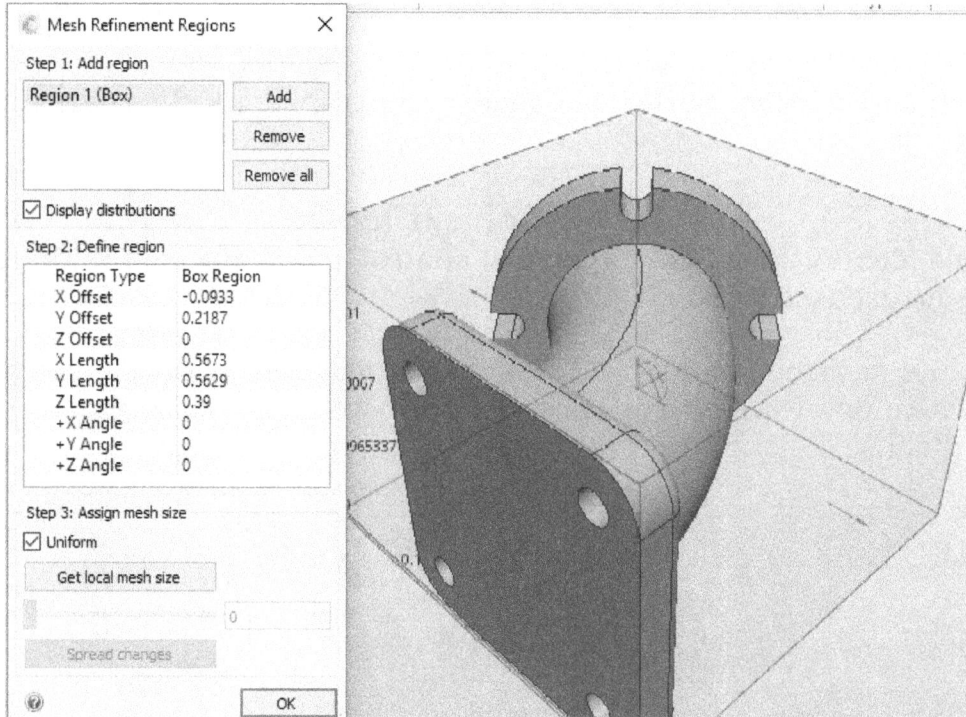

Figure-34. Mesh Refinement Regions dialog box

- The basic guidelines for mesh distribution is that it must be efficient to resolve the flow and temperature gradient effectively. In some regions, the coarser mesh is sufficient where the flow moves in single direction. But in case of various direction, the fine mesh is required.
- The **Mesh Refinement Regions** tool is used to create a mesh in a particular area, where geometry of design is not available. It is important to note that refinement regions are not real geometry, and cannot hold any other settings like boundary conditions and material.
- Click on the **Add** button from **Mesh Refinement Regions** dialog box, the **Region 1 (Box)** will be created and displayed on the model.
- To add more box, click again on the **Add** button.
- Click in the **Region Type** drop-down from **Step 2: Define region** area of the **Mesh Refinement Regions** dialog box and select the shape of region from the list; refer to Figure-35.

Figure-35. Selecting region type

- Click in the edit boxes from **Step 2: Define region** area section of **Mesh Refinement**

Regions dialog box and enter the desired values to set the shape & size of refinement region.

- You can also adjust the shape and size of refinement region by moving the drag handle from Graphics window.
- Select the **Uniform** check box from **Step 3: Assign mesh size** area section to create a mesh with single size element because the mesh in the selected region is based on geometry enclosed within the region.
- Clear the **Uniform** check box to allow the mesh size to produce more efficient mesh.
- Click on the Get local mesh size button from Mesh Refinement Regions dialog box to define a varying mesh. The mesh size edit box will be activated.
- The default value is adjusted to 1. You can enter the desired value from 0 to 1 in the respective edit box or specify the value by moving the mesh size slider. The lower the size, more coarse the size of **Mesh Size Refinement** region.
- Click on the **Spread Changes** button from **Mesh Refinement Region** dialog box to propagate the effect of mesh in the selected region.
- To remove the desired region, select the region box from **Mesh Refinement Regions** dialog box and click on the **Remove** button. The selected region will be removed.
- If you want to remove all the region, click on the **Remove All** button from **Mesh Refinement Region dialog** box.
- After specifying the parameters, click on the **OK** button from **Mesh Refinement Region** dialog box. The refinement region will be created on the model; refer to Figure-36.

Figure-36. Selected mesh refienemnt region

- The created refinement region will be added in Design Tree with the name as Automatic size and Region (Box).

Identify potential problem areas

The **Identify potential problem areas** tool is used to run a diagnostic on the model to identify the problems of mesh like problematic surfaces. Identifying these problems and locating them before running an analysis is necessary to reduce the effort and wasted time. The procedure to use this is discussed next.

This diagnostic function searches for surfaces and edges that are extremely thin & small relative to other parts of model. These entities are caused by poor geometric design or the result of multiple design format conversion throughout the life of model designing.

- Click on the **Identify potential problem areas** button from **Meshing Context Toolbar**. The **Diagnostics** dialog box will be displayed; refer to Figure-37.

Figure-37. Diagnostics dialog box

- The **Edge** tab is active by default in **Diagnostics** dialog box.
- Select the **Arrows** check box to view the arrows upon the affected edges; refer to Figure-38.

Figure-38. Arrows on highlighted reas

- Click in the **Highlight edges** edit box and enter the value to highlight the edges of smaller values as per entered value. You can also specify the value by moving the **Highlight Edges** slider.

- Click in the **Max size** edit box and enter the maximum value to locate the edges of size less than entered value. Edges will be highlighted accordingly.
- Click on the **Restore default max** button to reset maximum value for edges.
- Click on the **Save to a text file** button to save the data of displayed edge in a format of text file. The **Save File** dialog box will be displayed. Specify the desired location and click on the **Save** button.
- Click on the **Save to a group** button from **Diagnostics** dialog box to save the displayed edge to a group. The **Add to Group** dialog box will be displayed.
- Click in the **Min refinement length** edit box and enter the desired value of edge length.
- Click on the **Use highlight length** button to select the length of highlighted edges of the model in the **Min refinement length** edit box.
- Click on the **Restore minimum length scale** button from **Diagnostics** dialog box to reset the entered data.
- Click on the **Surfaces** tab from **Diagnostics** dialog box, the tools to detect the thin surfaces will be displayed; refer to Figure-39. Options in the **Surface** tab are used to identify potentially problematic surface that may cause problem while generating mesh, like silvers surface, thin annular surface, and surface with the cusp.

Figure-39. Surfaces tab of Diagnostics dialog box

- Move the **Highlight surfaces** slider or enter the value manually in the **Highlight Surfaces** edit box to specify the value for detecting the surfaces with edge length less than the entered value.
- Check the **Status** after specifying the value. When status shows "**No Problems Found**" then there is no problem in the design of model. But, if status shows "**Potential Problems Found**" then some surfaces of model are less than the entered value in **Highlight Surfaces**.
- Other tools of **Surfaces** tab are same as discussed in **Edge** tab.
- After specifying the parameters, click on the **Close** button.

Suppress (no mesh)

The **Suppress** tool is used to suppress the selected body. The suppressed body is removed temporarily from the model so that it cannot interfere in analysis. The procedure is discussed next.

- Click on the selected part of model. The **Meshing Context Toolbar** will be displayed.

- Click on the **Suppress** button from the displayed menu. If you had not created any mesh on the selected part then the selected part will be suppressed. But if, you had created any mesh on the selected part, the **Suppress Confirmation** box will be displayed; refer to Figure-40.

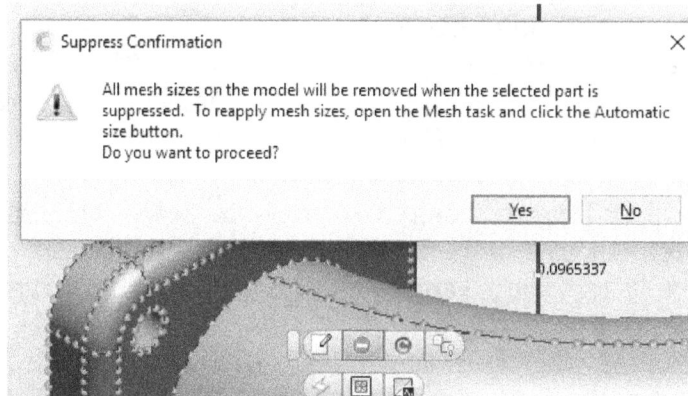

Figure-40. Suppress Confirmation box

- Click on the **Yes** button to confirm, the part will be suppressed.

*** End of Chapter ***

FOR STUDENTS NOTES

FOR STUDENTS NOTES

Model Setup in Autodesk CFD

Chapter 3

Topics Covered

The major topics covered in this chapter are:

- *Applying Materials*
- *Boundary Conditions*
- *Initials Conditions*
- *Generating Mesh*
- *Motion tool*

INTRODUCTION

In the last chapter, we have learned the interface of software and tools for navigation through the model. In this chapter, we will learn the procedure of applying material, boundary condition, initial Conditions, etc. on the model.

APPLYING MATERIALS

Material is a key input for any analysis. The result of analysis is directly related to material of the object. There are few properties of material like, ultimate strength, hardness, and young's modulus which play important role in success/failure of the object under specified load. Also, material determines the application of object in real world. For example, we do not use glass to make pistons in engine. That's why, the selection of material should be good enough to perform the analysis. The procedure to apply material is discussed next.

- Open the Autodesk CFD 2018 from Start menu or from Desktop icon. The Autodesk CFD 2018 will be opened and welcome screen will be displayed.
- Click on the **New** button from **Ribbon** and open the desired part file which is compatible with Autdodek CFD to work with. The part file will be displayed along with all activated tools for creating an analysis; refer to Figure-1. The procedure to create a new analysis has been discussed in previous chapter.

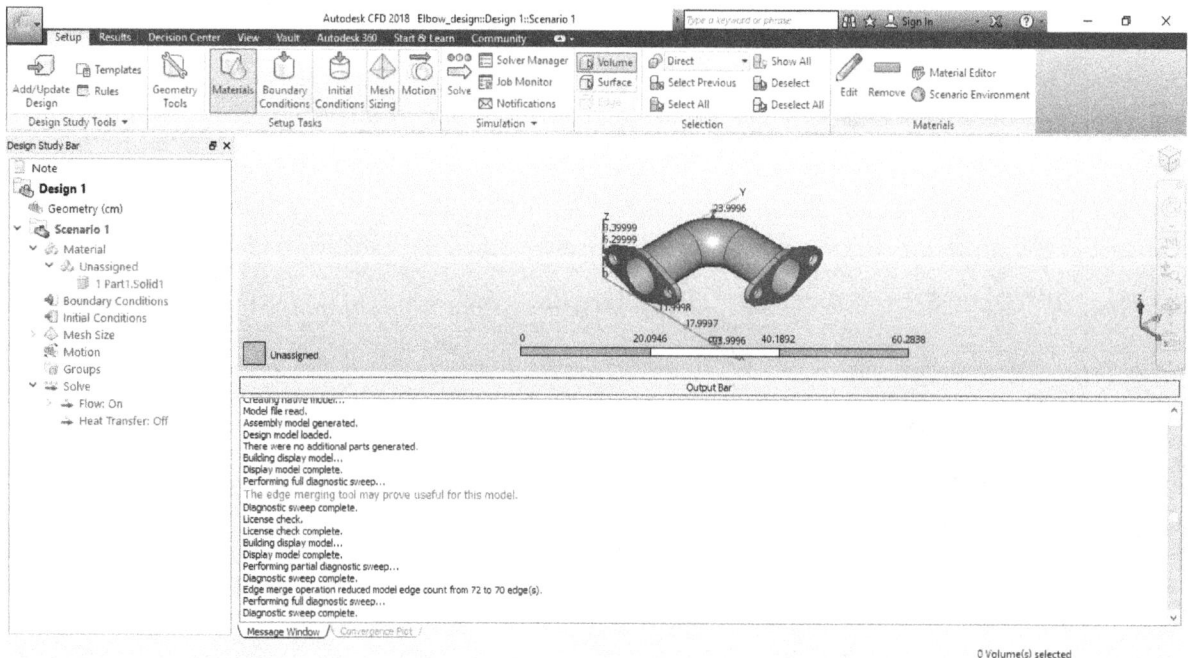

Figure-1. Welcome screen for elbow design

- On starting the analysis, the **Design Study Bar** will be displayed at the left in the application window. Various options are available in **Design Study Bar** to assign material, apply boundary condition, create mesh, and so on.
- After adding model in Autodesk CFD 2018, the first step for running an analysis is to assign material to the model. Either it is blank space in the form of air or a metal part, you need to assign proper material to the model. The analysis of model depends on the type of material assigned to various components of model.

Method First

- Click on the **Materials** button from **Setup Tasks** panel of **Setup** tab and then click on the **Edit** button from **Materials** panel; refers to Figure-2. The **Materials** dialog box will be displayed; refer to Figure-3.

Figure-2. Setup tab

Figure-3. Materials dialog box

- The parameters and details of **Materials** dialog box will on discussed later in this chapter.

Second Method

- Right-click on the unassigned part of model from **Design Study Bar**. The right-click menus will be displayed; refer to Figure-4

Figure-4. Material right-click menu

- Click on the **Edit** button from the displayed menu. The **Materials** dialog box will be displayed.

Third Method

- Click on the **Materials** button from **Setup Tasks** panel of **Setup** tab. The material options will be activated.
- Left-click on the model, the context toolbar will be displayed. Click on the **Edit** button from the displayed toolbar; refer to Figure-5. The **Materials** dialog box will be displayed.

Figure-5. Context toolbar of model

- When we click anywhere in the graphic window then the context toolbar for material is displayed because we have selected the **Materials** tool from **Setup Tasks** panel. If we were selected the **Boundary Conditions** button or **Initial Conditions** button or any other tool, the context toolbar related to that selected parameter will be displayed instead of **Materials** dialog box.

Forth Method

- After selecting **Materials** tool from **Setup Tasks** panel in the **Ribbon**. Right-click anywhere on the Graphics window. The right-click menus will be displayed; refer to Figure-6.

Figure-6. Right-click menus for Material

- Click on the **Edit** button from right-click menu. The **Materials** dialog box will be displayed.
- Make sure, the **Default** option is selected in **Material DB Name** drop-down, because the default list contains all the materials which are going to be used while analysis.
- Click in the **Type** drop-down from **Materials** dialog box and select the required material type; refer to Figure-7.

Figure-7. Material type drop-down

- Each material type list contains various materials of same kind. Click in the **Name** dialog box from **Materials** drop-down and select the required material; refer to Figure-8.

Figure-8. Selecting material for model

- Click on the **Set** button for **Environment** option, the **Material Environment** dialog box will be displayed; refer to Figure-9. The environment settings are only applicable to solid and fluid materials.

Figure-9. Material Environment dialog
box

- For some analysis, material property are constant with respect to time and for other simulations, material property needs to vary with time, like natural convection, and high-speed compressible simulations.
- To simulate these types of analysis, the material properties must be allowed to vary. The default material type list contains a single version of each material which can be applied to model.
- On selecting a material in the **Material Environment** dialog box, the properties of selected material will be displayed.
- Select the **Fixed** radio button from **Material Environment** dialog box to keep environment properties constant.
- Select the **Variable** radio button from **Material Environment** dialog box to vary properties as defined in the material. Note that, only properties defined with a variable method will vary.
- By default, the **Use scenario environment** check box from **Material Environment** dialog box will be selected which means it uses the data specified in **Scenario Environment** dialog box. Clear the **Use scenario environment** check box to set the temperature different from **Scenario Environment** dialog box.
- Click in the **Temperature** edit box and specify the required value.
- Click on the **Temperature unit** drop-down and select the desired unit.
- Similarly, specify pressure and pressure unit as required.
- Click on the **OK** button from dialog box to apply parameters.

Scenario Environment

The **Scenario Environment** dialog box is used to set the environment conditions for an individual material. Sometime, the scenario environment value is not sufficient to define the material property, if materials operates at different conditions, like two types of fluid flowing in a model. The procedure to use this is discussed next.

- Click on **Scenario Environment** tool from **Materials** panel of **Setup** tab, the **Scenario Environment** dialog box will be displayed; refer to Figure-10.

Figure-10. Scenario Environment

- Click in the **Pressure** edit box from **Scenario Environment** dialog box and enter the desired value.
- Click on the **Pressure unit** drop-down and select the desired unit for pressure from the displayed list.
- Click in the **Temperature** edit box from **Scenario Environment** dialog box and enter the desired value.
- Click on the **Temperature unit** drop-down and select the desired unit for pressure from the displayed list.
- After specifying the parameters, click on the **OK** button. The parameters for scenario environment will be specified.
- After specifying the desired parameters from **Material Environment** dialog box, click on the **OK** button.

Material Editor

- Click on the **Edit** button from **Materials** dialog box; refer to Figure-11. The **Material Editor** will be displayed; refer to Figure-12.

Figure-11. Edit button from Material dialog Box

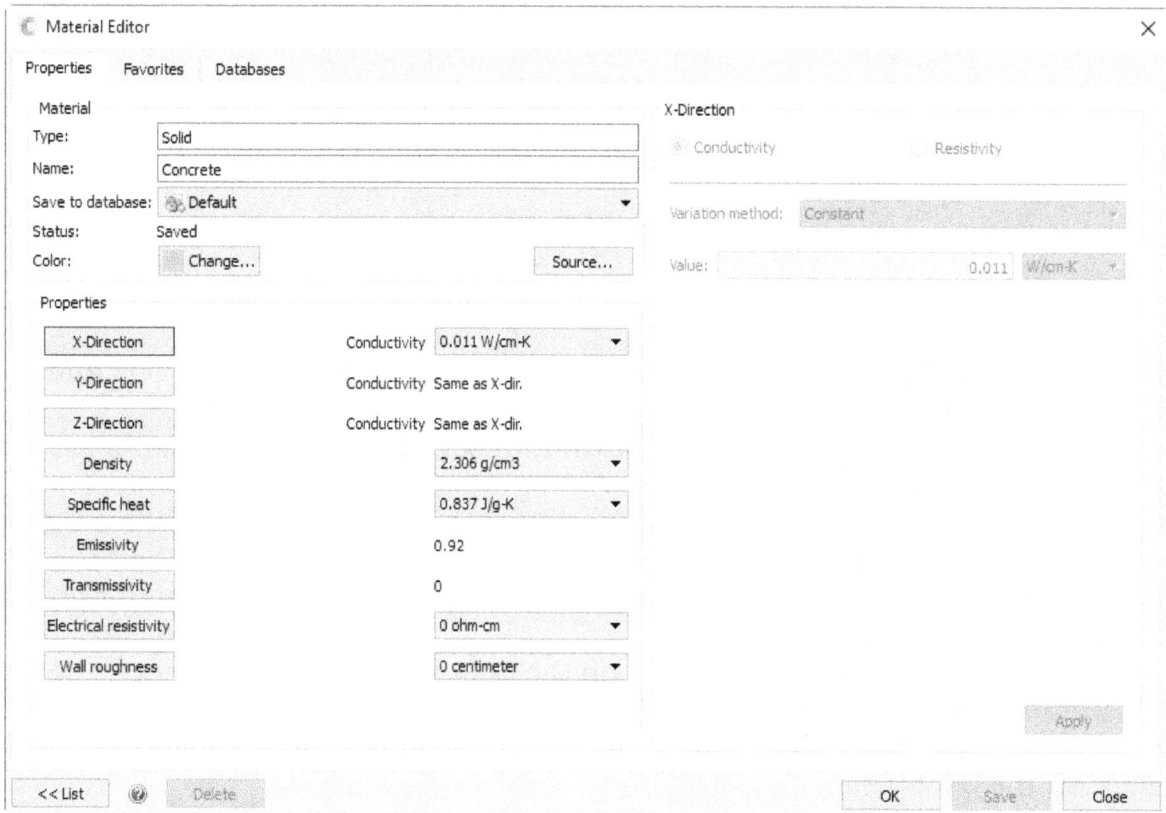

Figure-12. Material Editor dialog box

- You can also open the **Material Editor** dialog box from **Materials** panel of **Setup** tab by clicking on **Material Editor** button; refer to Figure-13

Figure-13. Material Editor
button

- The **Material Editor** dialog box is used to view the parameters of default fluid. You can also create a new material as per your desired parameters in **Material Editor** dialog box.
- There are three tabs in the **Material Editor** dialog box, i.e. **Properties** tab, **Favorites** tab, and **Database** tab. The options in these tabs are discussed next.

Properties tab

- By default, the properties tab is selected in **Material Editor** dialog box. In the **Properties** tab, you cannot change the parameters of a material, you can check the parameters.
- The name of selected parameter for a specific model will be displayed in **Name** edit box.
- The **Save to database** option shows the location, where the selected material is saved.
- Click on the **Change** button next to **Color** option to change the color of model..
- Click on the **Source** button from **Material Editor** dialog box to view the source

of material. The **Material Values Source** dialog box will be displayed; refer to Figure-14

Figure-14. Material Values Copper box

- View the source of material and click on the **OK** button. You will be returned to **Material Editor** dialog box.
- The parameters of selected material are shown under **Properties** section.
- Click on the **<<List** button from **Material Editor** dialog box to view the list of all fluid present in Autodesk CFD 2018; refer to Figure-15.

Figure-15. List button

- If you want to search a material from list of material to save time, click in the **Search** edit box and enter the name of desired material.
- Click on the **Type** drop-down from **Select** section and select the desired type of material type. After selection of material type, the materials of selected type will be displayed.

- Click on the **Database** drop-down from the **Refine selection** section and select the desired database to only view the material of selected database.
- Click on the desired material from the list. The properties will be displayed at right.
- If you use some of the materials frequently for analyses then you can add these material to your favorite material list. To do so, right-click on the material, a right-click menus will be displayed; refer to Figure-16.

Figure-16. Add to favorities button

- Click on the **Add to favorites** button from the displayed list, the selected material will be added to favorite material list and a red star will be displayed on the material icon.
- You can also save the selected material to **My Material** database by clicking on the **My Materials** button from **Save to** cascading menu of right-click shortcut menu.

Adding New Material

To add new material, right-click on the **My Materials** node. The right-click menus will be displayed; refer Figure-17.

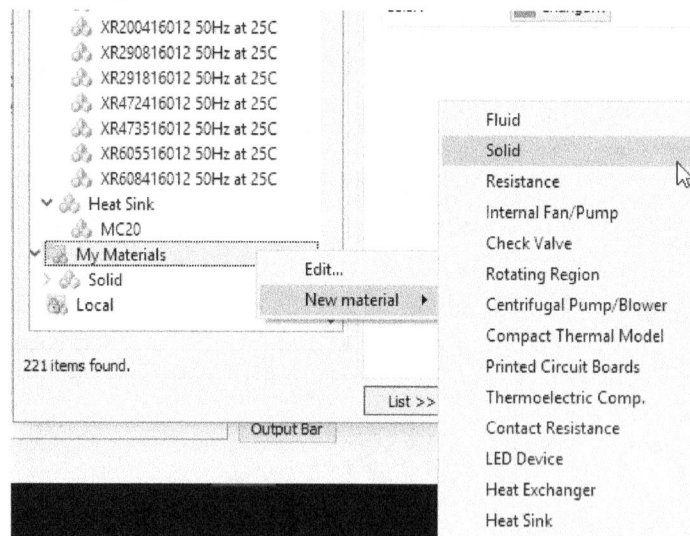

Figure-17. Adding new Material

- Hover the cursor to **New Material** option. The cascading menu will be displayed.
- Click on the desired material type. The **Properties** tab will be displayed; refer to Figure-18

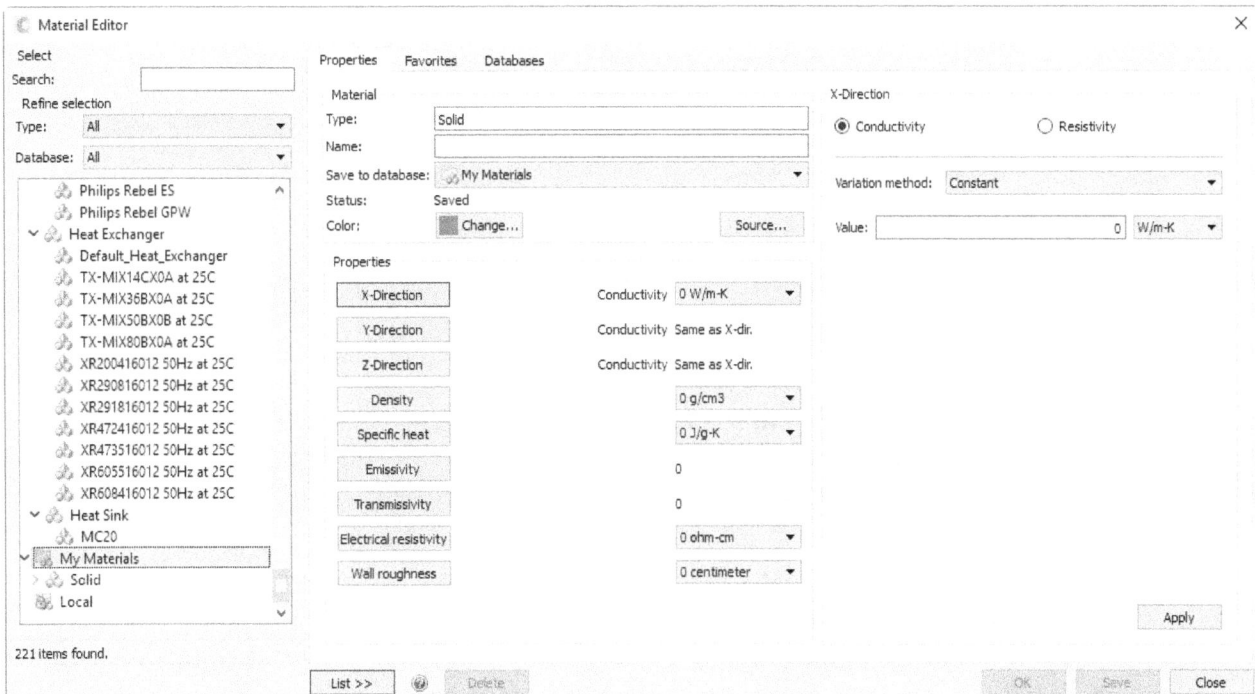

Figure-18. Specifying properties of new material

- Now, specify the properties & parameters as required in **Material Editor** dialog box to create a new material and click on the **Apply** button to apply parameters to new material.
- Click on the **Save** button from **Material Editor** dialog box. The material will be created and could be used in current analysis. The newly created material will be added under **My Material** database.
- If you want to remove the selected material then, click on the **Remove** button from **Material** dialog box. The material will be removed from model and model material will be **Unassigned**.
- After specifying the parameters, click on the **Apply** button from **Materials** dialog box. The selected material will be applied on the model.

APPLYING BOUNDARY CONDITIONS

The **Boundary Conditions** option is used to create flow inlet and outlet boundary conditions as well as wall conditions of selected fluid-contacting faces for both internal and external flow analyses. Also, thermal wall conditions can be created on selected external walls for internal flow analyses with enabled heat conductions in solid. For 3D models, you can apply these conditions to model surfaces and for 2D models, you can apply boundary conditions to edges.

Boundary conditions connect the model with surroundings. Without boundary conditions, the analysis cannot be defined. Mostly boundary conditions can be defined in two state i.e. steady state and transient state. Steady state boundary condition persist throughout the analysis process and transient boundary condition vary with time throughout the process. The procedure to use this tool is discussed next.

- Open the desired model in Autodesk CFD 2018 and apply the material as required.
- Before applying the boundary conditions on the surface of model, you need to enable the **Boundary Conditions** task by clicking on it from **Setup Tasks** panel of **Setup** tab; refer to Figure-19. The **Boundary Conditions** tool will be enabled.

Figure-19. Boundary Condition tool

- When you are applying **Boundary Conditions** in a fluid flow model then you need to make sure you apply proper lids on the openings of model.
- There are various methods to apply the boundary conditions to the model which are discussed next.

First Method

- After activating the **Boundary Conditions** tool from the **Setup Tasks** panel and click on the **Edit** button from **Boundary Conditions** panel of **Setup** tab; refer to Figure-20. The **Boundary Conditions** dialog box will be displayed; refer to Figure-21.

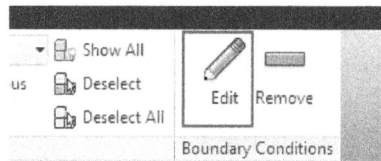

Figure-20. Edit button of Boundary conditions tool

- Set the desired parameters for boundary conditions in the dialog box.

Figure-21. Boundary Conditions dialog box

- To apply the boundary condition on a particular surface, you need to click on the surface from model before clicking on **Apply** button from **Boundary Conditions** dialog box.

Second Method

- Right-click on the **Boundary Conditions** option from **Design Study Bar**, the right-click menus will be displayed; refer to Figure-22.

Figure-22. Edit button from Boundary Conditions option

- Click on the **Edit** button from displayed menu, the **Boundary Conditions** dialog box will be displayed as discussed earlier with parameters of earlier specified boundary conditions.

- Click on the **New BC** tool from displayed right-click menu to create a new boundary condition. The **Boundary Conditions** dialog box will be displayed.
- To apply the boundary condition on a particular surface, you need to click on the surface from model before clicking on **Apply** button from **Boundary Conditions** dialog box.

Third Method

- After activating **Boundary Conditions** tool from **Setup Tasks** panel, left-click on the surface on which you want to apply boundary condition. The **Context Toolbar** will be displayed; refer to Figure-23.

Figure-23. Context Toolbar for Boundary Condition

- Click on the **Edit** button from displayed menu, the **Boundary Conditions** dialog box will be displayed; refer to Figure-24.

Figure-24. Boundary Conditions dialog box after selecting face

- There are various types of boundary conditions available in Autodesk CFD 2018, which you can apply on boundaries as required. Some important boundary conditions are given below.

Velocity

Velocity boundary condition is commonly used as inlet boundary condition in a model. Velocity boundary condition can be specified as normal to the selected surface. You can apply the velocity to outlet of a model but, direction should be out of the model.

Rotational Velocity

The Rotational Velocity boundary condition apply rotational velocity to a wall and is used for simulating a rotating object surrounded by the selected fluid, like a rotating plate in a fluid.

Volume Flow Rate

The Volume Flow Rate Boundary Condition is applied to planer openings of model. Generally, it is used in inlet conditions and also when the density of fluid is constant throughout the analysis. This boundary condition can also be applied to flow outlet, if the direction of flow is out of model. When applying this boundary condition to multiple surfaces of the model at same time, the flow direction must be the same.

Mass Flow Rate

The Mass Flow Rate boundary condition is applied to planer inlets and outlets. It is generally used as inlet boundary condition. This boundary condition can also be applied to flow outlet, if the direction of flow is out of model. If you are applying this boundary condition to multiple surfaces of the model at same time then the flow direction must be the same.

Pressure

The Pressure boundary condition is generally used as outlet condition. The recommended outlet condition is static atmospheric pressure of 1 atm for open environment.. After applying this condition, no other condition are needed to apply at outlet.

Temperature

The Temperature boundary condition is used to apply temperature condition at desired location on the model.

Slip/Symmetry

The Slip/Symmetry boundary condition causes the fluid to flow along a wall instead of stopping. Slip walls are useful for defining symmetric planes. The Slip condition can be used with a very low fluid viscosity to simulate Euler flow. In case of axisymmetric analysis, you do not need to apply symmetric condition manually because it is set automatically along the axis.

Unknown

The Unknown boundary condition is used when you have to apply open boundary condition where no other constraints are applied. Mostly, this boundary condition is used at the outlet of compressible flow analysis like for supersonic flow, where neither the outlet pressure nor the velocity are known. There is no value associated with unknown condition.

Scalar

The Scalar boundary condition is a unitless quantity ranging between 0 and 1 that represent the concentration of the scalar quantity for tracking concentrations.

Humidity

The Humidity is a unitless quantity ranging between 0 to 1 that represent relative humidity. Here, 1 represent a humidity level of 100%.

- Click on the **Type** drop-down from **Boundary Conditions** dialog box and select the required boundary condition. In our case, we are selecting **Velocity** boundary condition.
- Click on the **Unit** drop-down from **Boundary Conditions** dialog box and select the desired unit. In our case, we are selecting **mm/min** unit.
- Click on the **Time** drop-down from **Boundary Conditions** dialog box and select the required option. Select **Steady State** option if you want to set fixed values of boundary conditions with respect to time. Select the **Transient** option if you want to specify time curve for variation of boundary condition values.
- Click on the **Method** drop-down from **Boundary Conditions** dialog box and select the **Normal** button to apply velocity normal to the selected surface and select the **Component** button to specify velocity along three major axes..
- Click on the **Reverse Normal** button from **Boundary Conditions** dialog box to reverse the direction of fluid velocity. On clicking this button, you could notice the change in direction of Normal arrow pointing toward or away from the selected surface.
- Click on the **Spatial Variations** drop-down from **Boundary Conditions** dialog box and select **Constant** button to define the variations as constant. Select **Fully Developed** button to specify the entrance of the model as fully developed. Pipe and ducts flow are assumed to be fully developed. The fully developed flow profile is more realistic than a uniform (slug) profile.
- Click on the **Spatial Variations** drop-down from **Boundary Conditions** dialog box and select **Linear Variations** button to vary a velocity or temperature boundary condition in one dimensional across a boundary surface.
- Click in the **Velocity Magnitude** edit box from **Boundary Conditions** dialog box and specify the value of boundary condition.
- After specifying the parameters, click on the **Apply** button to create the boundary condition on the selected surface; refer to Figure-25. A colored line will be created on the selected surface and the created boundary condition will be mentioned at lower left of the screen; refer to Figure-26.
- If you want to delete the boundary current condition, click on the **Remove** button from **Boundary Conditions** dialog box. The current boundary condition will be deleted from the selected surface.

Figure-25. Applied boundary condition

Figure-26. Colored stip

- Similarly, create the boundary condition at outlet of the model; refer to Figure-27.

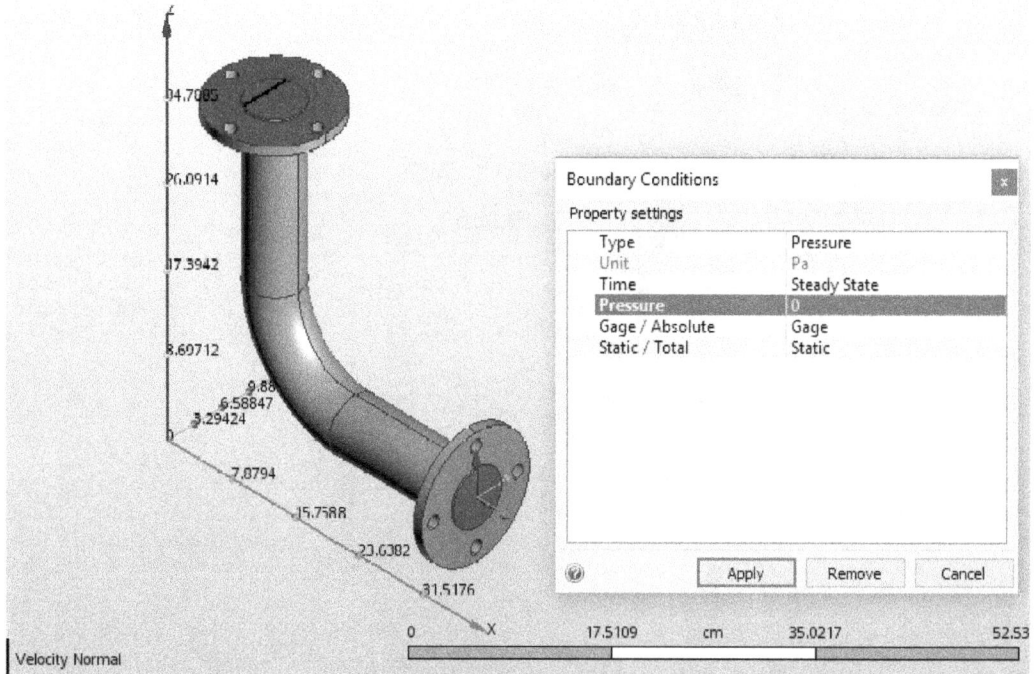

Figure-27. Outlet condition

- In most fluid flow cases, we use **Pressure** boundary condition at outlet for a natural outlet.
- The colored strip will be created after clicking on **Apply** button from **Boundary Conditions** dialog box; refer to Figure-28.

Figure-28. Colored strips of boundary conditions

INITIAL CONDITIONS

The **Initial Conditions** tool is used to apply initial conditions in an analysis. These conditions are different from Boundary Conditions because these conditions are only applicable at the beginning of analysis. These conditions are primarily used for transient analysis, but sometimes these could be used for steady state analyses under some circumstances.

Sometimes, the **Initial Conditions** tool is not visible to Autodesk CFD 2018 **Ribbon**. To activate this, you need to follow these following steps:

- Click on the **Application** button at the top left corner of application window, the **Application** menu will be displayed; refer to Figure-29.

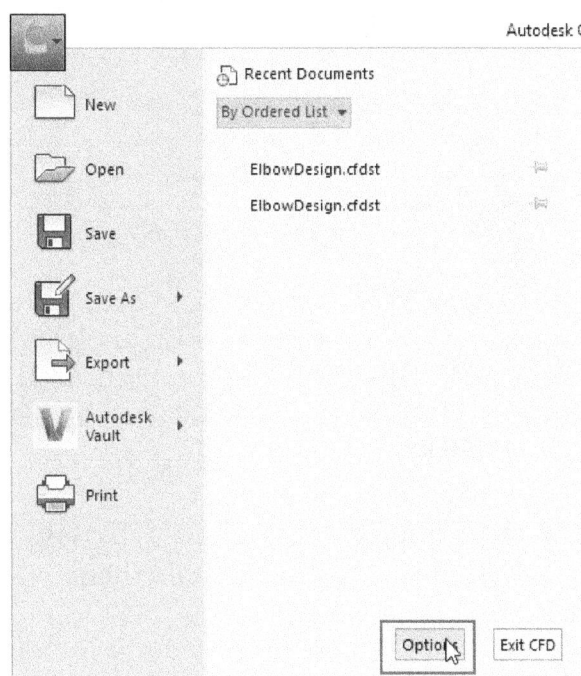

Figure-29. Application menu

- Click on the **Options** button from menu, the **User Interface Preferences** dialog box will be displayed; refer to Figure-30.

Figure-30. User Interface Preferences dialog-box

- Click on the **Show Initial conditions task icon** drop-down from **User Interface Preferences** dialog box and click on the **Yes** button. You can also set the desired settings and parameters from this dialog box as required.
- After specifying the parameters, click on the **OK** button. The **Initial Conditions** tool will be activated in **Ribbon**.

Applying Initial Conditions

- Click on the **Initial Conditions** button from **Ribbon**. The **Initial Conditions** tool will be activated.
- The method of opening the **Initial Conditions** dialog box is similar to the methods which were discussed in last section, i.e. by **Edit** button.
- Click on the **Edit** tool from **Initial Conditions** panel of **Setup** tab; refer to Figure-31. The **Initial Conditions** dialog box will be displayed; refer to Figure-32.

Figure-31. Edit button of Initial Conditions tool

Figure-32. Initial Conditions dialog box

- Click on the surface of the model where you want to apply initial boundary condition.

Note: You can apply the initial boundary condition to a specific volume of model. What you have to do is select the **Volume** button from **Selection** panel in place of **Surface** button; refer to Figure-33. In our case, we are selecting the **Surface** button to apply initial condition.

Figure-33. Selection panel

- Click on the **Type** drop-down from **Initial Conditions** dialog box and select the desired initial boundary condition. These conditions have already been discussed earlier.
- Click on the **Unit** drop-down from **Initial Conditions** dialog box and select the desired unit of selected condition type.
- The **Re-initialize** check box of **Initial Conditions** is activated when you had done a simulation before. This tool is used to reset the condition on the selected parts, like to re-initialize the temperature after flow simulation to see how the temperature varies with time.
- Click on the **Method** drop-down from **Initial Conditions** dialog box and select the required option.
- Click in the **Velocity Magnitude** edit box from **Initial Conditions** dialog box and specify the desired value of the selected conditions. The name of this edit box will be changed as per selected condition.
- Click on the **Direction** drop-down and select the required option.
- After specifying the parameters, click on the **Apply** button from **Initial Conditions** dialog box; refer to Figure-34. The initial condition will be created and added in **Design Study Bar**.

Figure-34. Applying Initial conditions

GENERATING MESH

The **Mesh** tool is used to display the computational mesh cells and mesh related parameters at the calculation moment selected for getting the results. The software estimates a global element size for the model taking into consideration its volume, surface area, and other geometric details. The size of the generated mesh (number of nodes and elements) depends on the geometry and dimensions of the model, element size, mesh tolerance, mesh control, and contact specifications. In the early stages of design analysis where approximate results may suffice, you can specify a larger element size for a faster solution. For a more accurate solution, a smaller element size may be required.

Meshing generates 3D tetrahedral solid elements, 2D triangular shell elements, and 1D beam elements. A mesh consists of one type of elements unless the mixed mesh type is specified. Solid elements are naturally suitable for bulky models. Shell elements are naturally suitable for modeling thin parts (sheet metals), and beams and trusses are suitable for modeling structural members.

The procedure to create the mesh of the solid is given next.

* Click on the **Mesh Sizing** tool from **Setup Tasks** panel to activate mesh tool; refer to Figure-35. The **Mesh Sizing** tool will be activated and other tools related to mesh will be displayed.

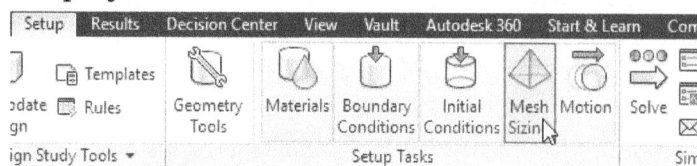

Figure-35. Mesh Sizing tool

Automatic Mesh Generation

- Click on the **Automatic** button from **Type** panel of **Setup** tab to enable automatic mesh sizing of the model; refer to Figure-36.

Figure-36. Type panel

- Click on the **Autosize** button from **Automatic Sizing** panel to generate mesh automatically. The mesh will be generated in the form of blue dots on the edges of model; refer to Figure-37.

Figure-37. Automatically generated mesh

- The generated mesh will also be displayed in **Design Study Bar**; refer to Figure-38.

Figure-38. Automatic mesh in
Design Study Bar

- If you want to refine the mesh of the model, right-click on the **Surface Refinement** option from **Design Study Bar** and click on the **Edit** button; refer to Figure-39. The **Mesh Sizes** dialog box will be displayed; refer to Figure-40.

Figure-39. Edit button of Surface refinement

Figure-40. Mesh Sizes dialog box

- Select the **Surface Refinement** check box from **Automatic sizing refinement** section, the **Refine** button to refine the surface will be activated.
- Click on the **Refine** button, the mesh will be refined at its best.
- Select the **Gap Refinement** button from **Automatic sizing refinement** section to refine the gap present in the model. You can also open the **Mesh Sizes** dialog box by clicking on the **Edit** button from right-click menus of **Gap Refinement** option of **Design Study Bar**.
- Click on the **Refine** button, the mesh will be refined.
- After specifying the parameters, click on the **Apply** button from **Mesh Sizes** dialog box. The changes will be updated.

Manual Mesh Generation

- Click on the **Manual** button from **Type** panel of **Setup** tab; refer to Figure-41. The tools will be updated in the **Ribbon** as per **Manual** tool.

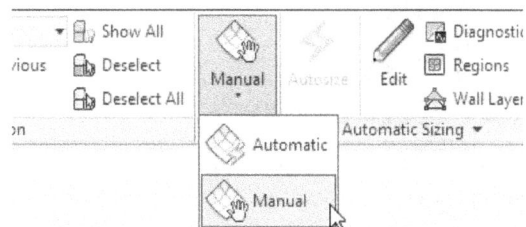

Figure-41. Manual button Type panel

- Click on the **Edit** button from **Automatic Sizing** panel of **Setup** tab, the manual **Mesh Sizes** dialog box will be displayed; refer to Figure-42

Figure-42. Manual Mesh Sizes dialog box

- To create mesh manually, you need to select the Surface, Volume, or Edge separately from the model to create the mesh of that selected part.
- To select the **Surface**, **Volume**, or **Model**, you will need to activate the respective button from **Selection** panel; refer to Figure-43.

Figure-43. Selection panel

- Click on the **Element Size** edit box from **Mesh Sizes** dialog box and enter the value; refer to Figure-44. Less the value of **Element Size**, more coarse the mesh will be.

Figure-44. Entering value for manual mesh

Wall Layers

The **Wall layers** tool is used to add element layer along all fluid walls and solid-fluid interface. It increases the original size of mesh to a great extent to produce a smooth distribution along corners, where original mesh is unable to reach. The **Wall layer** tool ensures proper spreading of mesh across small gaps and corners. This tool create layers before construction of 3D mesh. A gradual transition between surfaces ensure gradual variations in element height throughout the mode. The procedure to use this tool is discussed next.

Note: It is not possible to add layers to imported mesh, because wall layers are added before the generation of mesh.

- Click on the **Wall layer** button from **Mesh Sizes** dialog box, the **Wall Layer** dialog box will be displayed; refer to Figure-45

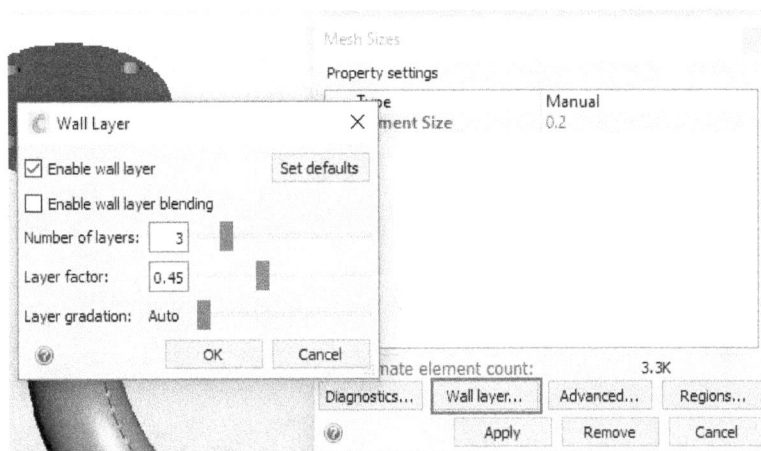

Figure-45. Wall Layer dialog box

- Select the **Enable Wall Layer** check box from **Wall Layer** dialog box to activate the tools related to wall layer. This check box is activated by default.
- Select the **Enable Wall Layer** blending check box from **Wall Layer** dialog box to create a more gradual transition in the selected region. By default, the transition between wall layer region and original mesh is instantaneous from highly anisotropic to isotropic.
- Click in the **Number of layers**: edit box and enter the value to control the number of layers of prismatic element. In some rotating-region analyses, you can improve the stability of layers by entering the value to 1. You can also set the **Number of Layers** by moving the respective slider.
- Click in the **Layer factor** edit box from **Wall Layer** dialog box and enter the value to control the thickness of layer. The method of determining the layer height of a particular surface is by multiplying the Layer factor by the local isotropic length scale. You can also specify the value of **Layer Factor** by moving the respective slider.
- Move the **Layer gradation** slider from **Wall Layer** dialog box to control the rate of growth of wall layers near wall. More the wall layer, more will be computational time. As the number of wall layers increases, the layer thickness often has a tendency to become uniform.
- Click on the **Set Defaults** button from **Wall Layer** dialog box to reset the entered parameters of **Wall Layer** dialog box.
- After specifying the parameters, click on the **OK** button from **Wall Layer** dialog box. You will be returned to **Mesh Sizes** dialog box.

Advanced

The Advanced button is used to specify several additional parameters for controlling mesh distribution over a selected part, surface, edge, and model. The procedure to use this button is discussed next.

- Click on the **Advanced** button from **Mesh Sizes** dialog box, the **Advanced Meshing Controls** dialog box will be displayed; refer to Figure-46.

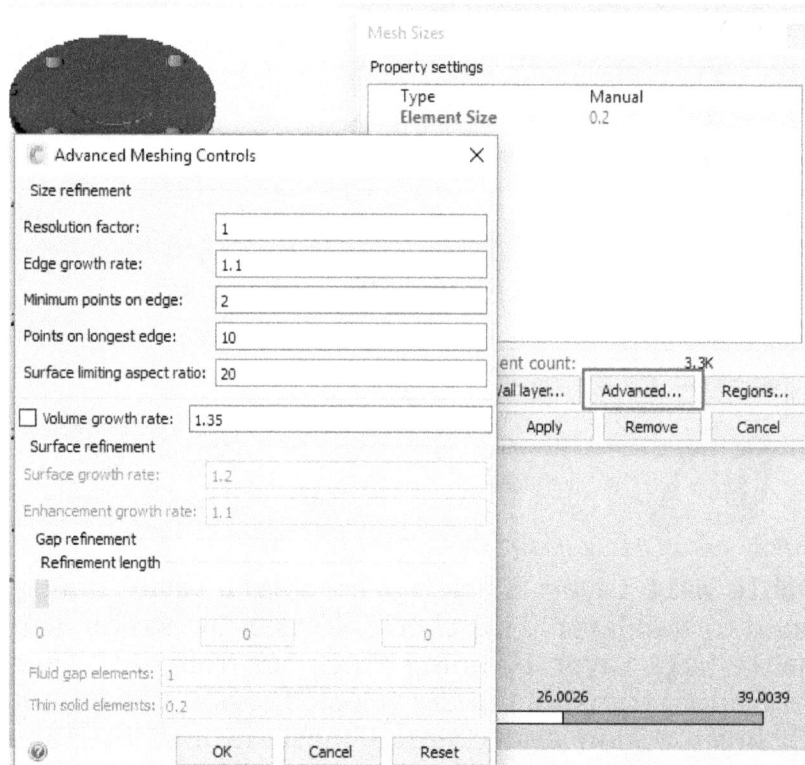

Figure-46. Advanced Meshing Controls dialog box

- Click in the **Resolution factor** edit box from **Advanced Meshing Controls** dialog box specify desired the value to control the relative fineness of the mesh in response to the curvature of model entities. The effects of Resolution factor are localized to region of high curvature. Smaller the value of Resolution factor, more fine will be the mesh on model with curvature. The model regions without curvature are not affected by this parameter. The acceptable range of this parameter is from 1 to 3. Beyond this range, values are rejected.
- Click in the **Edge growth rate** edit box and enter the value to control the quality of mesh distribution computed by automatic sizing. The smaller value of **Edge growth rate** cause slower variation in distribution from regions of high to low curvature. The 1.1 and 1.5 value of Edge growth rate represent 10% and 50% growth rate.
- Click in the **Minimum points of edge** edit box and enter the value to specify the minimum number of points on edge. For entities lacking curvature, a minimum level of resolution is guaranteed by this parameter.
- Click in the **Points on longest edges** edit box and enter the value to specify the points on longest edge of selected part. This tool is more relevant for geometry with no curvature, like surrounding box from external flow. This tool may create more points on longest edge as compared to the value specified in Longest Edge parameter.

- Click in the **Surface limiting aspects ratio** edit box and enter the value to introduce a constraint on length scale to ensure they are not larger than a specified factor of the dimensions of the surface. This tool is generally used in Automatic sizing of a mesh. This affects the distributions on edges bounding high aspect-ratio surfaces.

- Click in the **Volume growth rate** edit box and enter the value to control the volume elements grow. The range of entering the value is between 1.01 to 2.0. In this, the value of 1.1 and 1.4 cause the growth rate of 10% and 40% respectively.

- Other parameters of this dialog box were discussed earlier.

- After specifying the parameters, click on the **OK** button from **Advanced Meshing Controls** dialog box. You will be redirected to **Mesh Sizes** dialog box.

- The **Diagnostics** and **Regions** buttons were discussed earlier.

- After specifying the parameters, click on the **Apply** button from **Mesh Sizes** dialog box; refer to Figure-47. The mesh will be generated at selected part as per entered parameter. In our case, the coarser mesh is created; refer to Figure-48.

Figure–47. Mesh Sizes dialog box along with selected surface

Figure-48. Generated mesh

- The notification of created mesh will also be added in **Design Study Bar**; refer to Figure-49.

Figure-49. Mesh displayed in Design Study Bar

- If you want to delete any mesh then right-click on the **Surfaces** node of that mesh and click on the **Remove** button from displayed menu; refer to Figure-50. The selected mesh will be removed from model.

Figure-50. Right-click menu of mesh

- If you want to edit the parameters of mesh, then right-click on the desired mesh from **Design Study Bar** and click on the **Edit** button. The **Mesh Sizes** dialog box will be displayed.

- If you want to remove all the created mesh of a model then right-click on the **Mesh Size** option from **Design Study Bar** and click on the **Remove All** button from the displayed menu; refer to Figure-51.

Figure-51. Right-click menu of Mesh Size

- If you click on the **Generate mesh** button from right-click menus, the software start analysis of the model. The tools used to solve the analysis will be discussed in next chapter. So, hold on.

MOTION

The **Motion** tool is used to analyze the interaction between moving part of model to the surrounding fluid. The movement of the part could be angular and linear. With this tool, we can analyze the motion on fluid medium as well as flow induced forces on the model. The procedure to use this tool is discussed next.

- Click on the **Motion** button from the **Motion** panel in the **Ribbon** to activate the tool. The tools related to **Motion** will be displayed in **Motion** panel; refer to Figure-52.

Figure-52. Motion panel

- Click on the **Edit** button from **Motion** panel of **Setup** tab, the **Motion** dialog box will be displayed; refer to Figure-53.

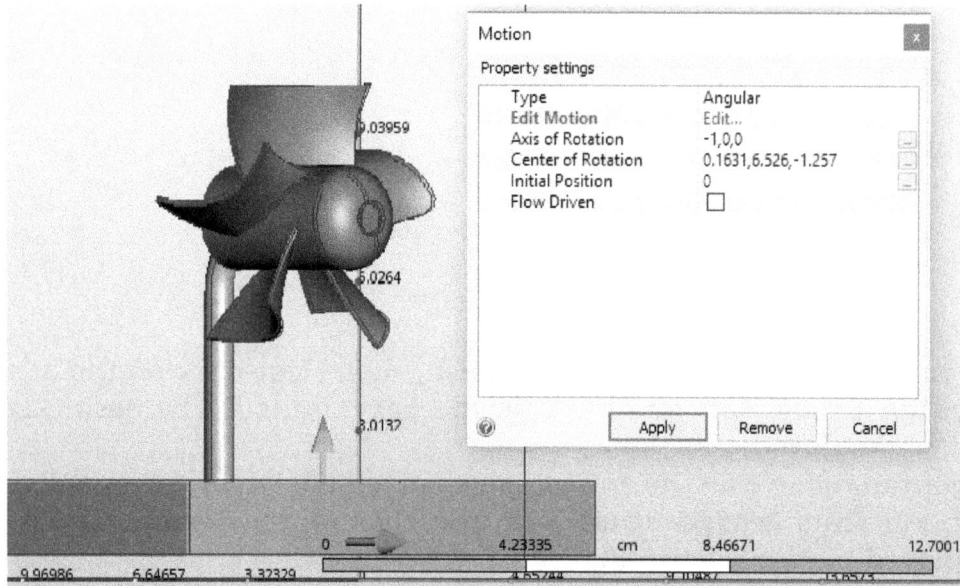

Figure-53. Motion dialog box

Types of Motion

Click on the **Type** drop-down from **Motion** dialog box, the motion type list will be displayed. There are seven types of motion available in Autodesk CFD 2018, which are discussed below.

Angular Motion

The **Angular** motion is the rotation of a part about an axis. Some examples are, displacement pumps, Gear pumps, check walls, Fan, Centrifugal pumps, Etc. The component in angular motion can have paths that interfere, like gear teeth, fan blades, Etc. The **Angular** motion dialog box is displayed as Figure-54.

Figure-54. Angular Motion dialog box

Linear Motion

The **Linear** motion is the motion of an object in a straight line. Some examples are, piston cylinder mechanism, values opening and closing, reciprocating motion, etc. The **Linear Motion** dialog box is displayed as Figure-55

Figure-55. Linear Motion dialog box

Combined Linear/Angular

The **Combined Linear/Angular** motion is used where we need to apply both the motions, i.e. angular motion and well as linear motion. The selected part will follow combined linear and angular motion. The directions of both the motions need to be specified in **Motion** dialog box. For flow indued rotation, developed torque is used to compute angular accelerations. The linear position of object is determined by user specifications or a result of flow induced forces.

If linear and angular motions are flow induced, it could be assumed that the two motions are uncoupled and work independently to each other. The axis of rotation is determined by translation of object. Some examples of Combined Linear/Angular motion are, rack and pinion gear, tightening screw.

The **Motion** dialog box for combined linear/angular motion is as shown in (Change all others in the same way) Figure-56.

Figure-56. Combined Linear/Angular dialog box

Combined Orbital/Rotational Motion

The **Combined Orbital/Rotational Motion** is used where the orbital motion and rotation motion works together. In this, the object rotates about its axis of rotation and also orbits about an axis parallel to its axis of rotation. Example like, epicyclic gear, solar system. The orbital speed of object is usually slower than the primary rotational speed. The **Combined Orbital/Rotational** motion dialog box for combined linear/angular motion is as shown in Figure-57.

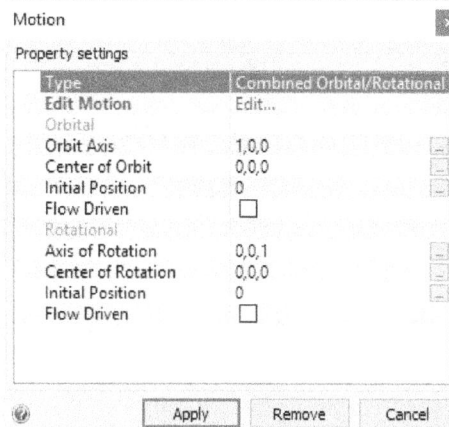

Figure-57. Combined Orbital Rotational motion dialog box

- The rotational and orbital motion of a component can either be user-prescribed or flow driven.

Nutating Motion

The **Nutating Motion** is used in several types of liquid flow meters. In Nutating motion, object is inclined at an angle to reference axis. When the normal vector of object rotates about the reference axis, the angle between normal vector and reference axis remains constant. The result is that the object actually wobbles about the reference axis, but does not change angular position relative to it. Example like, coin wobbling along its edge. In Nutating motion, the user needs to define three parameters to set-up nutating motion which are, tilt axis, the axis of nutation (Nutating axis), and centre of nutation. The **Nutating Motion** dialog box of combined linear/angular motion is as shown in Figure-58.

Figure-58. Nutating Motion dialog box

Sliding Vane Motion

Sliding Vane motion is a combination of angular motion and linear motion. In this, the path of linear translation is user defined , and is not changed by the rotational motion. The location of the axis of rotation is specified by the user. Example of this motion is, sliding-vane positive displacement pumps. In this type of pump, the pistons rotate about the center-line of the impeller, but translate radially. The direction of linear motion changes at every angular motion and the axis of rotation remains constant. The **Sliding Vane** dialog box of combined linear/angular motion is as shown in Figure-59.

Figure-59. Sliding Vane motion dialog box

Free Motion

The **Free Motion** allows motion of component in any direction. This is most easy type of motion from all and it can be used to stimulate partially constrained movement of objects within an active flow field. This motion type is flow driven and is defined by enabling or disabling any of the six degrees of freedom. The **Free Motion** dialog box of combined linear/angular motion is as shown in Figure-60.

Figure-60. Free Motion dialog box

Let's get back to specifying parameters for **Motion** dialog box.

- Click on the **Type** drop-down from **Motion** dialog box and select the required motion type. In our case, we are selecting **Angular** motion type.
- Click on the component from model at which you want to apply angular motion; refer to Figure-61.

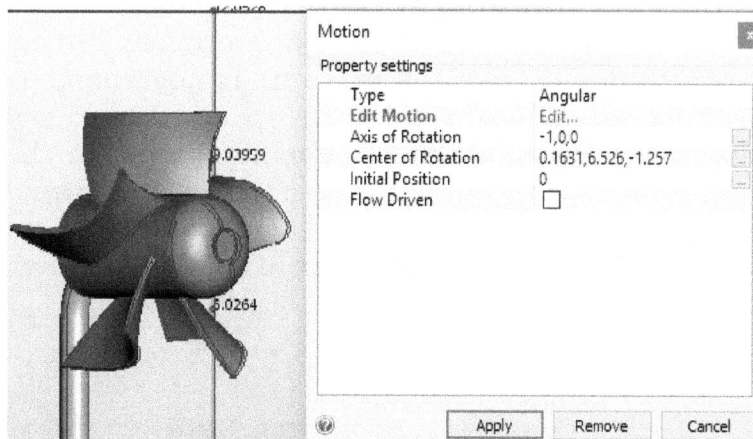

Figure-61. Selected component for angular motion

- Click on the **Edit** button of **Edit Motion** option from **Motion** dialog box, the **Motion Editor** dialog box will be displayed; refer to Figure-62.

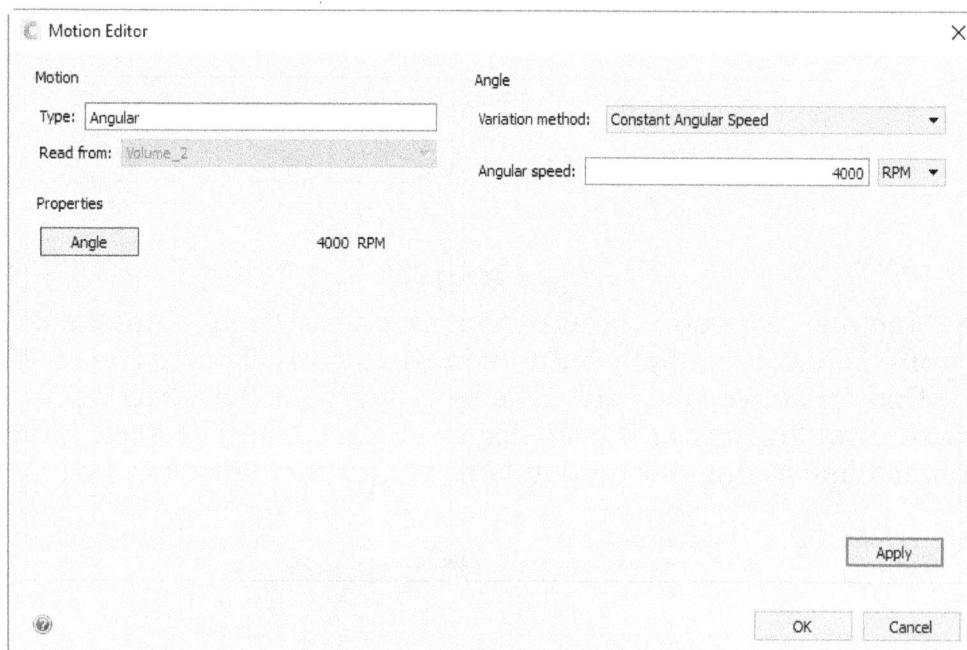

Figure-62. Motion Editor-dialog box

- The selected **Angular** motion type is displayed in **Motion Editor** dialog box. If we had selected any other motion type, then the selected motion type will be displayed here along with related parameters.
- Click on the **Variation method** drop-down from **Angle** section and select the **Constant Angular Speed** option to specify a constant angular speed for the selected part throughout the process.
- Click in the **Angular speed** edit box from **Angle** section and specify the rotation speed of selected part.
- Click on the **Units** drop-down and select the desired unit for rotation.
- Click on the **Variation method** drop-down from **Angle** section and select the **Oscillating** option to oscillate the selected component angularly through a prescribed angle, in a specified time. Parameters related to **Oscillating** option will be displayed in **Angle** section of **Motion Editor** dialog box.

- Click in the **Half period** time edit box from **Angle** dialog box and enter the value of time taken by object to rotate from start position to end position of angular displacement.
- Click in the **Angular Displacement** edit box and enter the value of included angle of stroke; refer to Figure-63.

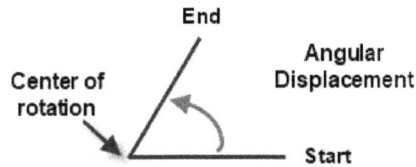

Figure-63. Angular Displacement

- Click on the **Variation method** drop-down from **Angle** section and select the **Table** option to specify angular position at specific times.
- Enter the data of Angle and Time in the table as desired.
- Select the **Cyclic** check box from **Motion Angle** section of **Motion Editor** dialog box to repeat only forward sweeps through the angle table.
- Select the **Reciprocating** check box from **Angle** section of **Motion Editor** dialog box to repeat forward and reverse sweeps through the angle table.
- After specifying the parameters from **Motion Editor** dialog box, click on the **Apply** button and then **OK** button, You will be redirected to **Motion** dialog box.

Axis of Rotation

- The **Axis of Rotation** button of **Motion** dialog box is used to set the axis of rotation of the selected component. The rotational direction of component is selected as per right hand thumb rule. You need to choose the X,Y, or Z axes to choose Cartesian direction as the axis of rotation.
- Click on the **Axis of Rotation** button from **Motion** dialog box, the **Axis of Rotation** box will be displayed; refer to Figure-64.

Figure-64. Axis of rotation box

- Click on the X,Y, or Z from **Axis of Rotation** box to set the direction of rotation of selected component as per right hand thumb rule; refer to Figure-65. In our case, we have selected the X axis.

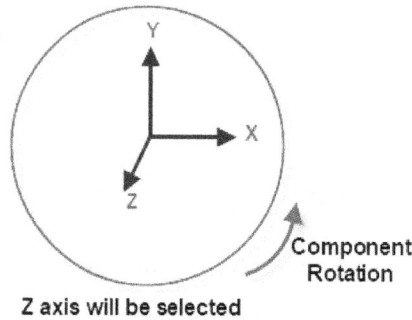

Z axis will be selected

Figure-65. Selection of direction

- Click on the **Inverse** button to reverse the rotation direction of selected component.
- The **(0,0,0)** from **Axis of Rotation** button of **Motion** dialog box is equals to **(X,Y,Z)** of **Axis of Rotation** box. Which means, when you select the X axis from **Axis of Rotation** box, **1** will be displayed in **Motion** dialog box in place of X, and if you also have selected the **Inverse** button from **Axis of Rotation** dialog box, **(-1,0,0)** will be displayed in **Axis of Rotation** button of **Motion** dialog box.
- Click on the **Select surface** button from **Axis of Rotation** dialog box to specify the rotation direction of component by selecting a surface from mode. The surface selection will be activated. The **Surface** will be selected and coordinates of surface will be displayed.

Center of Rotation

The **Center of Rotation** is used to specify the point through which axis of rotation passes. The procedure to use this is discussed next.

- Click on the **Center of Rotation** button from **Motion** dialog box, the **Center of Rotation** box will be displayed; refer to Figure-66.

Figure-66. Center of Rotation box

- Click on the **Select Surface** button from **Center of Rotation** box to specify the centre of rotation of component by selecting surface from model. The coordinates of selected surface will be displayed in **Motion** dialog box.

Initial Position

The **Initial Position** button is used to specify the initial angular position of the part from the as-built position of model. This tool is very helpful for fine tuning the model when the original position of the model is not appropriate. The procedure to use this is discussed next.

- Click on the **Initial Position** button from **Motion** dialog box. The **Initial Position** edit box will be activated and **Initial Position** box will be displayed; refer to Figure-67.

Figure-67. Initial Position box

- Enter the desired value in **Initial Position** edit box or move the **Initial Position** box slider to specify the initial position value. When you move the **Initial Position** slider, the selected component will also move, respectively.

Flow Driven

The **Flow Driven** check box from **Motion** dialog box is used to apply minimum and maximum limit of rotation to the selected component. In some cases, we don't want a full 360° rotation of component, what we want is a restricted rotation of component. In this type of condition, the **Flow Driven** tool is used. The procedure to use this is discussed next.

- Select the **Flow Driven** check box from **Motion** dialog box, the **Minimum Bound** and **Maximum Bound** options will be activated and displayed in **Motion** dialog box; refer to Figure-68.

Figure-68. Flow Driven check box

- The default value of **Maximum Bound** and **Minimum Bound** is set to **Unbounded** in **Motion** dialog box.
- Click on the **Minimum Bound** button, the **Minimum Bound** box will be displayed; refer to Figure-69.

Figure-69. Minimum Bound box

- Move the **Minimum Bound** slider to set the minimum rotation limit of the component.
- Click on the **Maximum Bound** button from **Motion** dialog box, the **Maximum Bound** box will be displayed; refer to Figure-70.

Figure-70. Maximum Bound box

- Move the **Maximum Bound** slider to set the maximum rotational limit of component. If you want to return back to unbound condition than click on the **Unbounded** button from **Maximum** Bound box.
- After specifying the parameters in **Motion** dialog box, click on the **Apply** button. The motion will be created and displayed in **Design Study bar**.
- Similarly, you can apply other types of motions to selected components.

*** End of Chapter ***

FOR STUDENTS NOTES

FOR STUDENTS NOTES

Solving Analysis

Chapter 4

Topics Covered

The major topics covered in this chapter are:

- *Control Tab*
- *Adaptation Tab*
- *Physics Tab*
- *Convergence Plot*

INTRODUCTION

In last chapters, we have learned the tools used for preparing the analysis. The understanding of those tools is vital to perform the analysis and generate valid result of an analysis. In this chapter, we will learn the tools used to perform analysis and check different results.

SOLVING ANALYSIS

To solve an analysis, you need to apply the materials and boundary condition to the model. These tools were discussed in last chapters. After applying the boundary condition, you need to create a mesh of required shape and size. This can be done automatically as well as manually as discussed in previous chapter. After creating the mesh, the next step is to solve the analysis, which is discussed next.

There are various methods to solve the analysis, which are discussed next.

Method 1

In this method, we will discuss the procedure of activating the **Solve** tool from **Design Study Bar**.

- Right-click on the **Solve** button from **Design Study Bar**, the right-click menu will be displayed; refer to Figure-1.

Figure-1. Right-click menu of Solve button

- Click on the **Solve** button from displayed right-click menu, the **Solve** dialog box will be displayed; refer to Figure-2.

Figure-2. Solve dialog box

Method 2

- Right-click on the canvas window outside the model, the right-click menu will be displayed; refer to Figure-3.

Figure-3. Right-click menu of graphics window

- Click on the **Solve** button from the displayed menu, the **Solve** dialog box will be displayed.

Method 3

- Click on the **Solve** button from **Simulation** panel of **Setup** tab; refer to Figure-4, the **Solve** dialog box will be displayed; refer to Figure-5.

Figure-4. Solve button from Simulation Panel

Figure-5. Solve dialog box along with model

Solve dialog box

The **Solve** dialog box is used to specify the parameters for performing a simulation. There are three tabs in this dialog box to specify the parameters, which are discussed next.

Control tab

The tools and parameters of **Control** tab are used to specify analysis parameters, like transient or steady state and set the number of iterations. The **Control** tab is by default selected in **Solve** dialog box.

- Click on the **Steady State** button from **Solution Mode** drop-down of **Control** tab to make the analysis independent of time.
- Click on the **Transient** button from **Solution Mode** drop-down of **Control** tab to make the analysis to be time-dependent. All motion analyses will run as a Transient analyses. You can switch between the two modes anytime during an analysis.

Save Interval

- Double-click on the **Save Intervals** node button from **Control** tab of **Solve** dialog box to specify the saving time of results and information in Autodesk CFD. The default value is specified at 0, which means result are saved only when the analysis completes the specified iterations or stops manually.
- Select the **Table** check box from **Save Interval** section to save iterations or time steps at varying interval. The **Table Editor** button will be displayed; refer to Figure-6.

Figure-6. Table Editor button

- Click on the **Edit** button of **Table Editor** option to specify the data, the **Results Output Frequency Editor** dialog box will be displayed.
- In **Results Output Frequency Editor** dialog box, you need to specify the data of number of iterations and save frequency; refer to Figure-7.

Figure-7. Adding data in Results Output Frequency Editor dialog box

- The result will be that, from step 0, output will be saved at every 10 iterations. At step 25, output will be saved at every 15 iterations. At step 65, the output will be saved at every 30 iterations. Finally, from step 100, output will be saved at every 100 iterations. If more than 100 steps are needed for analysis like 300 steps, than results will be saved at every 100 iterations.
- Click on the **Insert** button of **Results Output Frequency Editor** dialog box to insert a row above the selected row.
- Click on the **Delete** button to remove the selected row from the table.
- Click on the **Import** button to import the data for current analysis.
- Click on the **Save** button to save the table data. The **Save** dialog box will be displayed. Select the desired location from **Save** dialog box and click on **Save** button. The data will be saved at desired location.
- After specifying the parameters, click on the **OK** button. You will be redirected to **Solve** dialog box.

- Click on the **Solver Computer** drop-down and select the desired solver to solve the current analysis. You can also solve the current analysis using cloud solver if you have cloud credits. For cloud solver, you will need a internet connection.
- Click in the **Continue From** edit box and enter the desired iteration number from where solver will start solving analysis. Suppose, you have performed an analysis earlier on the current model, and after updating the model you want to continue the model from a specific value in between 1 to 100. Then, you can simply enter the desired value in **Continue From** edit box. The analysis will start from the entered value.

If a last iteration or time step is selected, then all selected saved iterations will be deleted from the current analysis. If you have changed mesh definitions, boundary conditions, or material of model then these are automatically incorporated into the analysis. After changing these parameters, you have to reset the **Continue From** value to 0, if not, following cases may arrive:

1. The current results are interpolated into new mesh
2. A new mesh will be generated.
3. The analysis iteration count reset to 0.

- Click in the **Iterations to Run** edit box from **Solve** dialog box and enter the value of iterations for current analysis.

Solution Control
- Click on the **Solution Control** button of **Control** tab from **Solve** dialog box to enable or disable the **Intelligent Solution Control** tool. The **Solution Controls** dialog box will be displayed; refer to Figure-8.

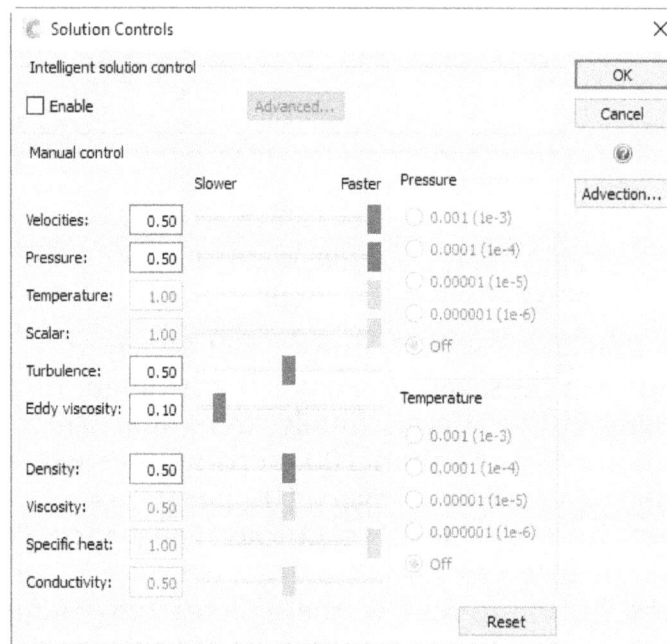

Figure-8. Solution Controls dialog box

- Select the **Enable** check box to control the convergence progression of the steady state stage of the analysis. Clear the **Enable** check box to disable **Intelligent Solution Control** tool.

- After clearing the check box, you need to specify various parameters manually to use **Solution Control** tool.
- Click on the **Advection** button from **Solution Controls** dialog box to control the solution progression rate so that chances of divergence are minimized.
- After specifying the parameters, click on the **OK** button from **Solution Controls** dialog box. You will be returned to **Solve** dialog box.

Result quantities

The **Result Quantities** button is used to view or hide the result parameters that are available after the analysis is complete. The procedure to use this is discussed next.

- Click on the **Result quantities** button from **Solve** dialog box, the **Result Quantities** dialog box will be displayed; refer to Figure-9.

Figure-9. Result Quantities dialog box

- Select the check boxes of those quantities which you want to view after analysis. If you want to view all parameters, click on the **All** button from **Result Quantities** dialog box.
- If you want to deselect all the quantities, then click on the **None** button.
- After selecting the required quantities, click on the **OK** button from **Result quantities** dialog box. You will be returned to **Solve** dialog box.

Physics tab

The **Physics** tab is used to define simulation conditions and solution parameters. The procedure to use this is discuss next.

- Click on the **Physics** tab from **Solve** dialog box, the **Physics** tab will be displayed; refer to Figure-10.

Figure-10. Physics tab

Flow

- Select the **Flow** check box from **Solve** dialog box to enable to fluid pressure and momentum equations. Clear the **Flow** check box for conduction-only heat transfer analysis. In case of natural convection, both flow and heat transfer must be enabled.

- Click on the **Compressibility** drop-down from **Physics** tab and select the **Incompressible** button to specify the flow whose maximum Mach number is less than 0.3.

- Click on the **Compressibility** drop-down from **Physics** tab and select the **Subsonic** button to specify the flow that is compressible but contain shock.

- Click on the **Compressibility** drop-down from **Physics** tab and select the **Compressible** button to specify the flow that has Mach number greater than 0.8 with or without heat transfer and shock.

- Select the **Hydrostatic Pressure** check box from **Physics** tab of **Solve** dialog box to specify the weight of fluid as an important factor in the current analysis, whether fluid is at rest or moving. On activating this check box, the Gravity Method and Gravity Direction options will be activated.

- Click on the **Gravity Method** drop-down from **Physics** tab and select the **Earth** button, when you are taking earth as a reference for creating analysis. In this case, you need to specify the direction of gravity by entering the value in **Gravity Direction** button. Suppose your model is constructed such that "down" in negative Z direction, the unit vector for gravity should be (0,0,-1). If you are selecting **Component** button in spite of **Earth** button, then you need to enter the magnitude and direction vector in **Gravity Components** field. The **Components** button is generally used in flows with hydrostatic pressure and buoyancy driven flows.

Heat Transfer

- Select the **Heat Transfer** check box from **Physics** tab of **Solve** dialog box to specify the transfer of heat in the flow. Clear this check box to specify the simulation to be adiabatic. On selecting **Heat Transfer** check box, more options related to this will be activated.

- Select the **Auto Forced Convection** check box from **Physics** tab to automatically stage a forced convection analysis into separate flow and heat transfer stages. Using this option, the flow and heat transfer can be solved separately because the flow does not depend on temperature distribution.

- Select the **Radiation** check box from **Physics** tab of **Solve** dialog box to include surface-to-surface radiation effects in heat transfer analysis. The **Radiation** option is generally used when field temperature near model is very high. On selecting this check box, the solar heating button becomes active. Click on this button to set solar radiation parameters. The **Solar Heating Dialog** box will be displayed; refer to Figure-11

Figure-11. Solar Heating Dialog box

Solar heating plays an important role in designing homes and building. Engineers need to understand and account for the effects of solar heating on performance and efficiency of structures. Solar heating works with Radiation solver, and supports radioactive heat transfer through transparent media. The procedure to use this is discussed next.

- Select the **Enable solar heating** check box from **Solar Heating Dialog** box. Tools of solar heating will be activated.
- Select the geographical location as selecting country from **Country** drop-down and city from **City** drop-down. The **Latitude**, **Longitude**, **GMT**, **DEG**, and **MIN** will be specified by default. If you want to set these parameters manually, select the **Manual** check box.

Note - **Latitude** must be between -90 to 90 degrees, **Longitude** must be between -180 and 180 degrees, and the **GMT** must be between -12 to 12.

- Set the date and time from **Date and Time** section of **Solar Heating Dialog** box by using up and down arrows.
- Select the required orientation of solar heating from **Orientation** section of **Solar Heating Dialog** box.
- Select the **Steady State** button from **Time** drop-down to assign temperature to the outer surfaces of the model. Click in the **Temperature** edit box and enter the desired value to specify ambient reference temperature.
- Select the **Transient** button from **Time** drop-down to specify how the **Ambient Temperature** varies with time using the **Time Curve** table. Click on the **Time Curve**

drop-down and select the required option to specify time curve.

- After specifying the parameters, click on the **OK** button from **Solar Heating Dialog** box. You would be returned to Solve dialog box.

Turbulence

The **Turbulence** tool is used to specify flow turbulence of model. The procedure to use this is discussed next.

- Click on the **Turbulence** button from the **Physics** tab of **Solve** dialog box, the **Turbulence** dialog box will be displayed; refer to Figure-12.

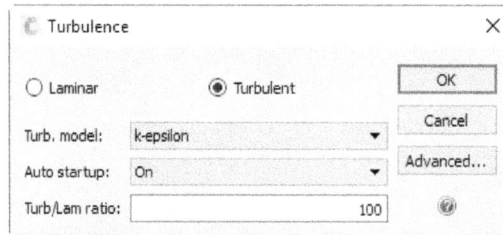

Figure-12. Turbulence dialog box

- Select the **Laminar** radio button from **Turbulence** dialog box to specify the flow as laminar flow. In laminar flow, the layers of fluid particles slide over the adjacent particle without disturbing the motion of others particles; refer to Figure-13.
- Select the **Turbulent** radio button from **Turbulence** dialog box to specify the flow as turbulent. In turbulent flow, the fluid properties of flow vary rapidly with time. The velocity, pressure, density, and other flow properties show random changes.

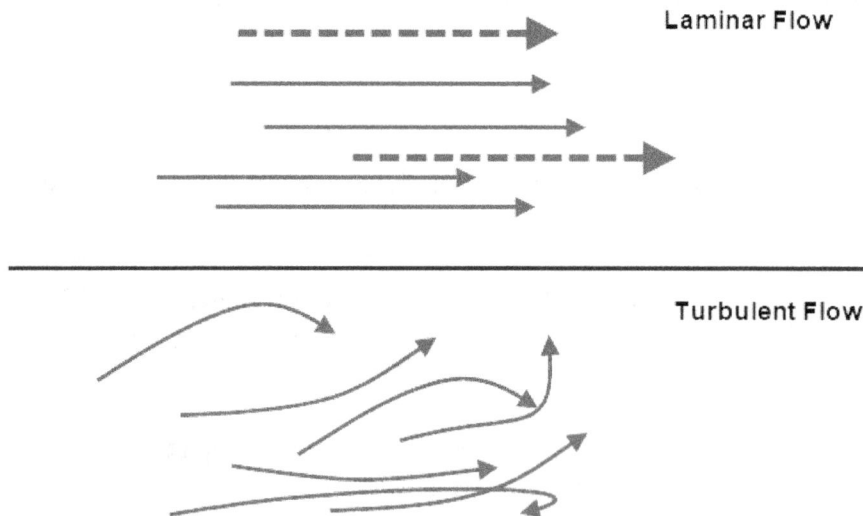

Figure-13. Laminar and Turbulent Flow

- Click on the **Turb. model** drop-down and select the desired turbulence model.
- Click on the **Auto startup** drop-down from **Turbulence** dialog box and select the required option to run **Automatic Turbulent Start-up** algorithm as per command.
- Select the **Lock On** button from **Auto startup** drop-down to keep ATSU on during the entire analysis until you shut it down. If you are having convergence difficulties after 50 iterations, then you must enable **Lock On** button. If ATSU is already

turned on, then you should run at least 200 iterations to ensure convergence of the turbulent flow simulation.

- Select the **Extended** option from **Auto startup** drop-down to activate an extended version of ATSU. This method is generally used for compressible analyses. At least 400 iterations should run in this algorithm.
- Click in the **Turb/Lam ratio** edit box from **Turbulence** dialog box and enter the ratio of value to estimate the effective viscosity at the beginning of turbulent flow analysis. The default value of this option is generally suitable for mostly flows.
- Click on the **Advanced** button from **Turbulence** dialog box to specify more parameters of turbulence flow.
- After specifying the parameters, click on the **OK** button from **Turbulence** dialog box. You will be returned to **Solve** dialog box.

Advanced

The **Advanced** button in the **Solve** dialog box is used to specify mixing humidity, quality, and cavitation properties. The procedure to use this button is discussed next.

- Click on the **Advanced** button from **Solve** dialog box, the **Advanced** dialog box will be displayed; refer to Figure-14.

Figure-14. Advanced dialog box

- Select the **No scaler** radio button from **Advanced** dialog box to not involve scalar calculation as a part of analysis.
- Select the **General scalar** radio button from **Advanced** dialog box to specify the value of scalar as a part of analysis. The **Diffusion Coefficient** edit box will be activated.
- Click in the **Diffusion Coefficient** edit box and specify the value to control the mass diffusivity of the scalar quantity into the surrounding field. The zero value of **Diffusion Coefficient** will prevent any diffusion of scalar quantity.
- Select the **Humidity (moist air)** radio button from **Advanced** dialog box to simulate moist gas. In this, both the relative humidity and condensed water can be visualized. Note that, in this software, condensation of moist gas can be modeled but it cannot be possible to model the evaporation of water into gas stream.
- Select the **Quality** radio button of **Advance** dialog box to simulate a homogeneous mixture of vapor and liquid. If scalar is 0, then there will be no vapor. If scalar is 1, there will be all vapors.
- Select the **Cavitation** radio button from **Advance** dialog box to predict the small collection of bubbles in a model due to fluid flow. When cavitation is selected, fluid pressure does not fall below the vapor pressure. If not selected, the fluid pressure will fall below vapor pressure.

- After specifying the parameters from **Advanced** dialog box, click on **OK** button. You will be returned to **Solve** dialog box.

Free Surface

The **Free surface** tool is used to simulate the interface between liquids and gases. This tool is generally used in modeling flow phenomena like sloshing, waves, and spilling. The procedure to use this tool is discussed next.

- Click on the **Free surface** tool from **Physics** tab of **Solve** dialog box, the **Free Surface** dialog box will be displayed; refer to Figure-15.

Figure-15. Free Surface dialog box

- The options of **Free Surface** dialog box will be activated on selecting **Enable free surface** check box.
- Click in the **Earth gravity directional unit vector** edit box from **Free Surface** dialog box and enter the value of X,Y, or Z to include the effects of elevation change on the liquid. You need to specify a unit gravity vector to indicate the direction of pull.
- The **Acceleration** section is used to specify body forces experienced by fluid, like a fluid transportation tank.
- Select the **Constant** option from component drop-downs to simulate a acceleration that does not vary with time and click in the adjacent edit boxes to specify acceleration values.
- Select the **Piecewise Linear** button from component drop-down to define a time variation of an acceleration component. The **Edit** button will be activated.
- Click on the **Edit** button to specify acceleration time data, the **Acceleration Curve Editor** dialog box will be displayed; refer to Figure-16.

Figure-16. Acceleration Curve Editor dialog box

- Enter the value of acceleration with respect to time in **Acceleration Curve Editor dialog** box and click on the **OK** button. You will be returned to **Free Surface** dialog box.
- After specifying the parameters from **Free Surface** dialog box, click on the **OK** button. You will be returned to **Solve** dialog box.

Adaptation tab

The options of **Adaptation** tab are generally used to improve the mesh by running the analysis multiple times. At the end of each run, this tool modifies the mesh as per result and uses this mesh for next cycle. The procedure to use this is discussed next.

- Click on the **Adaptation** tab from **Solve** dialog box. The **Adaptation** tab will be displayed; refer to Figure-17.

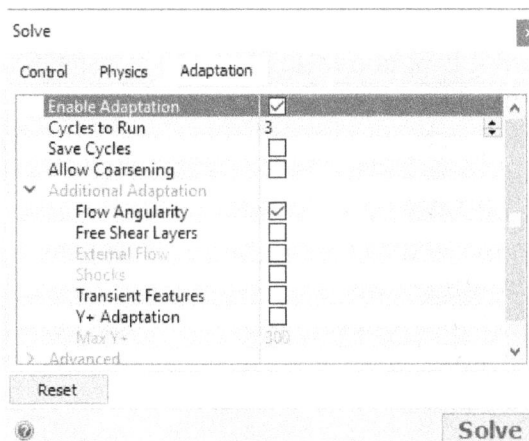

Figure-17. Adaptation tab of Solve dialog box

- Click on the **Enable Adaptation** check box from **Adaptation** tab of **Solve** dialog box to activate Adaptation for the current study. When it is enabled, a baseline scenario will run to completion.

- Click in the **Cycles to Run** edit box and specify the number of cycles which you want to run for refining mesh. By default, 3 cycles are specified for this. Note that the total number of scenarios includes a baseline plus specified number of cycles.
- Select the **Save Cycles** check box from **Adaptation** tab to save each intermediate mesh. Scenario will be automatically cloned on finish and the cycle number is appended to the base scenario name. Clear the check box to save only final mesh and results. For example: the default name is scenario 1 at the beginning of the process. Scenario 1 could run to completion and cloned, named as Scenario 1-Mesh 1. The mesh on scenario 1 is adapted to results, and run to completion. Scenario 1 is cloned again, named as Scenario 1 Mesh 2. This process will continue till specified number of cycles. At the end, Scenario 1 contains the final mesh, and intermediate cycles are saved in Scenario 1 - Mesh 1, Scenario 2 - Mesh 2, Scenario 3 - Mesh 3, etc. Throughout the process, scenario 1 will always the active scenario.
- Select the **Allow Coarsening** check box from **Adaptation** tab of **Solve** dialog box to make the mesh coarser than normal. By default, **Adaptation** tool only refines mesh and with the use of **Allow Coarsening** tab, it prevents the mesh from growing too fine.

Additional Adaptation

The **Additional Adaptation** option complements the primary options for defining mesh adaptation. The procedure to use these options are discussed next.

- Click on the **Additional Adaptation** node from **Adaptation** tab of **Solve** dialog box. The controls and parameters of **Additional Adaptation** will be displayed.
- Select the **Flow Angularity** check box from **Adaptation** tab to improve the resolution in areas that contain large amounts of flow separation and circulatory flow.
- Select the **Free Shear Layers** check box from **Adaptation** tab to sharply define velocity gradient within a flow stream in case pipe bend. The Free Shear Layers occurs at the intersection between slow velocity flow and free velocity flow, like separate region. For accurate flow prediction, it is important that the distribution of mesh is fine enough to capture the severe velocity gradient within the shear flow layers. In general, the free stream flow is pushed towards outside radius of pipe and flow separation region occurs at inside radius of pipe.
- The **External Flow** check box is available only if **Free Shear Layers** check box is selected in the dialog box. The external flow option tunes mesh adaptation to refine the mesh of the model in high velocity gradient regions occurring between viscous and free-stream flows in large unbounded flow domains, like aerodynamics flows.
- The **Shock** option is available in compressible flow. Select the check box to enable this option. This option is used to focus the mesh on location and gradients across a sudden barrier, like a shock wave.
- Select the **Transient Features** check box from **Adaptation** tab, if flow has dynamic region like flow reattachment or vortex shedding. This performs three adaptations per error criteria before proceeding to next criteria. The result is that dynamic

features are better resolved, but static regions are not.

- Select the **Y+ Adaptation** check box to specify the sensitivity of boundary element thickness. It is a non-dimensional distance between a wall node and its corresponding neighbor node.

- The **Max Y+** option is activated after selecting the **Y+ Adaptation** check box. Select the **Max Y+** check box to achieve desired accuracy by reducing or increasing the value. As per numerous study, the ideal range of **Max Y+** is between 35 and 350. The default value for **Max Y+** is 300.

Advanced

The tools of **Advanced** node are used to provide detailed control over the process of mesh generation. In the parameters of **Advanced** node, the parameters are provided with default values which were based of testing and most rigorous situation. The procedure to use this tool is discussed next.

- Click on the **Advanced** node from **Adaptation** dialog box of **Solve** dialog box. The advanced parameters will be displayed; refer to Figure-18.

Figure-18. Advanced node of Solve dialog box

- Click in the **Growth Rate** edit box from **Advanced** node and enter the value to modify the smoothness of volumetric mesh. The **Growth Rate** option works similar to **Mesh Autosize** tool.
- Click in the **Boundary Layer Growth** edit box and enter the value to modify the smoothness of boundary layer mesh.
- Click in the **Refinement Layer** edit box and enter the parameters to prevent over-refinement of mesh when wall layer is disabled. When wall layers is enabled, the boundary layer specify the minimum allowable length scale during adaptation, and **Refinement Layer** plays no role.
- Click in the **Resolution Factor** edit box and enter the value to make the mesh more finer. For greater refinement, specify a value less than 1.0. This reduces the error threshold by specified factor, resulting in finer mesh.
- If you want to reset the values of **Adaptation** tab to default, click on the **Reset** button. The entered values will be reset to default.
- After specifying the parameters, click on the **Solve** button from **Solve** dialog box. The analysis will be started in no time.
- On clicking the **Solve** button, the **Message Window** of **Output** bar will be opened and calculation will start displaying on the **Message Window**; refer to Figure-19.

Figure-19. Running calculations

- The **Message Window** is used to view the ongoing processes of current project. Whatever action you do in Autodesk CFD, the notification, action, and result will be mentioned in this window.

Convergence Plot

The **Convergence Plot** is used to view the convergence information and curves of each iteration throughout the entire calculation. After starting the calculation of analysis, you can view the ongoing iteration throughout the process with the help of curves; refer to Figure-19.

Figure-20. Curves plot

- The **Start** and **End** edit boxes in the **Plot** tab of **Convergence Plot** tab indicates the starting and ending number of iteration. If you want to see the iterations of the current plot from 10 to 70, then specify respective values in **Start** and **End** edit boxes. The graph will be displayed based on entered values; refer to Figure-21.

Figure-21. View particular number of Iteration

- The starting and ending number of iterations are displayed in the highlighted box.
- The highlighted box at the upper right corner of the above figure contains various parameters, as given below,

> **Vx Velocity** refers to velocity in X direction.
> **Vy Velocity** refers to velocity in Y direction.
> **Vz Velocity** refers to velocity in Z direction.
> **Pres**. refers to pressure
> **Temp** refers to temperature
> **TKE** refers to two equation Turbulence.
> **TED** refers to turbulent kinetic energy.
> **Scalar** refers to scaler quantity.

- The **Global** button on the right of **Convergence Plot** tab is used to view the graph of global parameters in convergence plot.
- If you want to view the graph of particular parameter, then click on the **All** drop-down and select the desired parameter. The graph related to that parameter will be displayed; refer to Figure-22.

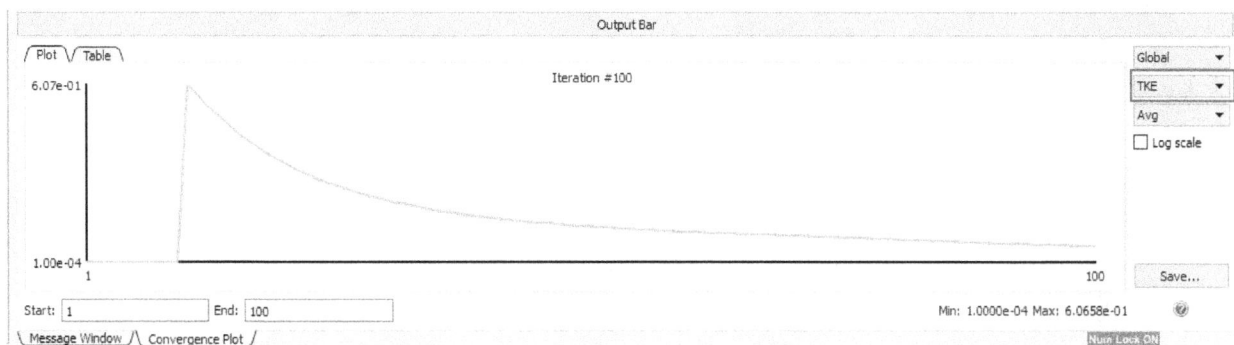

Figure-22. TKE graph

- You can also view the graph from a specific start and end value by entering the same in **Start** and **End** edit box.
- Click on the **Avg** drop-down from **Convergence Plot** tab to view the different values of plotted quantities.
- Click on the **Save** button to save the current data of iterations. The **Save Iteration History** dialog box will be displayed. Select the folder, where you want to save the data in **.CSV** format and click on the **Save** button. The file will be saved in specified folder.

- Click on the **Table** tab to from **Convergence Plot** tab to view the data of iterations. The data is all about parameters which we saw in **Plot** tab of **Convergence Plot** tab in the form of graph; refer to Figure-23. The data shown in **Plot** tab is graphical, and in **Table** tab the data is in the form of numerical values.

Figure-23. Table tab of Convergence tab

we will now discuss the **Results** tab. Process to analyze results with the help of tools of **Result** tab will be discussed in the next chapter.

Solve Manager

The **Solve Manager** is used to manage multiple scenarios in a queue. This tool is used, when we have to assign the processes to start in numerical order. The procedure to use this is discussed next.

- Click on the **Solve Manager** button from **Simulation** panel of **Setup** tab, the **Solve Manager** dialog box will be displayed; refer to Figure-24.

Figure-24. Solve Manager dialog box

- Select the desired check box from **Include in Solution Set** column to include the analysis to be solved. If you do not want to solve any of the analysis from **Solve Manager**, simply clear the check box.
- Click on the **Solver Computer** drop-down and selected the desired machine for solving analysis. You can select computer or Autodesk Cloud computer for solving analysis.
- Click on the **Start Time** drop-down and select the desired start time for the analysis.

- Select the order number from **Submit Order** drop-down to specify, which analysis to be solved first and which one should be solved last.
- Click on the **Select toggle** button from **Solver Manager** to toggle solver on or off.
- After specifying the parameters, click on the **Submit** button. The state will be changed from **Idle** to **Submitted** in **Solver Manager** and analyses will be start as per entered data.

Job Monitor

The **Job Monitor** is used to check real time information of analyses. It can be used to monitor the status of simulations running in the cloud, stops running simulations, and run simulation jobs in background . The procedure to use this is discussed next,

- Click on the **Job Monitor** button from **Simulation** panel from **Setup** tab, the **CFD 2018 Job Monitor** dialog box will be displayed; refer to Figure-25.

Figure-25. Job Monitor dialog box

- You can check the status of analyses in this dialog box. If you want to remove any of the analysis, right-click on the it and click on the **Remove Job** button. The result of the selected analysis will be lost.
- After checking the status of analysis, close the dialog box.

Notifications

The notifications are the e-mail sent by Autodesk CFD when your analysis has completed a specific milestone. The procedure to enable notification is discussed below.

- Click on the **Notifications** button from **Simulation** panel of **Setup** tab, the **Solver Notifications** dialog box will be displayed; refer to Figure-26.

Figure-26. Solver Notificaitons dialog box

- Click in the **SMTP Server** edit box and enter the name of your SMTP server. You can enter either the server or the server:port. Some common 3rd party servers are smtp.gmail.com:587 and smtp.mail.yahoo.com:465.
- Click in the **Username** edit box from **Solver Notifications** dialog box and enter the username as login id or domain name. For public email server, this is often your email address.
- Click in the **Password** edit box and enter the password of the username which you have entered above.
- Click in the **From** edit box and enter your email address. This email address must match the above entered username. This email address will appear in **From** field on emails sent through this service.
- Click in the **To** edit box and enter the target email address for notifications. You can enter multiple addresses in the edit box separated by comma.
- To receive notifications as a text message, enter the mobile number as per vendor specifications.
- Select the appropriate option check box from **Send messages** area of **Solver Notifications**, as per requirement.
- Select the **Send Convergence Plot** check box to select the events that trigger a notification. The **Iteration Interval** edit box will be activated. In this edit box, enter the number of iterations that should elapse between plot images.
- After specifying the parameters, click on the **Text message** button from **Solver Notifications** dialog box to confirm.
- After clicking **OK** button, notifications are sent for all subsequent analyses launched from your computer, under your window login. The analysis conclusion notification contains the status file. If an error occurs, this file includes the error message.

Note: If Notification e-mails are not delivered to Inbox, check your "Spam" or similar folder.

SMS Address for receiving text messages, by phone vendor.
- T-Mobile: phonenumber@tmomail.net
- Virgin Mobile: phonenumber@vmobl.com
- Cingular: phonenumber@cingularme.com
- Sprint: phonenumber@messaging.sprintpcs.com
- Verizon: phonenumber@vtext.com
- Nextel: phonenumber@messaging.nextel.com
- US Cellular: phonenumber@email.uscc.net
- SunCom: phonenumber@tms.suncom.com
- Powertel: phonenumber@ptel.net
- AT&T: phonenumber@txt.att.net
- Alltel: phonenumber@message.alltel.com
- Metro PCS: phonenumber@MyMetroPcs.com

These numbers are subject to change. Please consult your mobile number phone vendor for more information.

Monitor Point

The **Monitor Point** button is used to place some point in the model so that basic degree of freedom are plotted in convergence plot throughout the analysis. These points provides a way to track convergence at some specific location of the model. The procedure to use this is discussed next.

- Click on the **Monitor Point** button from **Simulation** panel drop-down of **Setup** tab. The **Runtime Monitor Points** dialog box will be displayed; refer to Figure-27.

Figure-27. Monitor Point button

- To add points, move the triad axis and click on the **Add** a point button from **Runtime Monitor Points** dialog box; refer to Figure-28.

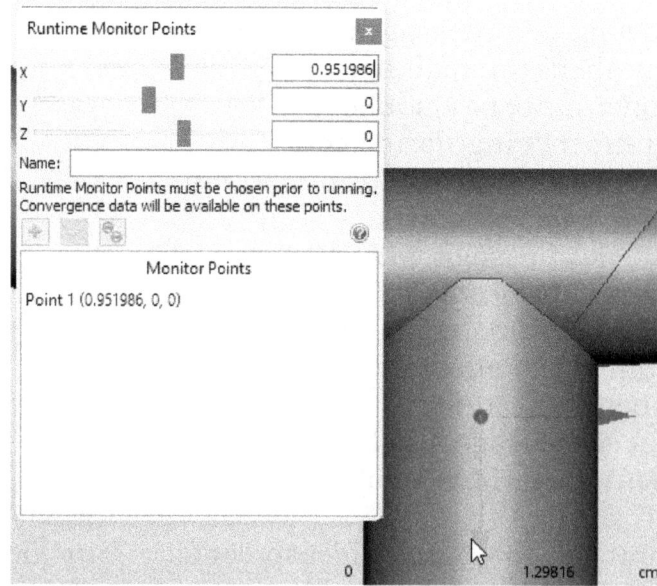

Figure-28. Adding Monitor points

- Similarly, you can add as many points as you want for convergence plot.
- You can create monitor points after the completion of iterations, and then run additional iterations. The plotted monitor point data will simply start at intermediate iteration, instead of at the beginning of the calculation.

Solver Computers

The **Solver Computers** tool is used to view and edit the configurations of solver computers. The procedure to use this tool is discussed next.

- Click on the **Solver Computers** button from **Simulation** panel drop-down in **Setup** tab, the **Solver Computers and Configurations** dialog box will be displayed; refer to Figure-29.

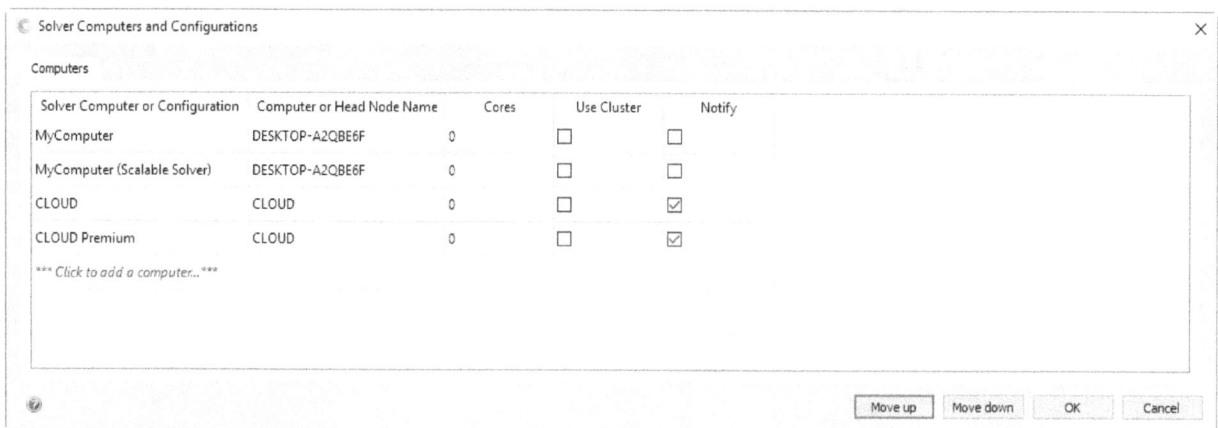

Figure-29. Solver computer and configurations dialog box

- Double-click in the **Cores** edit box and specify the cores which you want to use for solving analysis.

- Select the **Use Cluster** check box for desired solver to use the respective cluster to solve the analysis. Computer Clusters are set of computers that works together so that, they can be viewed and worked with single system.
- Select the **Notify** check box to get notify while using the respective solver.
- Click on the **Click to add a computer** button to add a custom solver as per requirement. The **Solver Computer** dialog box will be displayed; refer to Figure-30.

Figure-30. Solver Computer dialog Box

- Specify the desired parameters from **Solver Computer** dialog box and click on **OK** button. The solver will be added in **Computers** tab.
- After specifying the desired parameters in **Solver Computers and Configurations** dialog box and click on **OK** button.

Selection panel

The **Selection** panel contains various tools to select or deselect the model and its entity. The tools of this panel are discussed next.

- Click on the **Volume** button from **Selection** panel to enable volume selection. This tool is used, when you want to select volume from model to perform a function; refer to Figure-31.

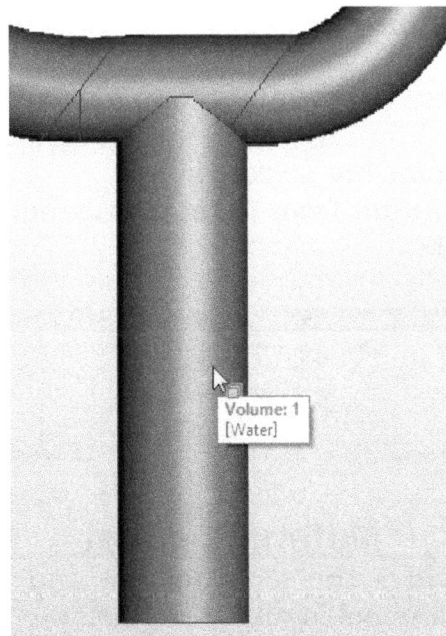

Figure-31. Selecting volume

- Click on the **Surface** button from **Selection** panel to enable volume selection. This tool is used, when you want to select surface of a model; refer to Figure-32.

Figure-32. Surface Selection

- Click on the **Edge** button from **Selection** panel to enable edge selection. This button is not available when working with 3D geometry.
- Click on the **Select by** drop-down and select the **Direct** option to select volume and surface. If you have selected **Volume** button then the volume of model will be highlighted. If you have selected **Surface** button, the surface of components will be highlighted on hovering the cursor on model.
- Click on the **Select Previous** button from **Selection** panel to select last previously selected item.
- Click on the **Select All** button from **Selection** panel to select every entity of current selection mode.
- Click on the **Show All** button from **Selection** panel to select resume the visibility of all hidden items.
- Click on the **Deselect** button from **Selection** panel to deselect the current selected entity. If you had selected multiple items, then this tool will deselect entities in reverse order in which items are selected.
- Click on **Deselect All** button from **Selection** panel to deselect all the selected entities; refer to Figure-33.

Figure-33. Selection panel

Materials panel

The **Materials** panel provides the tools to edit and remove the material from component. The tools of this panel is discussed below.

- Click on the **Edit** button from **Materials** panel to edit the material properties of selected component. Before clicking on **Edit** button, you will need to select the component. The **Materials** dialog box will be displayed. The options of this dialog box have already been discussed.

- Click on the **Remove** button to remove existing material from the component.
- Click on the **Material Editor** button from **Materials** panel to view the properties of material. The **Material Editor** dialog box will be displayed. The options of this dialog box have already been discussed.
- Click on the **Scenario Environment** button from **Materials** panel to edit the scenario environment. The **Scenario Environment** dialog box will be displayed which has been discussed earlier.

DESIGN STUDY TOOL PANEL

The **Design Study Tool** panel is used to define the structure of the design study. In this, you can add or update the design, and assign the structure of a fully defined scenario. The procedure to use this tool is discussed next.

Add/Update Design

The **Add/Update Design** tool is used to add or update the existing model. This tool is generally used, when we clone the design to make some more analysis after changing or modifying the component. The procedure to use this tool is discussed next.

- Click on the **Add/Update Design** button from **Design Study Tools** panel of **Setup** tab, the **Add Geometry File** dialog box will be displayed; refer to Figure-34.

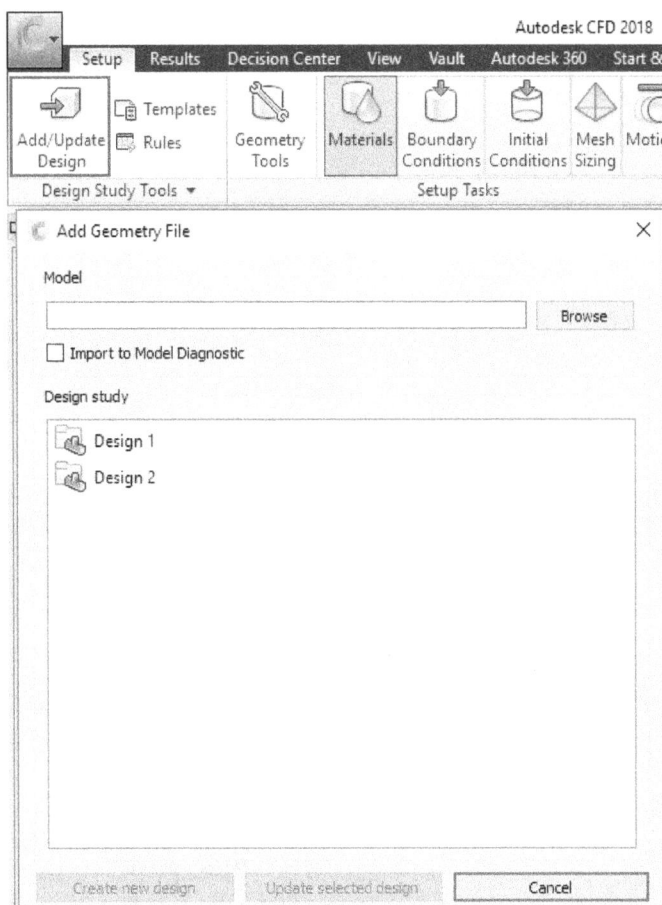

Figure-34. Add Geometry File dialog box

- Before proceeding to the next step, you should have a CAD model modified as required.
- Click on the **Browse** button from **Add Geometry File** dialog box, the **Add Geometry** dialog box will be displayed. Select the file, which you want to update and click on the **Open** button. The file will be displayed in **Model** edit box of **Add Geometry File** dialog box.
- Select the required design from **Design Study** section, which you want to update or modify the existing decision.
- Click on the **Create new design** button to create a new design using the geometry.
- Click on the **Update selected design** button to replace the geometry of the selected design with new geometry. The geometry will be updated and displayed.

Templates

A **Template** is a file that contains the model settings for one or more scenarios that define a design. Templates provide consistency for design studies that contain similar settings.

- Click on the **Templates** tool from **Design Study Tools** panel, the **Template Manager** will be displayed; refer to Figure-35.

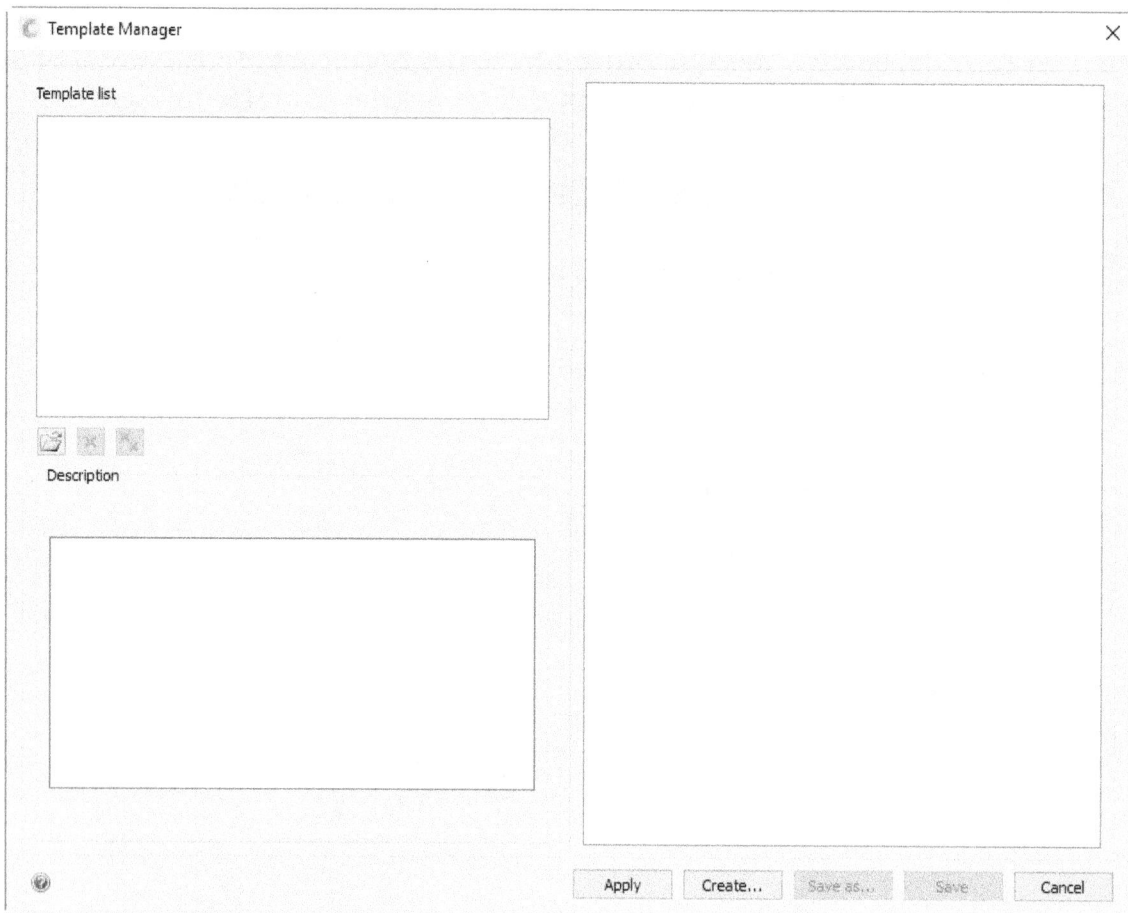

Figure-35. Template Manager dialog box

- Click on the **Create** button from **Template Manager** dialog box to create a new template file. The **Create a new template file** dialog box will be displayed. Specify the location of the file, where you want to save the template file. Specify the name of template and click on **Save** button. The template will be displayed in **Template list** section.

- Click on the desired template, the details will be displayed at the right of **Template Manager** dialog box; refer to Figure-36.

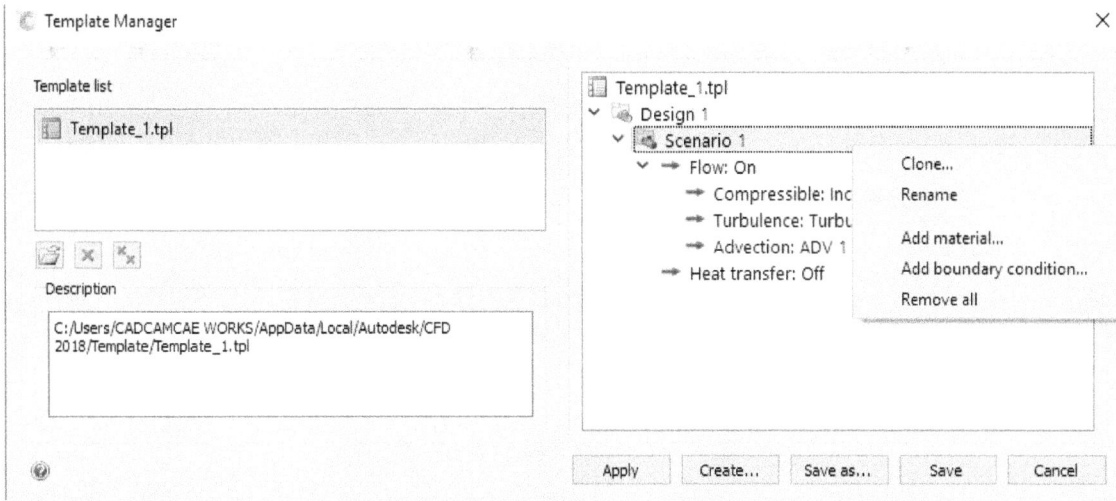

Figure-36. Added-template

- To add material, boundary condition, or clone the template, click on the respective button from right-click menu.
- After selecting the template, click on the **Apply** button to apply the selected template.

Rules

The **Rules** button is used to create associations between CAD and CFD settings. You can use these rules to automatically assign settings to frequently recurring CAD components. Rules are usually applied automatically when the design study is launched. The procedure to use this is discussed next.

- Click on the **Rules** button from **Design Study Tools** panel, the **Rule Manager** will be displayed; refer to Figure-37.

Figure-37. Rule Manager dialog box

- Click on the **Click to create a rule** button, the **Rule Creation** dialog box will be displayed; refer to Figure-38.

Figure-38. Rule Creation dialog box

- Enter the parameters to create rule and click on **OK** button from **Rule Creation** dialog box. The rule will be created and displayed in **Rule Manager** dialog box.
- Click on the **Select All** button from **Rule Manager** to select all the listed rules.
- Click on the **Remove all rules** button from **Rule Manager** to remove all created rules.
- Click on the **Import rules** button to import the pre-created rules. The **Open a setup file or rule file** dialog box will be displayed. Select the file and click on the **Open** button. The rule will be listed in **Rule Manager** dialog box.
- Click on the **Export Selected rules** button from **Rule Manager** to export the selected rule for future reference. The **Export a rule file** dialog box will be displayed. Select the desired folder where you want to save the rule file and click on **Save** button. The rule will be added in the list.
- Click on **Apply Now** button to apply the selected rule to current model.
- Click on the **Default material rule** button to apply or change the default material of the selected rule. The **Rule Creation** dialog box will be displayed. Modify the parameters as required.

Script Editor

The Autodesk CFD Application Programming Interface provides ways to work with Autodesk CFD functionality that are not readily available in the user interface. The API is a platform for customization, and can benefit design process. It is very flexible, and can be used for a wide variety of tasks, like, crating custom tasks, creating custom result quantities, etc. The procedure to use the script editor is discussed next.

- Click on the **Script Editor** button from **Design Study Tools** panel drop-down, the **CFD Script Editor** dialog box will be displayed; refer to Figure-39.

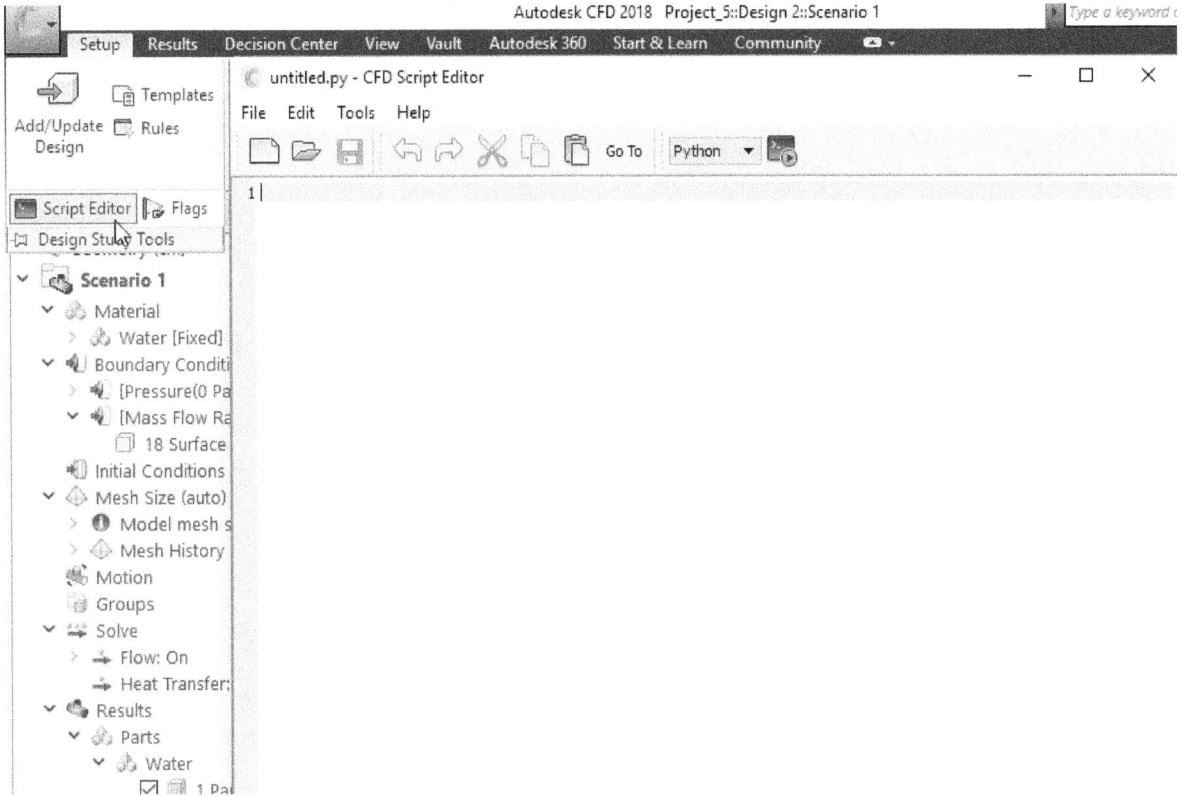

Figure-39. Script Editor

- Create the script as required.

Flags

The **Flags** button is used to modify many different aspects of Autodesk CFD. The procedure to use this button is discussed next.

- Click on the **Flags** button from **Design Study Tools** panel drop-down, the **Flag Manager** dialog box will be displayed; refer to Figure-40. The **Flag Manager** organizes and provides visibility to the collection of flags.

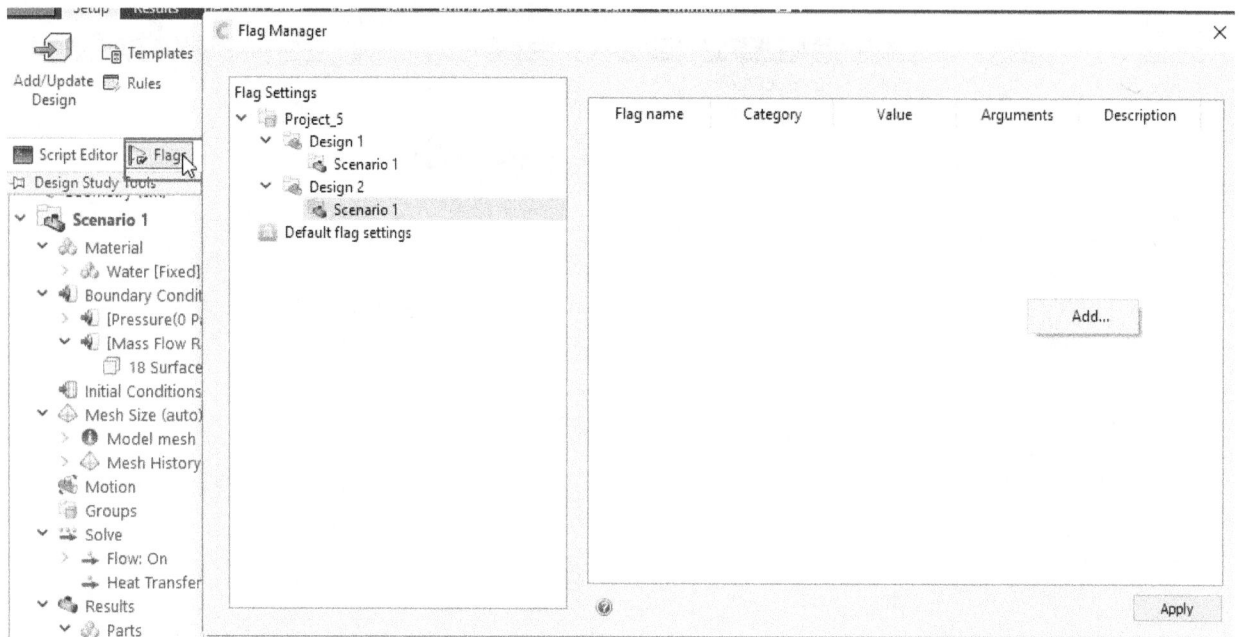

Figure-40. Flag Manager dialog Box

- You can add flag to the scenario by clicking on **Add** button from right-click menu. The **Add New Flag** dialog box will be displayed. Specify the flag name and click on **OK** button. The flag will be displayed.
- Select the flag and click on **Apply** button to apply the flag.

*** End of Chapter ***

FOR STUDENTS NOTES

FOR STUDENTS NOTES

Analyzing Results

Chapter 5

Topics Covered

The major topics covered in this chapter are:

- *Results tab*
- *Result Tasks panel*
- *Review panel*
- *Image panel*

INTRODUCTION

In the last chapter, we have learned the process to solve the analysis with the use of software. In this chapter, we will learn the processes to analyze results with the help of various tools.

RESULTS TAB

The **Results** tab is generally used to analyze the results of a simulation study with the help of various panels, like Image, Results Tasks panel, Reporting panel, Review panel, and Iteration/step panel; refer to Figure-1. These panels are discussed next.

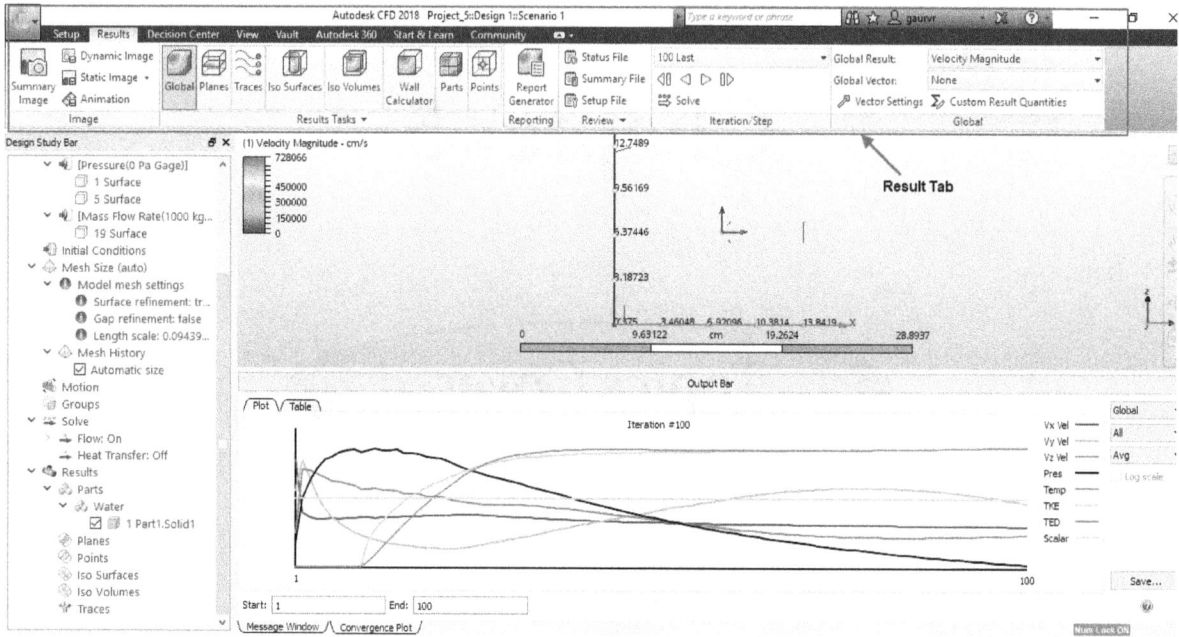

Figure-1. Result Tab

- You can check the process of analysis in **Output** tab. Every action of an analysis is displayed in **Output Bar**; refer to Figure-2.

Figure-2. Output Bar

Results Tasks panel

The **Result Tasks** panel is used to visualize the simulation results through various tools. These tools are discussed next.

Global

The **Global** tool is used to control the display of results and vectors on model surfaces.

The procedure is discussed next.

*   After the completion of analysis, click on the **Global** button from **Results Tasks** panel. The **Global** tool will be activated and **Global** context panel will be displayed at the right in **Ribbon**; refer to Figure-3.

Figure-3. Global tool

*   Click on the **Global Result** drop-down from **Global** context panel and select the required parameter which you want to display on the model surfaces; refer to Figure-4.

Figure-4. Global Result drop-down

*   On selecting any scalar quantity from **Global Result** drop-down, the plot will be displayed at the right of canvas screen as per analysis results; refer to Figure-5.

Figure-5. Plot Static Pressure

*   Click on the **Global Vector** drop-down from **Global** context panel and select the vector quantity to be displayed on surface of model; refer to Figure-6.

Figure-6. Global Vector drop-down

- The selected parameter of **Global Result** and **Global Vector** drop-downs will be graphically displayed.

Vector Settings

- Click on the **Vector Settings** button from **Global** context panel to specify the selected vector parameter. The **Vector Settings** dialog box will be displayed; refer to Figure-7.

Figure-7. Velocity Vector diaog box

- The **Vector Settings** dialog box is used to specify the length and intensity of vectors. Click on the **Results** tab and select the required vector. You can also specify the required vector from **Global Vector** drop-down. Vectors will be displayed as per selected vector.
- Select the **Same Length** radio button from **Vector Settings** dialog box to apply the same length to all the vectors.
- Move the length slider or enter the length value numerically in **Length** edit box to specify the length of vector. The maximum value of **Length** edit box is 0.999.
- Select the **Length Range** radio button from **Vector Settings** dialog box to display vector with different length; refer to Figure-8.

Figure-8. Length Range radio button

- Move the **Min** and **Max** slider to specify the length of vector. You can also specify the value of **Min** and **Max**, by entering the values in respective edit boxes.
- Click on the **More** button from **Vector Settings** dialog box to define advanced parameters for vectors; refer to Figure-9.

Figure-9. Parameters of More button

- Select the **Show arrowheads** check box from **Attributes** section to display the arrow head in vector arrows of result. Clear the check box to hide the arrow head.
- Click in the **Arrowhead size** edit box from **Attributes** section and enter the value to increase or decrease the size of arrowhead.
- Click in the **Scale factor** edit box from **Attributes** section and enter the value to increase or decrease the length of vector.
- Select the **Filtering** check box from **Vector Settings** dialog box to show regions where the active vector is within specified region.
- Click and enter the desired value in **Min** and **Max** edit boxes of **Filtering** section
- Click on the **Reset** button to reset the **Filtering** value.
- After specifying the parameters from **Vector Settings** dialog box, close the dialog box by clicking on the **Close** button. You will be returned to **Results** tab.

Custom Result Quantities

The **Custom Result Quantities** button is used to create custom result quantities to analyze and visualize results as per your requirement. Sometimes, we have to work on custom and different mechanism to find out the outcomes. In such a case, this tool is used to build a quantity which support mechanism and working of machine. The procedure to use this is discussed next.

- Click on the **Custom Result Quantities** button from **Global** context panel, the **Custom Result Quantities** dialog box will be displayed; refer to Figure-10.

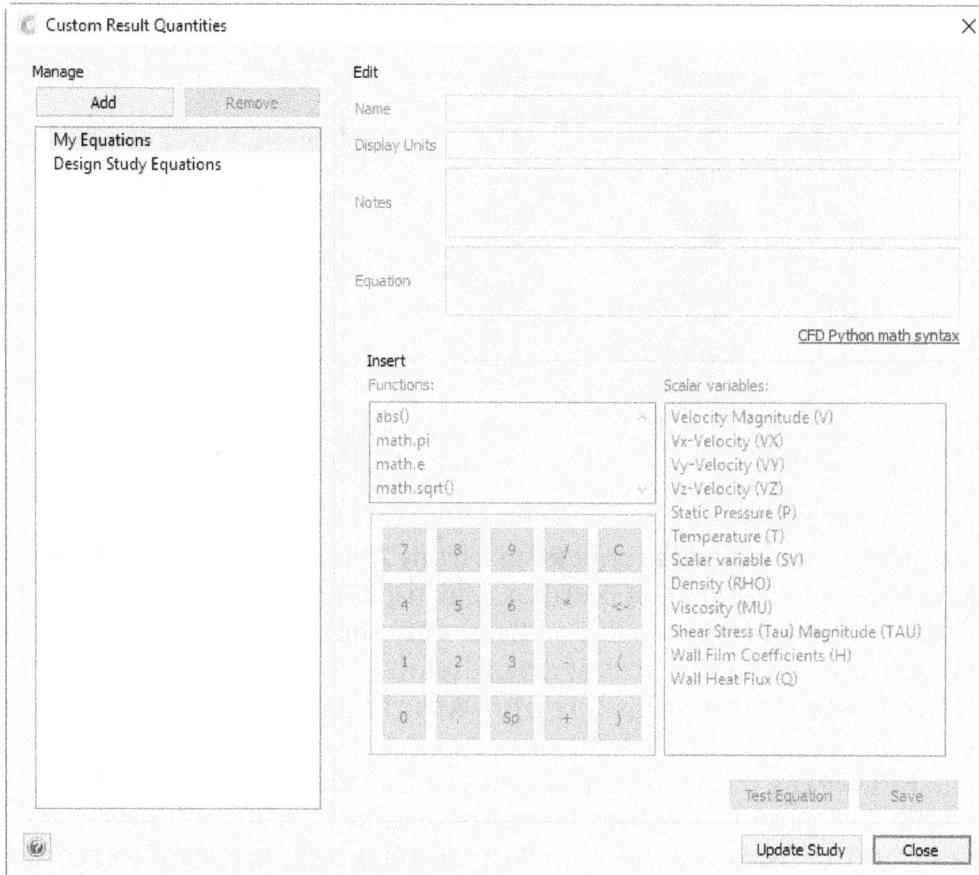

Figure-10. Custom Result Quantites dialog box

- Click on the **Add** button from **Custom Result Quantities** dialog box to add a new quantities. All the edit box of **Custom Result Quantities** dialog box will be enabled.
- Enter the required parameters in edit boxes and click on **Test Equation** button to test the equation.
- After testing, click on the **Save** button. The quantity will be created and displayed in **Global** context panel.
- After specifying the parameters, click on the **Close** button from **Custom Result Quantity** dialog box. You will be returned to **Result** tab.
- The total procedure to create custom quantity will discussed later in this chapter.

Planes

The **Planes** tool is used to visualize data in three dimensions. The procedure to use this tool is discussed next.

- Click on the **Planes** tool from **Results Tasks** panel of **Results** tab, the **Plane** tool will be activated and **Planes** context panel will be displayed at left in the **Ribbon**; refer to Figure-11.

Figure-11. Planes tool and panel

- Click on the **Add** button from **Planes** context panel to add a plane on the model to view the result. A plane will be displayed in the model and all tools of **Plane** context panel will be activated; refer to Figure-12.

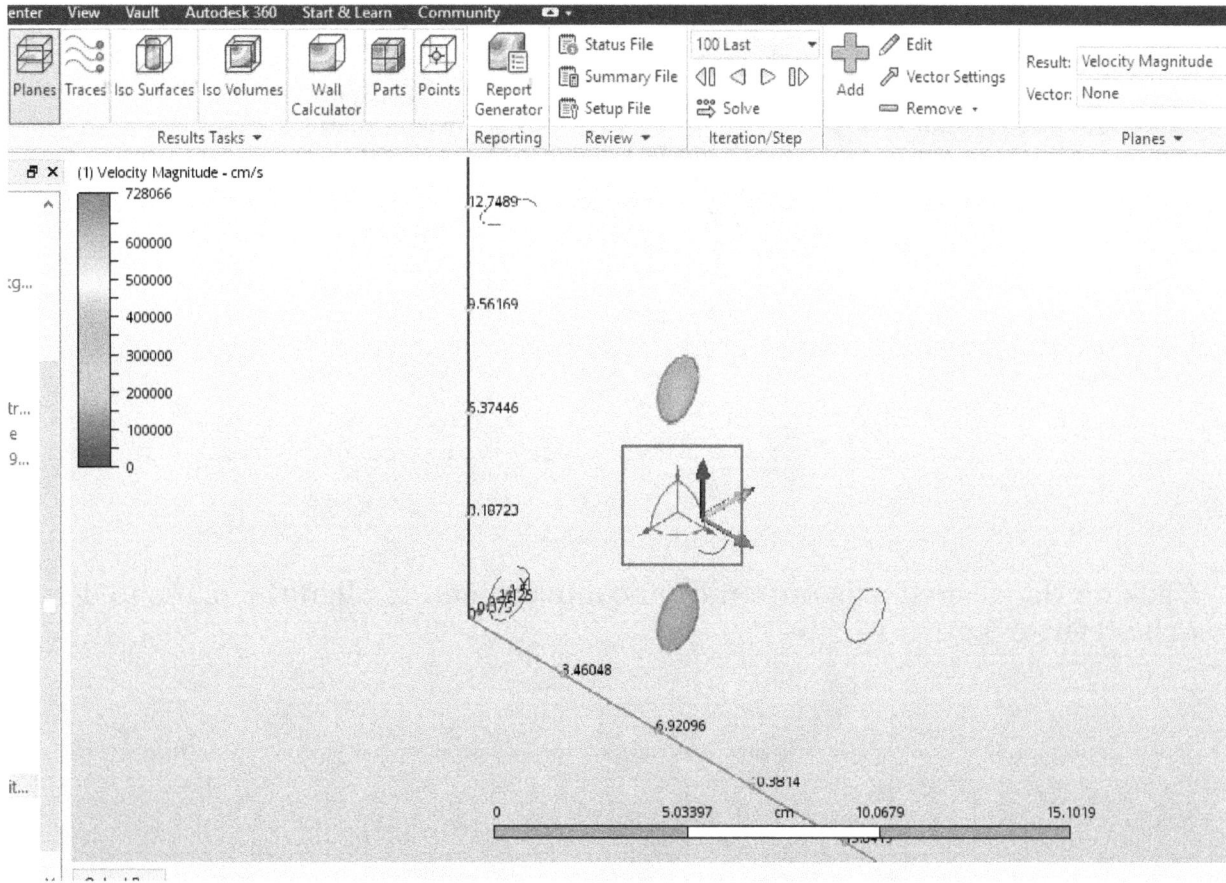

Figure-12. Adding plane

- You can move the added plane with the help of **Plane Controls**. What you need to do is, just grab the required arrow with left-click of mouse and drag to the position where you want to place your plane. The plane will start moving in perpendicular direction to itself.
- You can also change the plane angle or rotate plane by dragging the arc of **Plane Control**.
- If you want to align a plane to desired axis, left-click on the plane. A context menu will be displayed; refer to Figure-13

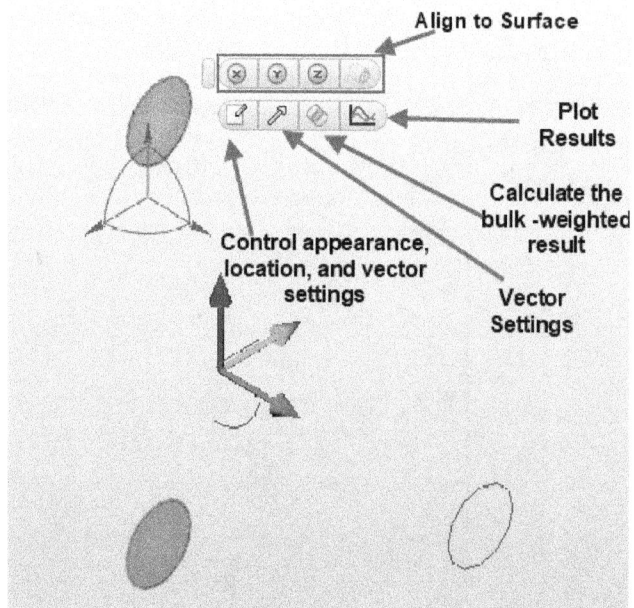

Figure-13. left-click plane context menu

- Click on the desired axis button from context menu to align the plane to desired axis; refer to Figure-14.

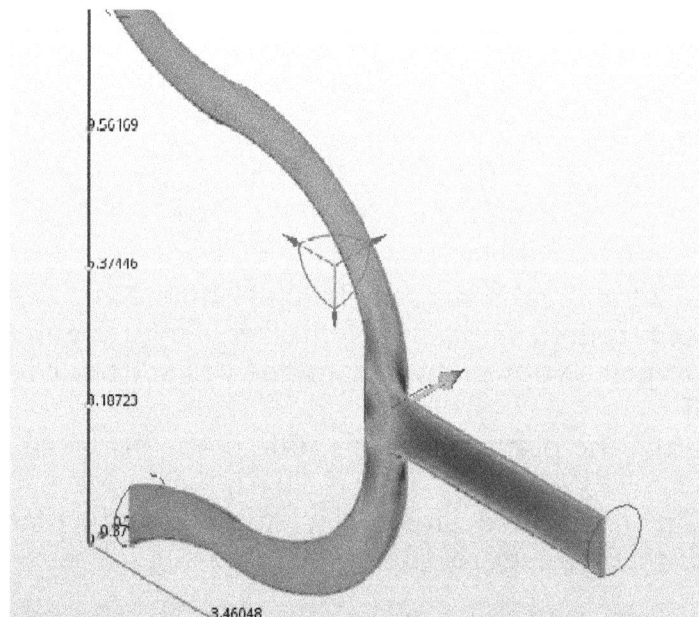

Figure-14. Plane aligned to Y axis

- Click on the **Align to Surface** button from context menu and click on the surface to align the added plane.
- Click on the **Control appearance, location, and vector settings** button from context panel to change appearance and location of plane. The **Plane Control** dialog box will be displayed; refer to Figure-15.

Figure-15. Plane Control dialog box

- The options of **Plane Control** dialog box will be discussed later in this chapter.
- Click on the **Vector Settings** button from context menu to change the plane vector setting with this tool. The **Vector Settings** tab of **Plane Control** dialog box will be displayed. The options of **Vector Settings** tab will be discussed later in this chapter.

Bulk Results

- Click on the **Calculate bulk-weighted results** button from context menu to calculate the bulk-weight results. The **Bulk Results** dialog box will be displayed; refer to Figure-16.

Figure-16. Bulk Results dialog box

- You can also open the **Bulk Results** dialog box by clicking on **Bulk** button from **Planes** panel; refer to Figure-17.

Figure-17. Bulk Button

- The **Bulk Results** dialog box calculates and shows bulk-weighted results on a result pane.
- Select the required check boxes of quantities from **Selection** tab of **Bulk Result** dialog box. If you want to change the unit of selected quantity, click on the unit near check box and select the desired unit from displayed unit list.
- Click on the **Reset** units button to reset the entered units of quantities in **Selection** tab.
- Click on the **All** button to select all the quantities and click on the **None** button to deselect all the quantities.
- After selecting the quantities, click on the **Calculate** button from **Bulk Result** dialog box. The bulk results will be added in **Output** tab; refer to Figure-18.

Figure-18. Output tab of Bulk Results dialog Box

- Click on the **Save** button from **Output** tab to save the current data of bulk result. The **Save Bulk Data** dialog box will be displayed.
- Select the desired location in your computer to save the file, and click on **Save** button. The data will be saved in selected location.
- Now, click on the **Close** button of **Bulk Results** dialog box. The dialog box will be closed and you will be returned to model.

XY Plot

The **XY Plot** is used to create graph of analysis result quantity. This tool is a convenient way to extract and present result data. The procedure to use this is discussed next.

- Click on the **XY Plots** button from left-click context menu after clicking on the added plane, the **XY Plot** dialog box will be displayed; refer to Figure-19. You can also open **XY Plot** dialog box by clicking on **XY Plot** button from **Planes** panel.

Figure-19. XY Plot

- Select the **Add by picking** radio button from **XY Plot** dialog box to add points by clicking on the plane.
- Click on the **Add points** button from **XY Plot** dialog box and click on the pre-created plane to specify points; refer to Figure-20. You can add as many points as you want, but the minimum value of adding points is 2 points.

Figure-20. Adding points

- The plot will pass through selected points location. Click on the **Points list** button from **XY Plot** dialog box to view the list of added points; refer to Figure-21. Again click on the **Point List** button to hide the shown list.

Figure-21. Points list

- Click on the **Plot** button from **XY Plot** dialog box to view the plot. The **XY Plot: Plot 1** will be displayed; refer to Figure-22.

Figure-22. XY Plot Plot 1

- You can customize the appearance of the plot by using the various button from dialog box.
- Click on the **Show points** button to view the points in graph and click again on the **Show Points** button to hide the points from graph.
- Click on the **Save data** button to save the current data for future reference. The **Save** dialog box will be displayed. Select the desired location and click on the **Save** button from **Save** dialog box.
- Click on the **Save image** button to save the current screen of graph. The **Save Image** dialog box will be displayed. Save the image in desired location. You can also select the desired file extension for image from **Save as Type** drop-down of **Save Image** dialog box. The default file extension for saving image is .bmp.
- Click on the **Save points** button to save the data of points. The file extension of points data file will be .xyp.
- Click on the top right corner drop-down to change the plotted result quantity and select the desired quantity from the displayed list.
- If you want to change the Y-axis unit, right-click on the plot window and select the desired unit from **Units** cascading menu; refer to Figure-23.

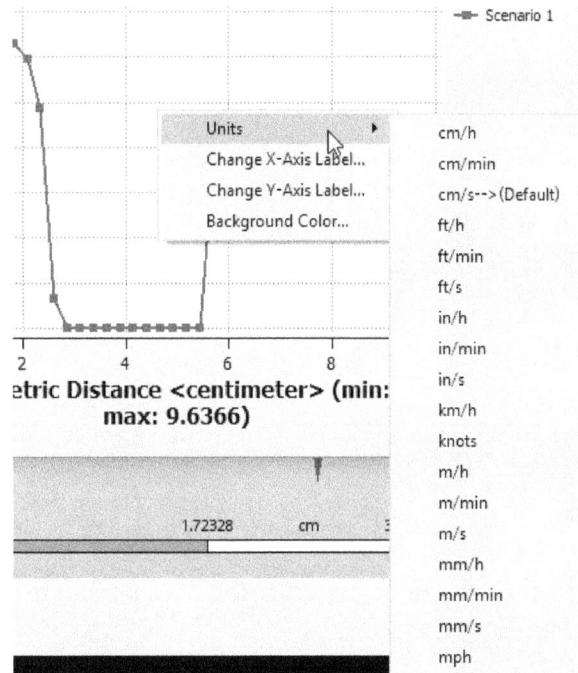

Figure-23. Selecting Units for Y-axis

• Click on the **Change X-axis label** button from right-click menu to change or create label. The **Edit X-axis Label** dialog box will be displayed; refer to Figure-24.

*Figure-24. The Edit X-Axis Label
dialog box*

• Enter the desired label and click on the **OK** button. The new label will be created and displayed in **XY Plot** dialog box.
• If you want to set the label to default, click on the **Set default** button from **Edit X-Axis** Label dialog box.
• Similarly you can change the Y-Axis label.
• Click on the **Background color** button from right-click menu to change the background color of graph. The **Select color** dialog box will be displayed; refer to Figure-25.

Figure-25. Select Color dialog

- Select the desired color and click on the **OK** button. The background color will be changed with the selected one.
- After checking the plot, click on the **Close** button from **XY Plot: Plot 1** dialog box. You will be returned to **XY Plot** dialog box.

Add by key-in

- Select the **Add by key-in** radio button from **XY Plot** dialog box to add the points by entering their particular X,Y, and Z coordinates values.
- Click in the **Add** edit box and enter the coordinates separated by comma. You can view the coordinates value of a particular point from **Status bar**; refer to Figure-26.

Figure-26. Entering coordinates value

- When you move the cursor on the added plane, the coordinates value of that particular point will be displayed in status bar. After entering the value, click on **Add** button of **XY Plot** dialog box. The point will be added.
- Similarly you can add as many points as you want.
- Click on the **Title** edit box and enter the name of title, which you want to give to the current plot.
- Click in the **Divisions per segment** edit box from **XY Plot** dialog box and enter the value to change the plot resolution. The default number of divisions between every point is 20.

- If you want to view the entered coordinates of points, click on **Points list** button from **XY Plot** dialog box. The list will be displayed; refer to Figure-27.

Figure-27. Points List for added coordinates

After specifying the parameters, click on the **Plot** button from **XY Plot** dialog box, the **XY Plot: Pot 2** will be displayed. This plot was discussed earlier.

Read from file

- Select the **Read from file** radio button from **XY Plot** dialog box to input the data from a previous saved file. The procedure to save a file was discussed earlier.
- Click on the **Browse** button from **XY Plot** dialog box, the **Open XYPlot Points File** dialog box will be displayed; refer to Figure-28.

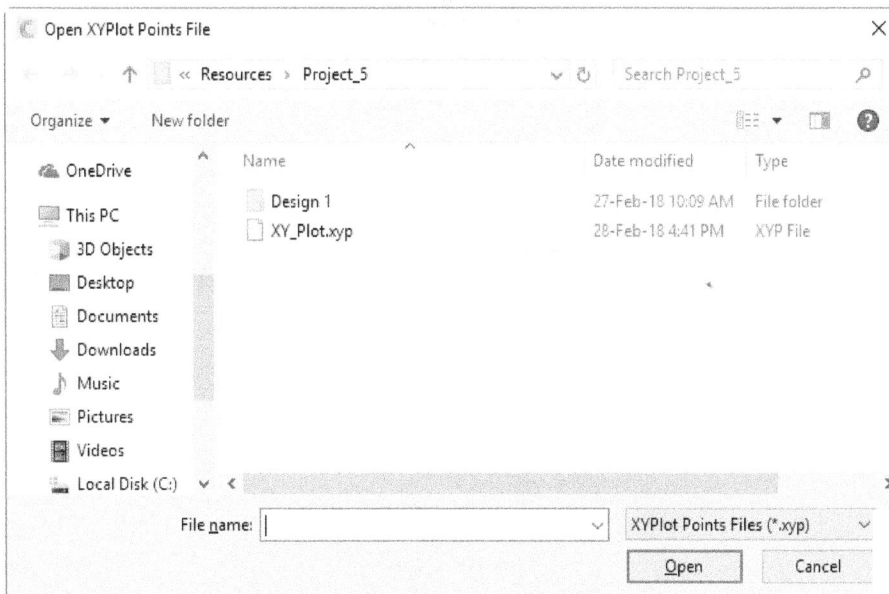

Figure-28. Open XYPlot Points File dialog box

- Select the desired file and click on the **Open** button, the file will be opened in **XY Plot** dialog box and the data related to this file will be automatically updated in **XY Plot** dialog box; refer to Figure-29.

*Figure-29. Updated XY Plot
dialog Box*

- Click on the **Plot** button from **XY Plot** dialog box to view the plot as per current coordinates.
- After checking the plot and performing required operation, close the **XY Plot** dialog box. You will be returned to **Results** tab.

Editing Plane for XY Plot

The **Edit** tool is used to align, move, and rotate the added plane. The procedure to use this is discussed next.

- Click on the **Edit** button from **Planes** panel of **Result** tab, the **Plane Control** dialog box will be displayed; refer to Figure-30.

Figure-30. Planes Control dialog box

- There are two tabs available in **Plane Control** dialog box, which are, **Controls** and **Vectors settings** tabs. First, we will discuss the **Controls** tab and then **Vector settings** tab.

Controls tab

- Click on the **Result** drop-down from **Plane Control** dialog box and select the desired quantity which you want to view on the added plane. On selecting the quantities, the visualization and appearance of plane also change.
- The coordinates in **Position** section show the exact location of plane. To change the location, click on the **Point on plane** button from **Position** section of **Plane Controls** dialog box. The **Edit point on Plane** dialog box will be displayed; refer to Figure-31.

Figure-31. Edit point on plane dialog box

- Enter the desired coordinates in X, Y, and Z edit box, and click on **OK** button. The plain will move to entered coordinates.
- Drag and move the **Move** slider in **Plane Control** dialog box to move the plane at desired location. You can also do the same by entering the value manually in **Move** edit box.
- If you want to rotate the plane in desired direction, click on the **Normal** button from **Move** section. The **Edit plane normal** dialog box will be displayed.
- Enter the desired values in X, Y, and Z edit boxes to define component of direction vector for plane. If you have entered 1 in **X** edit box then the plane will become perpendicular to X axis, if you specify 1 in Y edit box while others are 0 then plane will become perpendicular to Y axis.
- Move the **Rotate** slider to rotate the plane along selected axis. First, you need to specify the axis about which the plane should move using the **Rotation axis** button. The procedure to specify axis is same as discussed above.
- Click on the **Save table** button from **Plane Control** dialog box to save the plane table data. The **Save Plane Data** dialog box will be displayed. Specify the location and click on **Save** button. The file will be saved.
- Click on the **Appearance** drop-down and select the desired option to change the appearance of plane; refer to Figure-32.

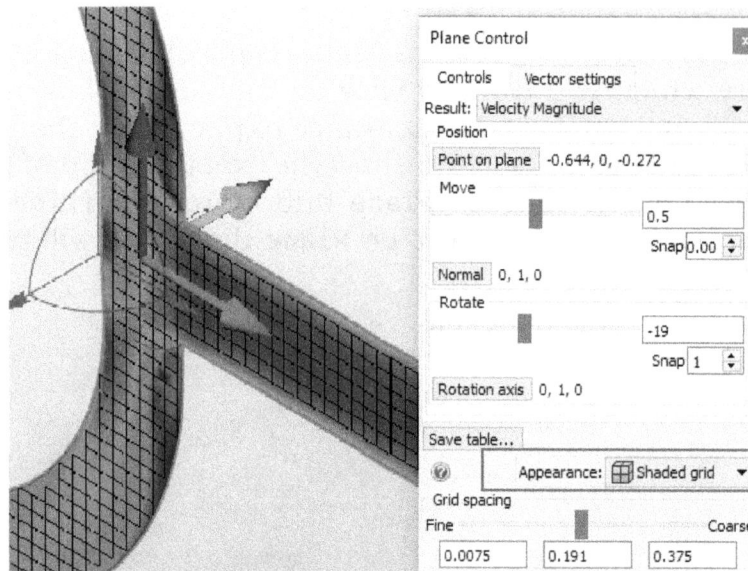

Figure-32. Selecting Appearance of plane

- The **Grid spacing** section is only available on selecting **Shaded grid** and **Outline grid** option.
- Move the **Grid spacing** slider to specify the spacing between grids. Move the slider towards **Fine** option to decrease the spacing between grids and move the slider towards **Coarse** option to increase the spacing of grids. You can also specify these values manually.

Vector Settings tab

The **Vector settings** tab is used to apply and modify the vector on a plane. The procedure to use this tool is discussed next. It is generally used to observe the flow of particles inside a model.

- Click on the **Vector settings** tab of **Plane Control** dialog box. The parameters related to **Vector Settings** tab will be displayed; refer to Figure-33.

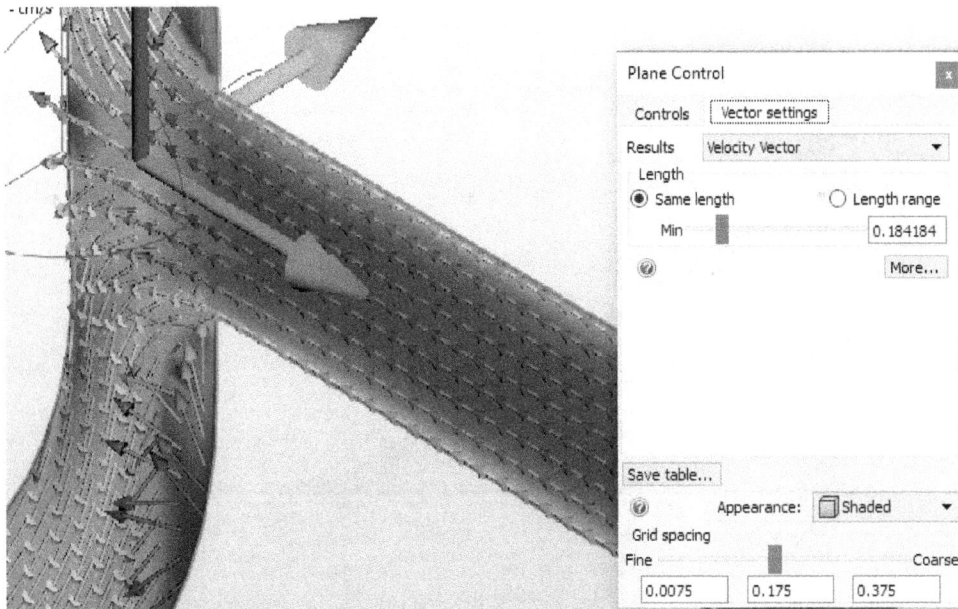

Figure-33. Vector settings tab

- The **Vector Settings** tab was discussed earlier in **Global** section in this chapter.
- You can also open the **Vector Settings** tab by clicking on **Vector Settings** tool from **Planes** panel; refer to Figure-34.

Figure-34. Vector Settings button

- After specifying the parameters in **Plane Control** dialog box, close the dialog box. You will be returned to **Results** tab.
- Click on the **Remove** button from **Plane** panel to remove the planes from the model. If you had added multiple planes to the model, click on the **Remove All** button by clicking on little arrow of **Remove** button. All planes will be deleted.
- Select the **Show Outline** check box from **Planes** panel drop-down to view outline of plane appearance; refer to Figure-35.

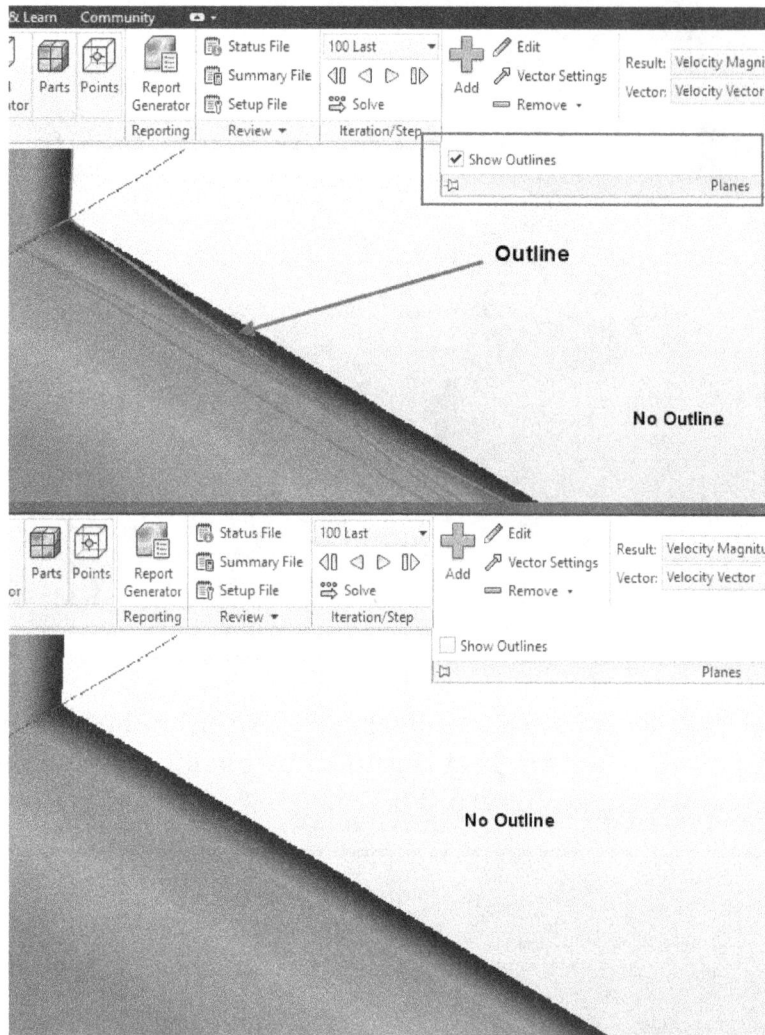

Figure-35. Outline of plane

- Click on the **Make Summary** button from **Planes** panel to make the selected plane as summary plane for results comparison in the **Decision centre**. The **Decision centre** will be discussed later.

Traces

The **Traces** tool is used to understand the behavior of flow inside the model, around the corners, and near edges. **Traces** tool acts like some colored droplet injected into flow. We can use these droplet to identifies the location where fluid changes its direction and how it moves. The procedure to use this is discussed next.

- Click on the **Traces** tool from **Results Tasks** panel of **Results** tab. The tools for applying **Traces** will be activated; refer to Figure-36.

Figure-36. Traces tool

- To apply **Traces** tool, you will need to add a plane near the inlet flow of the model. The reason behind this is to place some colored particles on that plane so that the placed particles will move as per the given flow in and around the model.

Create Set panel

The **Create Set** panel is used to specify the basic parameters of adding traces to a plane. These parameters are discussed next.

- Click on the **Seed Type** drop-down and select **Point** option to display flow of single point as per analysis. Click on the **Add** button from **Create Set** panel and click on the plane at desired locations, the flow will be traced automatically; refer to Figure-37. You can add as many points as required on the plane.

Figure-37. Traces with Point option

- Click on the **Seed Type** drop-down and select **Line** option to add a line of points on the plane. Click on the **Add** button from **Crate Set** panel and click to specify end points of line. The particles will be traced; refer to Figure-38.

Figure-38. Line option of traces

- Click on the **Seed Type** drop-down and select **Ring** option to add points in ring like structure on the plane. Now, click on **Add** button and click on the plane to specify center point of ring. Click again at desired location to define the diameter of ring. The particles will be traced in or around model as per flow; refer to Figure-39.

Figure-39. Ring option of traces

- Click on the **Seed Type** drop-down and select **Circular** option to add points in circular structure. The points will combine to form a circular shape of points.
- Click on the **Seed Pattern** drop-down and select the desired pattern in which points will be placed inside the circle; refer to Figure-40.

Diamond pattern   **Grid pattern**   **Hexagon pattern**

Figure-40. Seed pattern

- Click in the **Seed Density** edit box from **Create Set** panel and specify the density of points or seed. The limit of density value is in between 0 to 10. Higher the density value, more will be the gap between seeds or points.
- After specifying the required parameters, click on the **Add** button from **Create Set** panel and click on the plane to specify center of the circle and click again to specify the diameter of circle. The seeds will be traced as per flow inside the model; refer to Figure-41.

Figure-41. Circular Shape

- Similarly, you can create rectangular shape of seeds using **Rectangular** option of **Seed Type** drop-down from **Create Set** panel.
- Click on the **Seed Type** drop-down and select **Region** option to generate trace for whole selected face/surface. Now, you need to click on the plane, the particles will displayed as per the parameters set in **Create Set** panel of **Ribbon** while tracing the path; refer to Figure-42.

Figure-42. Region option of traces

- Click on the **Seed Type** drop-down and select the **Key in** option to create the seeds by entering the coordinates. Click on the **Add** button, the **Key In Trace Set** dialog box will be displayed; refer to Figure-43.

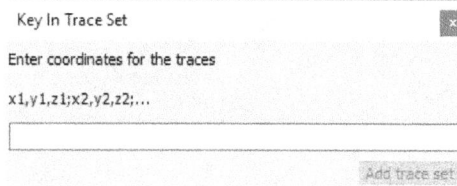

Key In Trace Set

Enter coordinates for the traces

x1,y1,z1;x2,y2,z2;...

Add trace set

Figure-43. Key In Trace Set dialog Box

- Specify the coordinates and click on the **Add trace** set button. The trace point will be added and displayed. Note that the entered coordinates should lie on plane, then only traces will work.

Modify Set panel

The **Modify Set** panel is used to edit and remove the existing traces. The procedure to use tools in this panel is discussed next.

- Click on the **Edit** button from **Modify Set** panel, the **Edit Traces Set** dialog box will be displayed; refer to Figure-44.

Edit Trace Set - Set 1

Set properties

Trace ID	Residence time (sec)
1	3.8195e-05
2	3.1670e-05
3	3.0331e-05
4	3.1049e-05
5	3.6636e-05

Delete   Delete set

Color
◉ Results   Velocity Magnitude ▼
○ Solid   ☐

Properties
Appearance: Cylinders ▼
Range: Full range ▼
Width: 100% ▼
Steps: 5000
☐ Mass   Mass properties

Close

Figure-44. Edit Trace Set dialog box

- The number of **Trace ID** from **Set Properties** section refers to the number of seeds on a plane. In our case, there are 45 seeds or points created on the plane with the help of **Region** option.
- If you want to delete any seed, select the seed and click on the **Delete** button. If you want to delete a set of seeds, select the seeds and click on the **Delete set** button.

- Click on the **Results** drop-down and select the desired result quantity which you want to see. Select the **Result** radio button to activate this drop-down.
- Select the **Solid** radio button from **Color** section to specify a desired color to the traces. The default color of traces is white.
- To change the color, click on the **Solid** check box which is placed in front of **Solid** radio button. The **Select Color** dialog box will be displayed; refer to Figure-45.

Figure-45. Select Color dialog box

- Select the color and click on the **OK** button from **Select Color** dialog box. The color of traces will be changed to your selected color.
- Click on the **Appearance** drop-down from **Properties** section of **Edit Trace Set** dialog box and select the required appearance of traces. There are 5 types of appearances available in **Appearance** drop-down.
- Click on the **Range** drop-down from **Properties** section to select the required range of traces. Select the **Forward** button to view traces towards the fluid flow. Select the **Backward** button to view traces against the fluid flow; refer to Figure-46. Select the **Full Range** button to view trace in both direction i.e. forward and backward direction.

Figure-46. Forward and backward range

- Click on the **Width** drop-down from **Properties** section and select the width of traces appearance.
- Click in the **Steps** edit box and specify the value of traces. Here, steps implies the length of traces inside the model; refer to Figure-47.

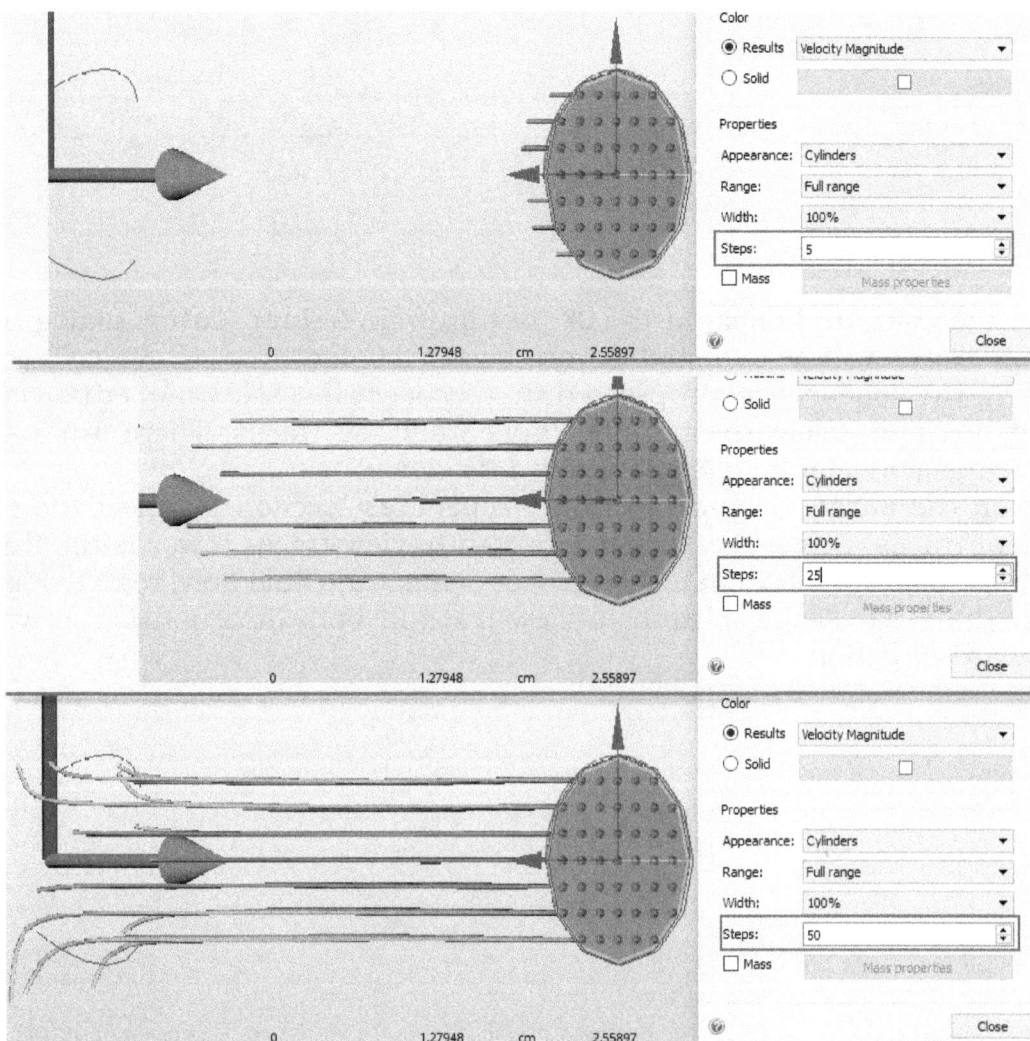

Figure-47. Steps

- Select the **Mass** check box from **Properties** section to apply some mass to the particles or seeds. This tool help us to observe the real time condition by applying mass to the seeds which are flowing along the flow inside the model. The resulting trace behaves like a physical substance within a flow system; refer to Figure-48.

Figure-48. Mass enabled and disabled

- You can see the difference in above figure. In left figure, the particles are acting like they are containing some mass and are flowing in a restricted manner inside the boundary of model. In right figure, you can see the particles are moving freely.
- On selecting the **Mass** check box, the **Mass properties** button will be activated. Click on the **Mass properties** button to view and edit the mass properties of the particles, the **Mass** dialog box will be displayed; refer to Figure-49.

Figure-49. Mass dialog box

- Click in the **Coefficient of restitution** edit box from **Mass** dialog box to specify the coefficient value. It is the measure of bounce amount between two objects, or we can say the ratio of velocities of objects before and after collision. Mathematically it can be described as:

$$C = \frac{V_{2f} - V_{1f}}{V_{2i} - V_{1i}}$$

V_{1f} - Velocity of first object
V_{2f} - Velocity of second object
 i - initial velocity
 f - final velocity

- The default value of **Coefficient of restitution** is 0.5 and can be specify in between 0.01 to 1. The value 0.01 implies the inelastic collision and the particles stick on hitting the wall. The value of 1 implies as perfectly elastic collision, and the particles has the same velocity before and after collision.
- Select the **Set initial velocity** check box from **Initial path** section of **Mass** dialog box to specify the initial velocity and direction of trace. The magnitude and direction (unit vector) option will be activated.
- Specify the **Magnitude** and **Direction (unit vector)** for initial velocity as desired.
- Select the **Enable gravity for massed particles** check box from **Gravity** section of **Mass** dialog box to include the body forces on the particles throughout the process. The X, Y, and Z components edit box will be enabled to enter the force value. Enter the value as required to specify the body forces on particle.
- Select the **Earth** check box from **Gravity** section of **Mass** dialog box to enable the earth's gravity on the trace particle. Now, you need to enter the unit vector in X, Y, and Z component to specify the direction of earth's gravity.
- The **Drag Correlation** characteristics of each particle only affect the motion not the flow of particle. Particle traces are purely a post processing tool and does not effect the flow field at all. The drag correlation is basically used for massed particles. The equation of **Drag Correlation** is given in **Mass** dialog box itself. What you need to do is enter the values of a, b, and c in respective edit boxes to change the drag as required.
- Click on the **Enable/Update Erosion** button from **Mass** dialog box to reduce erosion reduction for the sake of design improvement. The erosion will be updated automatically on the model.
- After specifying the parameters, click on **Apply** button and then click on the **Close** button from **Mass** dialog box, you will be returned to **Edit Trace Set** dialog box.
- After specifying the parameters from **Edit Trace Set** dialog box, click on the **Close** button. You will be returned to **Results** tab along with updated model.
- Click on the **Remove** button from **Modify Set** panel to remove the last added trace particles. If you want to remove all the added traces, click on the **Remove All** button from **Remove** drop-down in **Modify Set** panel of **Ribbon**; refer to Figure-50.

Figure-50. Remove and Remove All button

Project Seeds panel

The tools of **Project Seeds** panel are used to allow traces to be placed on desired surfaces or plane. These tools are generally used to position the traces on a desired location to visualize flow very close to model boundaries and edges.

Down to Shaded Surface

The **Down to Shaded Surface** button from **Project Seeds** panel is used for concentrating traces off the solid. This condition is used where flow is very close to the model and we need to study the effects of flow on the solid. The procedure to use this is discussed next.

- Create a seed distribution near the object that exceeds the size of object. You may have to create the seed grid off the solid and then move it near the object with the help of triad axis; refer to Figure-51.

Figure-51. Creating seed distribution

- This tool works by projecting the seed traces in the negative direction of the yellow axis. If necessary, rotate the triad axis to ensure the correct orientation.
- Now, select the model from **Results** of **Design Study Bar** and click on **Shaded** button from right-click menu; refer to Figure-52. The model will be displayed in shaded mode.

Figure-52. changing appearance

- Select the traces from **Results** and click on the **Down to Shaded Surface** button from **Projector Seeds** panel. The seeds will projected to the first shaded surface in line with negative yellow axis of triad; refer to Figure-53.

Figure-53. Seeds projected to surface

- To view the flow, hold and move the triad axis to a small distance away from model. The flow of traces will be displayed; refer to Figure-54. If no traces can be projected onto a surface, the trace distribution remains unchanged.

Figure-54. Flow as per traces

Up to Seed Plane

The **Up to Seed Plane** tool is used to project trace seeds that are distributed across a curved surface onto a plane. Click on **Up to Seed Plane** tool from **Project Seeds** panel, it moves the seed points to the plane defined by two blue axes in the triad; refer to Figure-55. This tool is used after applying the **Down to Shaded Surface** tool.

Figure-55. Before and after Up to seed plane tool

Process Traces panel

The **Process Traces** panel is used to animate the created traces and to extract data to external file. The **Process Traces** panel is generally used after applying traces to the model for watching the traces process in animation mode. The tools of this panel are discussed next.

- The **Animate** tool is used to view animation of existing traces. The procedure to animate is simple. Just click on the **Animate** tool, the **Animate Traces** dialog box will be displayed; refer to Figure-56.

Figure-56. Animate Traces dialog box

- Click in the **Animation Time (sec)** edit box and enter the value of duration to play the animation of traces.

- The other tools in **Animate Traces** dialog box are common play & pause tools with which you are already familiar.
- After specifying the duration of animation, click on the **Play** button. The animation starts playing; refer to Figure-57.

Figure-57. Playing animation

- If you want to save the animation video file, click on the **Save avi.** button from **Animate Traces** dialog box, the **Save AVI File** dialog box will be displayed.
- Specify the desired location and click on the **Save** button. The file will be saved in desired location.
- Click on the **Save Data Table** tool from **Process Traces** panel to save the data of all traces from initial position to final position off all particles as per animation of traces. The **Save Trace Data** dialog box is displayed.
- You need to specific the location to save the **Trace Data** file and click on the **Save** button. The file will be saved at specified location. You can view this file in MS Excel and other database processing software.

Iso Surfaces

The **Iso Surfaces** tool is a 3D visualization tool that shows a value as well as physical shape of flow characteristics. The physical shape of flow is useful for visualizing velocity distribution and thermal distribution in complicated flow paths of model. The **Iso Surfaces** tool is also used for determining the minimum and maximum values of quantity. An iso surface is a surface of constant value. The procedure to use this is discussed next.

- Click on the **Iso surfaces** tool from **Result Tasks** panel of **Results** tab, the **Iso Surfaces** panel will be displayed; refer to Figure-58

Figure-58. Iso surfaces tool and panel

- Click on the **Add** button from **Iso Surfaces** panel, the iso surface will be added on model and in **Results** of **Design Study Bar**; refer to Figure-59.

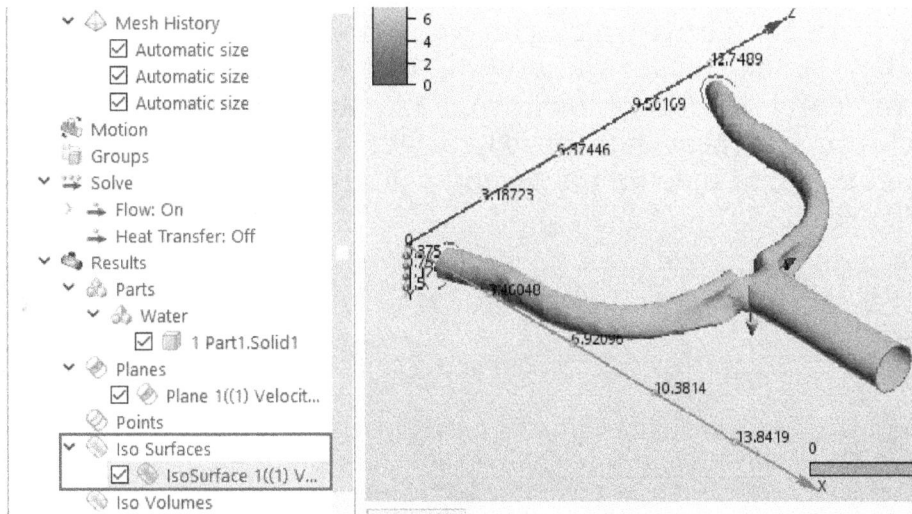
Figure-59. Iso surface

- Click on the **Edit** button from **Iso Surfaces** panel to edit quantity and appearance of the iso surface, the **Iso Surface Control** dialog box will be displayed; refer to Figure-60.

Figure-60. Iso Surface Control dialog box

- You can also open the **Iso Surface Control** dialog box by clicking on **Edit** button from after activating **Iso Surfaces** panel; refer to Figure-61.

Figure-61. Right click menu of iso surface

- The **Quantity** option is the scalar result that determines the shape of iso surface, and **Color By** option determines the color. By default, these two options are same. If you want to see two different results together, you need to select different scalar results.

- Click on the **Quantity** drop-down from **Iso Surface Control** dialog box and select the desired quantity which you want to view in iso surface. As you change the quantity, the iso surface will automatically change as per selected quantity.
- Click on the **Color By** drop-down from **Iso Surfaces Control** dialog box and select the desired appearance for iso surface. If you select any parameter other than **Velocity Magnitude** then a legend will also displayed on graphics window; refer to Figure-62.

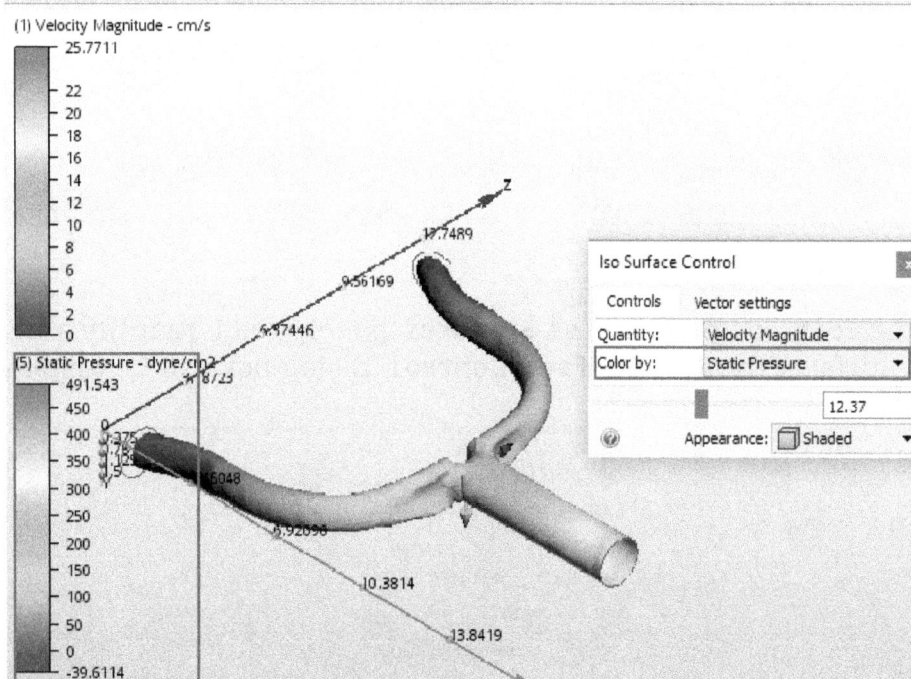

Figure-62. Chaning color of iso surface

- The above figures shows the velocity magnitude at all location of model that have same static pressure.
- Move the slider to change the location of iso surface in the model. You can also enter the value manually.
- Click on the **Appearance** drop-down from **Iso Surface Control** dialog box and select the required appearance of model.
- Click on the **Vector Settings** tab of **Iso Surface Control** dialog box to change the vector settings. **Vector Settings** tab will be displayed; refer to Figure-63.

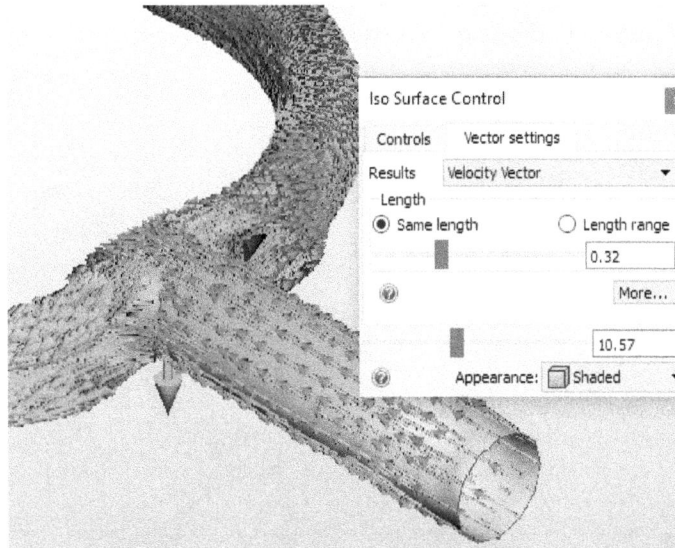

Figure-63. Vector Settings tab1

- The options in this tab are same as discussed earlier.
- After specifying the parameters, close the **Iso Surface Control** dialog box. The applied changes will be reflected on the model.
- You can also do the same using **Quantity**, **Color By**, and **Vector** drop-downs in **Iso Surfaces** panel of **Result** tab; refer to Figure-64.

Figure-64. Tools of Iso Surfaces panel

- To remove a single iso surface or all iso surfaces, click on the **Remove** and **Remove All** button respectively from **Iso Surfaces** panel. The iso surfaces will be deleted.

Iso Volumes

The **Iso Volumes** tool is used to display the result in the form of iso volume based on selected result parameters. Like you can create an iso volume for velocity result so that you can check the change in velocity of fluid at different locations in the model. The procedure to use this tool is discussed next.

- Click on the **Iso Volumes** tool from **Results Tasks** panel of **Results** tab, the tool will be activated and **Iso Volumes** panel will be displayed; refer to Figure-65.

Figure-65. Iso Volumes tool and panel

- Most of the tools in **Iso Volumes** panel are disabled by default. To enable them, you need to add an iso volume by clicking on **Add** button. Iso volume will be displayed on model.

- Click on the **Edit** button from **Iso Volumes** panel to edit the iso volume parameters, the **Iso Volume Control** dialog box will be displayed; refer to Figure-66.

Figure-66. Iso Volume Control dialog box

- Set the **Minimum** and **Maximum** value by moving the slider respectively. The iso volume as per specified minimum and maximum values of the result quantity will be displayed.
- Adjust the parameter of **Vector Settings** tab of **Iso Volume Control** dialog box as per requirement.
- After specifying the parameters, close the **Iso Volume Control** dialog box. The iso volume will be displayed as per specified parameters.
- The other tools is **Iso Volumes** panel are similar to **Iso Surfaces** panel, which were discussed earlier.

Wall Calculator

The **Wall Calculator** tool is used to calculate flow-induced forces on solid and wall surfaces. These forces are useful in many situations, like calculating the lift and drag on aerodynamics bodies. This tool can calculate pressure, wall temperature, heat flux, etc. The procedure to use this tool is discussed next.

- Click on the **Wall Calculator** button from **Result Tasks** panel of **Results** tab, the **Wall Result** dialog box will be displayed; refer to Figure-67.

Figure-67. Wall Results dialog box

- Select the **Volume** or **Surface** radio button from **Model entity selection** section to select entities of model for wall results.
- If you have selected **Volume** radio button, then hover the mouse on model, the volume will be highlighted. Click to select the highlighted model.
- If you have selected **Surface** radio button then hover the mouse on the model, the surfaces start to highlight. Click on the surface to assess wall results; refer to Figure-68.

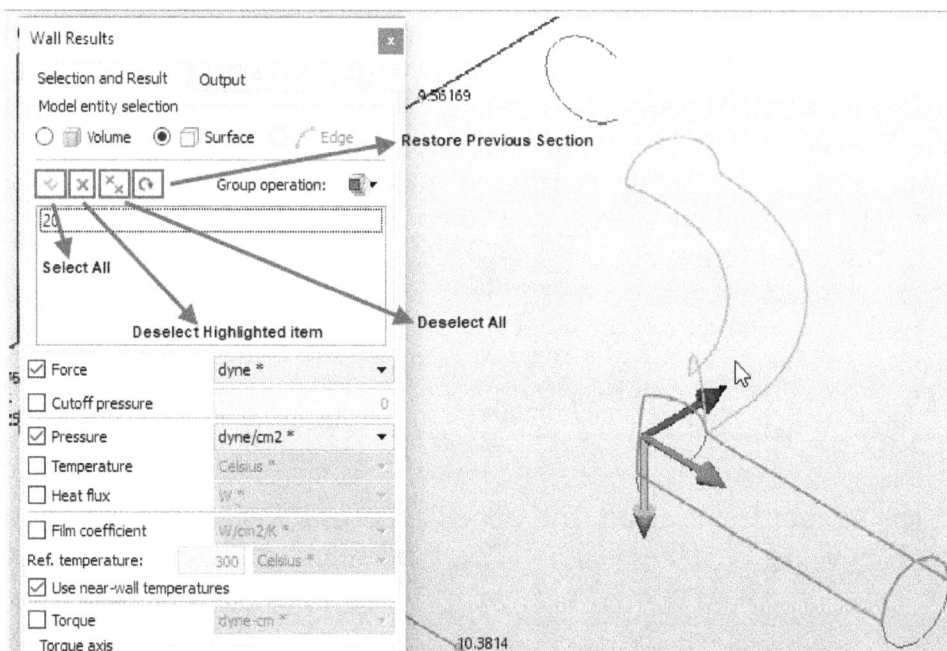

Figure-68. Selecting surfaces

- On selecting entities, the surfaces will be displayed in **Wall Results** dialog box.

- Click on the **Select All** button to select all the surfaces/volumes present in model.
- Click on the **Deselect Highlighted Items** button to deselect the highlighted surface/volume.
- Click on the **Deselect All** button to deselect all the selected surface/volume.
- Click on the **Restore Previous Selection** button to restore the last deleted selection.
- Select the **Force** check box from **Wall Results** dialog box to calculate the force. Force components and magnitude are computed for each selected surface and the total force for all selected surfaces is also computed. Select the desired unit for force from the unit drop-down.
- Select the **Cutoff Pressure** check box from **Wall Results** dialog box to remove very low wall pressure from the force calculation. The **Cutoff pressure** edit box will be activated. Click in the edit box and enter the minimum pressure value. This value will be assigned to all locations with pressures.
- Select the **Pressure** check box from **Wall Results** dialog box to display the pressure for wall results. Specify the unit of pressure from pressure drop-down.
- Select the **Temperature** check box from **Wall Results** dialog box to display unit on wall surface. Specify the unit of temperature from temperature drop-down. Temperature values on walls are not available during the analysis. They are computed after the analysis is completed.
- Select the **Heat Flux** check box from **Wall Results** dialog box to display heat flux in wall results. **Heat Flux** is based on thermal residual from heat transfer solution. The values of heat flux is not accessible from intermediate saved iterations or time steps on the **Wall Result** dialog box.
- Select the **Film Coefficient** check box from **Wall Results** dialog box, if you want to calculate film coefficient on wall.
- Click and specify the **Ref. temperature** value to calculate film coefficient which is based on heat flux and temperature difference between the specified reference temperature and wall temperature. Note that this edit box is not available if **Use near-wall temperatures** check box is stopped.
- Select the **Use near-wall temperatures** check box from **Wall Results** dialog box to use wall temperature at every wall node as the local reference temperature for calculating **Film Coefficient**.
- Select the **Torque** check box from **Wall Results** dialog box to calculate torque around an axis. Click on the **Point on Axis** button, the **Torque axis point** dialog box will be displayed. Specify the coordinates in as required and click on **OK** button; refer to Figure-69.

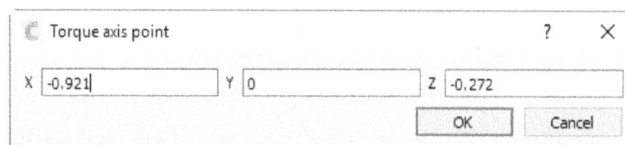

Figure-69. Torque axis point dialog box

- Click on the **Direction** button and specify the unit vector to specify direction of torque in **Torque axis direction** dialog box; refer to Figure-70.

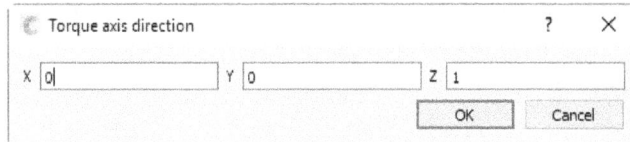

Figure-70. Torque axis direction edirt box

- After specifying the parameters in **Wall Result** dialog box, click on the **Calculate** button to calculate the wall results. The result of all selected surfaces will be displayed in **Output** tab; refer to Figure-71.

Figure-71. Output tab of Wall Results dialog box

- Click on the **Write to file** button from **Wall Results** dialog box to save this data to an excel .CSV file. The **Save Wall Data** dialog box will be displayed. Specify the desired location and click on the **Save** button. The file will be saved at specified location.
- Click on the **View File** button from **Wall Results** dialog box to open an existing .CSV file. The data of selected file will be displayed in **Output** tab.
- Click on **Close** button to close the **Wall Results** dialog box. You will be returned to **Results** tab.

Parts

The **Parts** tool is used to assess results on selected parts. The procedure to use this tool is discussed next.

- Click on the **Parts** tool from **Results Tasks** panel of **Result** tab; refer to Figure-72. The **Parts** panel will be activated and **Parts** dialog box will be displayed; refer to Figure-73.

Figure-72. Parts panel

Figure-73. Parts dialog box

- To compare parts, you need to click on the component from model, the selected part will displayed in **Parts** dialog box and the boundaries of selected parts will be highlighted in pink color; refer to Figure-74.

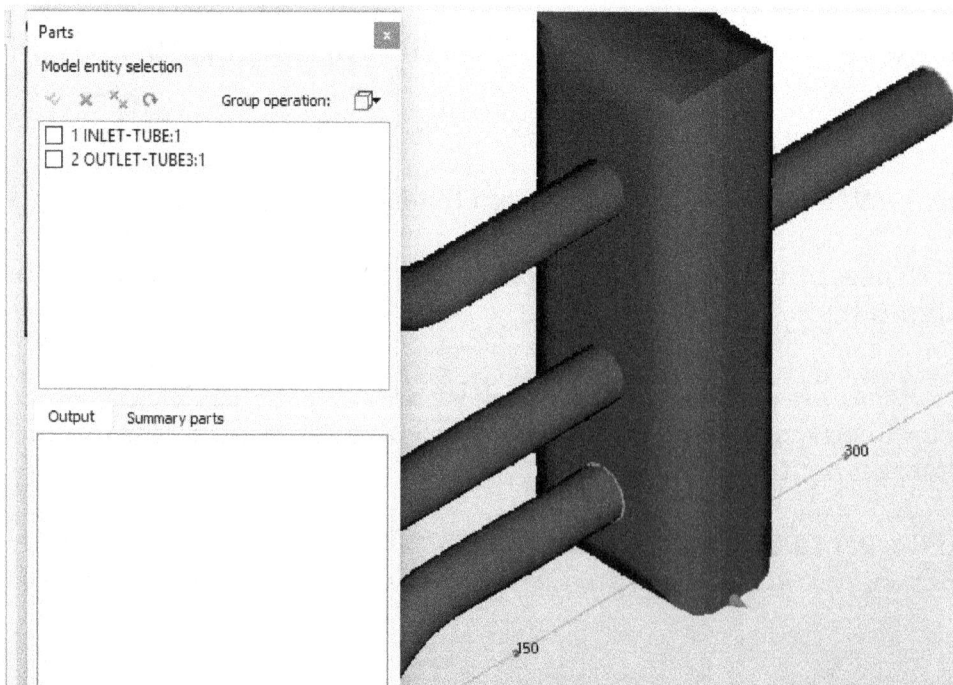

Figure-74. Selected parts

- Select the check box of components from Parts dialog box to select or deselect the parts for comparison.
- Click on the **Calculate** button from **Parts** dialog box, the result will be displayed in **Output** tab; refer to Figure-75.

Figure-75. Calculated results of parts

- Click on the **Make Summary** button from **Parts** panel to designate a part as a summary part.
- Click on the **Summary Parts** tab of **Parts** dialog box to view the list of summary parts; refer to Figure-76.

Figure-76. Summary Parts tab

- Click on the **Save** button from **Parts** dialog box to save the summary part data. The **Save Summary Part Data** dialog box will be displayed. Specify the desired location to save the file and click on the **Save** button. The data will be saved in .TXT format file.

Points

The **Points** tool is used to plot the time or iteration history at a specific location in model with Result Points. These result points act as summary points to assess critical values and to compare result with other scenarios. The procedure to use this tool is discussed next.

Before starting this tool, you need to specify a result save interval in **Solve** dialog box; refer to Figure-77. This cause the software to save intermediate time steps throughout the calculation. You may need to run the analysis again.

Figure-77. Save Intervals form

- Click on the **Points** tool from **Results Tasks** panel of **Results** tab, the **Points** dialog box will be displayed; refer to Figure-78.

Figure-78. Points dialog box and Points panel

- Move the **X**, **Y**, and **Z** slider to specify a point. You can also specify a point by moving triad axis. If you want to manually enter the coordinates for result point, then click in **X**, **Y**, or **Z** axis edit box and specify the value respectively.
- After specifying the location of point, click on the **Add** button from **Points** dialog box or **Points** panel or left-click menu; refer to Figure-79. The coordinated of points will be mentioned in **Points** dialog box; refer to . Figure-80.

Figure-79. Add button

Figure-80. Added points

- If you want to create a point on geometry surface, then left-click off the model and click on **Align to Surface** button. This tool will be activated; refer to Figure-81.

Figure-81. Align to surface button

- The **Align to Surface** tool gives priority to shaded surface. Always remember, not to click too close to a shaded surface while positioning a monitor point.
- After creating points, click on the **Plot** button from **Points** dialog box to view plot. The **XY Plot: Point 2** will be displayed along with the plot; refer to Figure-82.

Figure-82. XY Plot Point 2 dialog box

- The tools of **XY Plot** dialog box were discussed earlier.

Report Generator

The **Report Generator** tool is used to create a final report of your simulation. Earlier, you need to spend a significant amount of time for generating report in a presentable format. Now, with the help of this tool, you can easily create or customize the report to communicate and share with others. The procedure to use this tool is discussed next.

- Click on the **Report Generator** tool from **Results Tasks** panel of **Result** tab, the **Simulation Report** dialog box will be displayed; refer to Figure-83.

Figure-83. Simulation Report dialog box

- The **General** tab of **Report Generator** dialog box contains the information relating to input and modify. With the help of this tab, you can enter the data to make cover page of report.
- The **Contents** tab is used to create summary and content selection, which you want to include in your force.
- The **Simulations** tab is used to select designs and scenarios to include in your report.
- To reset the entered data, click on the **Reset** button.
- After specifying the parameters, click on the **Generate** button from **Simulation Report** dialog box. The report will be generated and displayed in Microsoft word or other word processor; refer to Figure-84.

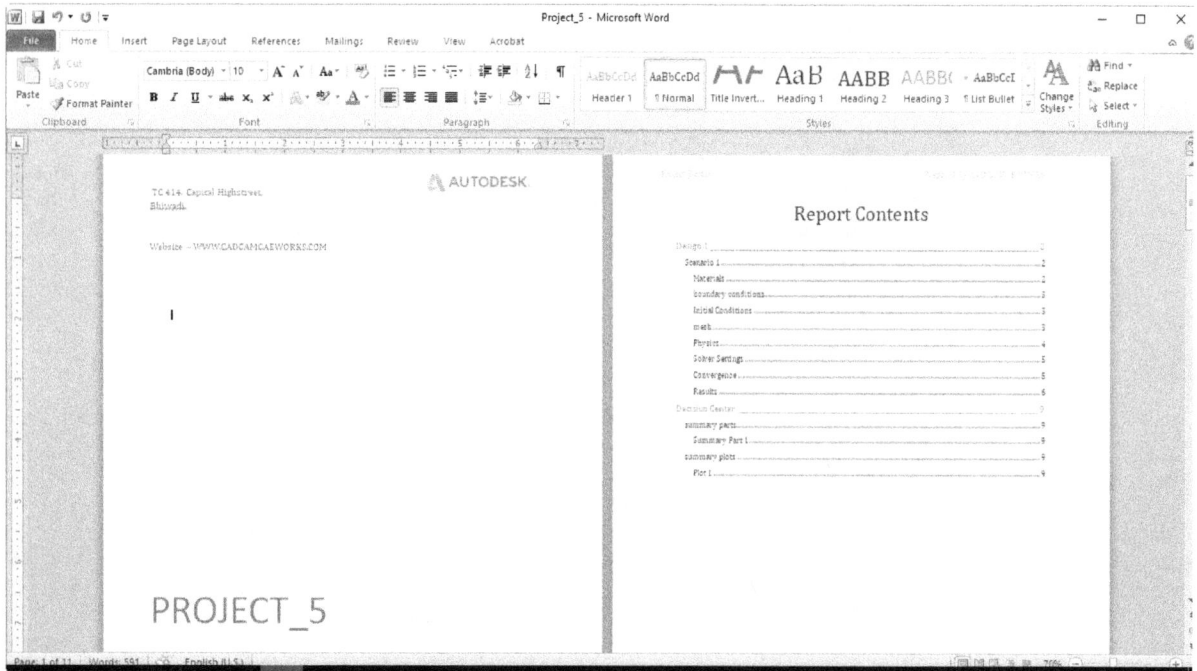

Figure-84. Generated report

- Save the file at desired location.
- Click on the **Save and Close** button from **Simulation Report** dialog box to save the data and close the dialog box.

Review Panel

The **Review** panel is used to view several information files produced during and end of the simulation process. The tool of this panel are discussed next.

Status File

- Click on the **Status File** button from **Review Panel** to view information related to trouble shooting of an error occurred during analysis. The **Status** dialog box will be displayed; refer to Figure-85.
- The convergence data in each degree of freedom is reported numerically for every iteration in status file. This data is useful for tracking convergence progress, and complement the data displayed in the Convergence Plot.

Figure-85. Status dialog box

- Click on the **Save** button to save the data.

Summary File

The **Summary File** button is used to view various types of informations, like Tabulated minimum, maximum, and average nodal values for computed field variables, bulk pressure, temperature, wall heat transfer, and summary of fluid-induced forces.

- Click on the **Summary File** button from **Review** panel, the **Summary** dialog box will be displayed containing data; refer to Figure-86. Save the file as required.

Figure-86. Summary dialog box

Setup File

The **Setup File** button is used to view a data containing the summary of boundary conditions, materials, and solver options. The data of setup file is automatically saved at the conclusion of every simulation. The procedure to use this tool is discussed next.

- Click on the **Setup File** button from **Review** panel, the **Setup Parameters** dialog box will be displayed; refer to Figure-87. Save the data as required.

Figure-87. Setup Paramaters dialog box

Summary History File

The **Summary History File** is used to view the summary information. Every time, when a simulation is stopped, the summary information of simulation is written to the summary file. This file can be used to view the history of summary information of each continuation of the simulation. Use Summary History File to understand the progression from one set of iterations to the next. The procedure to use this tool is discussed next.

- Click on the **Summary History File** button from **Review** panel drop-down; refer to Figure-88.

Figure-88. Summary History File button

- On clicking, the **Summary History** dialog box will be displayed; refer to Figure-89.

Figure-89. Summary History dialog box

- Save the file, if required.

Component Thermal Summary File

The **Component Thermal Summary File** button is used to view the component thermal summary file which contains the mean, maximum, and minimum temperatures for each solid part of model. This data is provided for each time step in a transient analysis. The component thermal summary file also contain temperature and heat flux data for compact thermal models and thermoelectric components. The procedure to use this is discussed next.

- Click on the **Component Thermal Summary File** button from **Review** panel drop-down by clicking on **Review** slide-out arrow. The **Component Thermal Summary** dialog box will be displayed; refer to Figure-90.

Figure-90. Component Thermal Summary dialog box

- Save the file as required.

Iteration/Step

The **Iteration/Step** panel is used to view or animate the saved results set for scenario. Each time an iteration is stopped, the results from last iteration are automatically saved. The procedure to use this is discussed next.

- Click on the **Iteration/Step** drop-down from **Iteration/Step** panel and select the required iteration, which you want to see on graphics window; refer to Figure-91. The selected iteration will be displayed.

Figure-91. Iteration Step panel

- By default, results from last saved iterations are displayed in graphics window.
- You shall be familiar with rest of the buttons of **Iteration/Step** panel.

Image Panel

The **Image** panel is used to create and share images of analyses for design collaboration and design comparison. The tools of the **Image** panel are discussed next.

Summary Image

The **Summary Image** tool is used to create snap of analysis in current orientation and visualization. With the help of this tool, you can compare results of different scenario using **Design Review Center** tool. This tool automatically compares the current configuration (orientation, result quantity, visualization features, etc.) to all selected scenario in the design study. The procedure to use this tool is discussed next.

- To compare, you need to make separate analysis for the same model. Like, removing a outlet from the model or adding an inlet, etc. You can modify the model as per your requirement.
- After the first analysis, perform a result task, like Global, planes, Iso surfaces, etc, and click on the **Summary Image** button from **Image** panel; refer to Figure-92. The snap will be captured and added in **Summary images** of **Decision Center** tab; refer to Figure-93.

Figure-92. Summary Image button

Figure-93. Decision Center tab

- The snap of current analysis will only be captured, if you are at last iteration number. You can snap as many images as you want.
- The snapped images will be stored in **Decision Center** tab. Added images will not be activated until you update the data.
- To update, right-click on the **Summary Images** from **Design Study Bar** of **Decision Center** tab and click on the **Update all images** button; refer to Figure-94. The images will be updated and displayed in **Output Bar**; refer to Figure-95.

Figure-94. Updating images

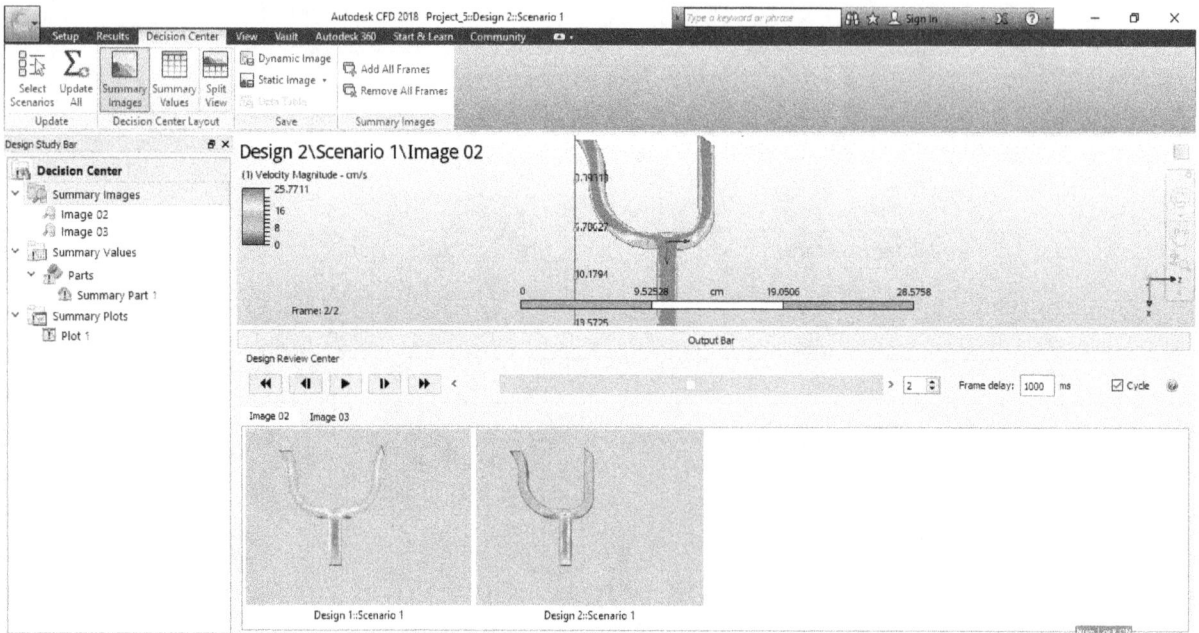

Figure-95. Comparing result

- Now, you can compare the results of a model, before and after changing the shape or after certain modification.
- The tools of **Decision Center** tab will be discussed in next chapter.

PRACTICAL

Let's create a custom quantity as **Kinetic Energy**.

Kinetic energy is the energy of object has when it is in motion. The kinetic energy can be easily determined by an equation using the mass and velocity of that object.

$$KE = 0.5 \times \rho v^2$$

$$m = mass\ of\ object$$
$$\rho = density\ of\ fluid$$

The standard unit of kinetic energy is joules (J), which is equivalent to

$$1\ kg * m^2/s^2$$

- Let us assume a fluid of density 20 kg/m³ moving with the velocity of 1.26 m/s. Determine the kinetic energy of box with Autodesk CFD.
- You need to create a model which contains moving fluid. Add **External Volume** with the help of **Geometry Tools** dialog box.
- Specify the required material to the fluid and surroundings.
- Now, we are going to create result quantity for fluid to determine its kintetic energy, and the procedure is given below.

- Click on the **Custom Result Quantities** button from **Global** panel of **Results** tab, the **Custom Result Quantities** dialog box will be displayed; refer to Figure-96.

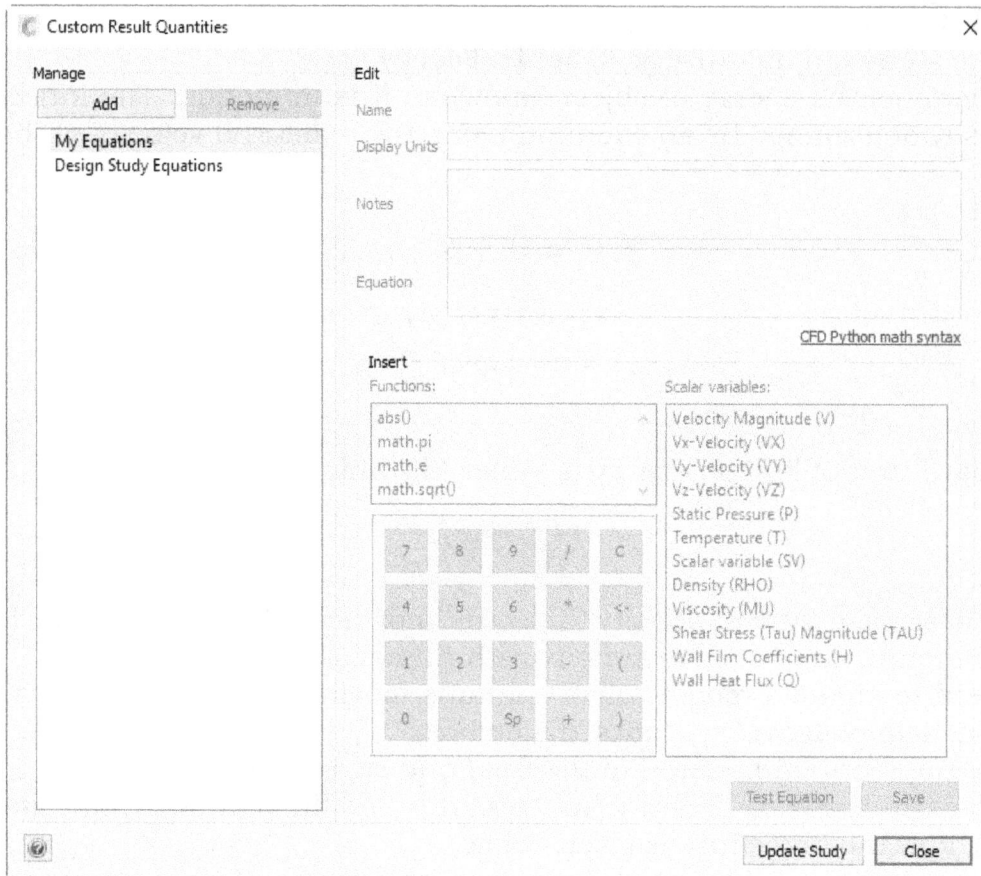

Figure-96. Custom Result Quantites dialog box

• Click on **Add** button to activate other parameters and enter the data as displayed in below figure; refer to Figure-97.

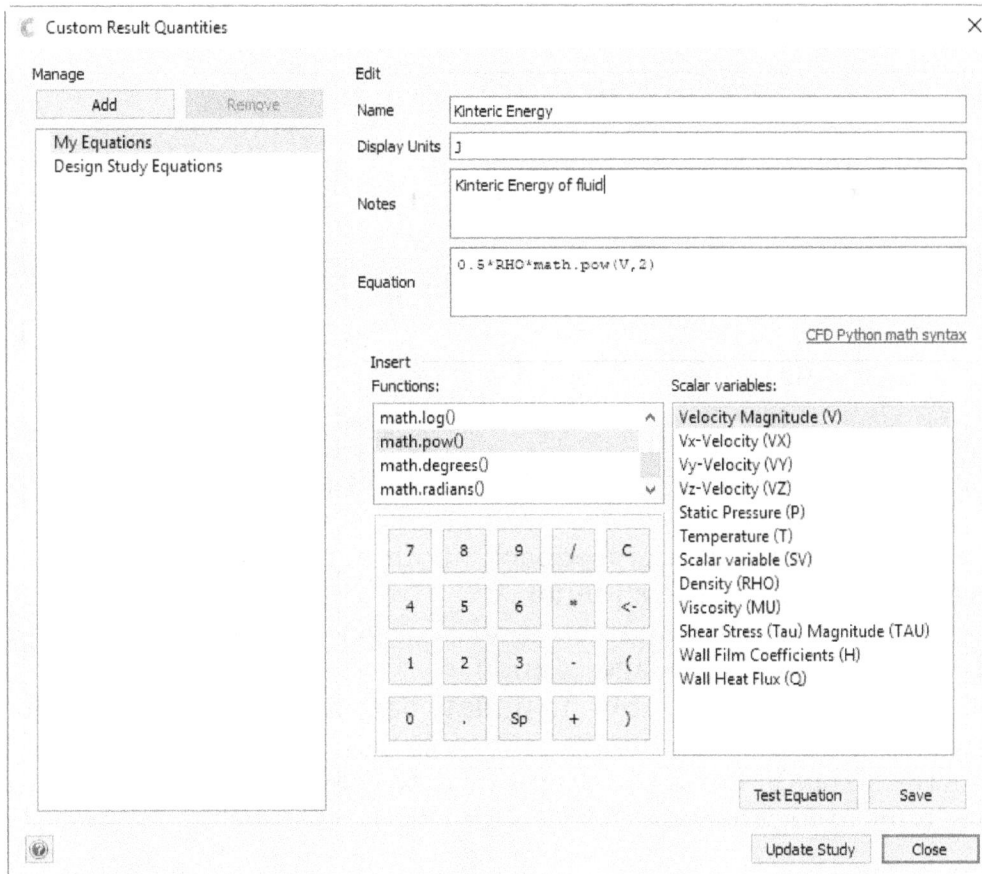

Figure-97. Added parameters for kinetic energy

- Click in the **Name** edit box and enter the name of custom result quantity.
- Click in the **Display** unit edit box and enter the unit of custom result quantity.
- Click in the **Notes** edit box and enter the notes as required.
- Click in the **Equation** edit box and enter the equation of quantity. For creating an quantity, you need to gather and understand the information of equation and its component. Like, what is velocity and its unit.
- To enter the variable in **Equation**, you need to double-click on the required variable from **Scalar** variables section.
- To apply math power, click on **Math.pow** button from **Functions** section and enter **(variable,variable unit)** inside brackets.
- After specifying the parameters, click on the **Test Equation** button from **Custom Result Quantities** dialog box, the **Custom Result Quantities - Test Equation** dialog box will be displayed; refer to Figure-98.

Figure-98. Custom Ressult Quantities Test Equation dialog box

- Click on the **Test** button, the feedback about equation will be displayed. Click on **Close** button to close the equation.
- Modify the data as per requirement and click on the **Save** button. The custom quantity will be added in **Manage** section.
- Click on the **Update Study** button to update data and click on **Close** button. You will be returned to **Results** tab.
- Click on the **Global Results** drop-down to view the recently created result quantity; refer to Figure-99.

Figure-99. Kinetic Energy

- Now, you can use this result quantity in analysis of your model.

FOR STUDENT NOTES

FOR STUDENT NOTES

Comparing and Visualization

Chapter 6

Topics Covered

The major topics covered in this chapter are:

- *Decision Center*
- *Update Panel*
- *Decision Center Layout*
- *Save panel*
- *View tab*
- *View Settings panel*

INTRODUCTION

In this last chapters, we had discussed the various tools of result tab for analyzing the result and creating the summary file. In this chapter, we will learn the tools used to comparing results and visualizing results.

DECISION CENTER

The **Decision Center** tab is used to compare results form multiple scenarios. There are various panels containing tools to compare results, which are discussed next.

Update Panel

The tools in **Update** panel are used to specify the selected scenario which are reported in the Summary items. It is also used to ensure all summary items as current. The tools of **Update** panel are discussed below.

Select Scenarios

The **Select Scenarios** button is used to select or deselect the scenarios. The procedure to use this tool is discussed below.

- Click on the **Select Scenarios** button from **Update** panel of **Decision Center** tab, the **Select Scenarios** dialog box will be displayed; refer to Figure-1.

Figure-1. Select Scenarios dialog box

- Select the check box of desired scenario, which you want to keep. Less number of scenario selected, more time would be saved to perform simulation.
- Click on the **Select All** button to select all scenario, and to clear all selected scenario, click on **Clear All** button.
- After selecting the required scenario, click on **OK** button. The selected scenario will be displayed.

Update All

The **Update All** tool is used to update all the summary data at once. The procedure to use this tool is discussed next.

- The exclamation symbol in **Design Study Bar** as displayed in Figure-2, means that a summary item has not mapped to other scenarios, or results has changed and not mapped, which means it requires update. To update these scenarios, click on **Update All** button.

Figure-2. Scenarios to update

Decision Center Layout

The **Decision Center Layout** panel is used to configure the appearance of scenario as per your requirement. The tools of this panel are discussed below.

Summary Images

- Click on the **Summary Images** button from **Decision Center Layout** panel of **Decision Center** tab to view the **Design Review Center**. The **Design Review Center** and **Summary Images** panel will be displayed; refer to Figure-3.

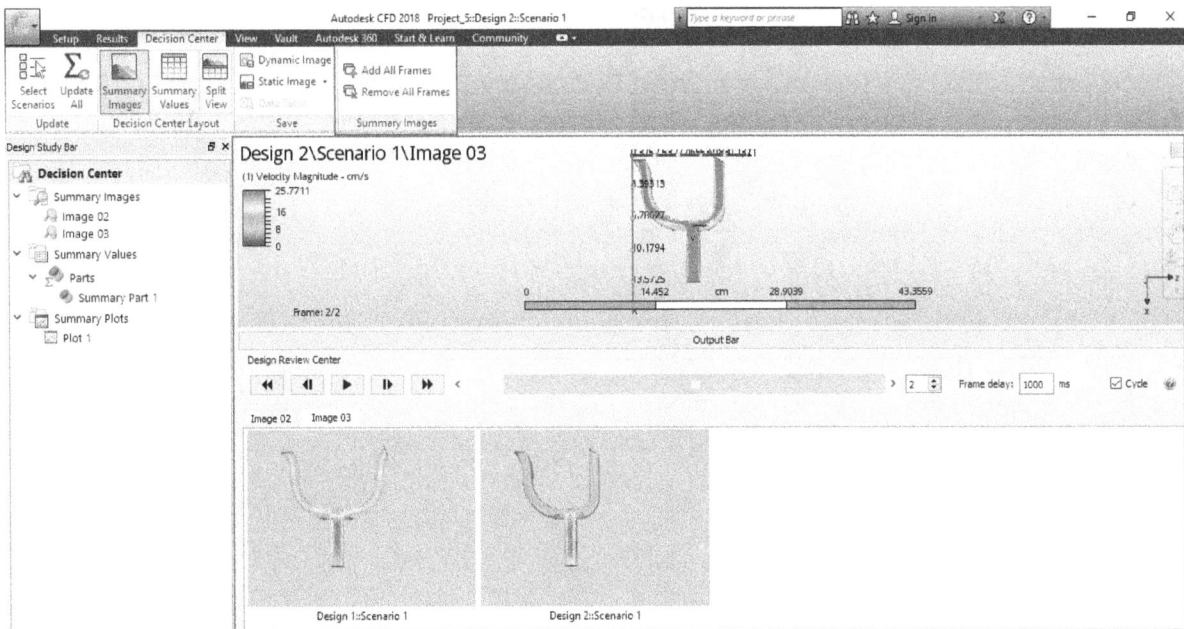

Figure-3. Summary Images button

- You can view and edit the summary images for comparison. Use the **Design Review Center** tools to play the video for comparison.

- Click on the **Add All Frames** button from **Summary Images** panel of **Decision Center** tab to add all frames in **Design Review Center**, and to remove, click on the **Remove All Frames** button.

Summary Values

The **Summary Values** button is used to review only tabular data. The procedure to use this tool is discussed next.

- Click on the **Summary Values** button from **Decision Center Layout** panel of **Decision Center** tab, the tabular data will be displayed; refer to Figure-4.

Figure-4. Summary Values buttonpng

- The tabular data hides the summary images from the view.

Split View

The **Split View** tool is used to view summary images and summary values together. The procedure to use this tool is discussed next.

- Click on the **Split View** button from **Decision Center Layout** panel of **Decision Center** tab, the **Summary Images** and **Summary Values** tab will be displayed; refer to Figure-5.

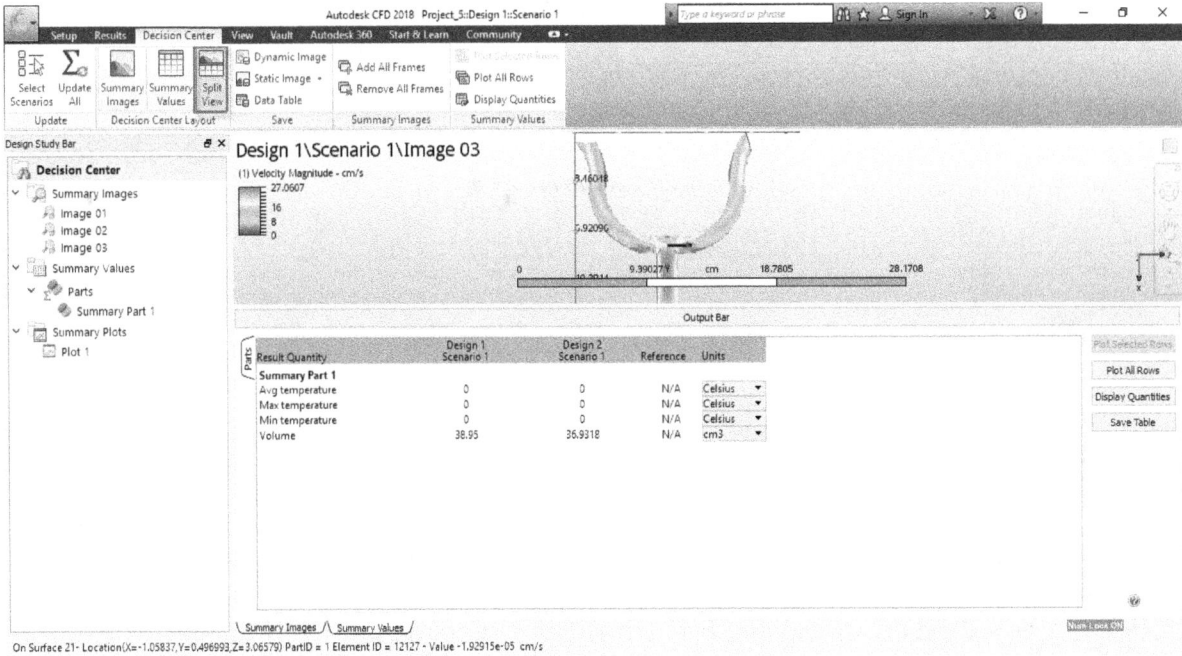

Figure-5. Split View button

Save panel

The **Save** panel is used to export visual and tabular data for sharing with others. The procedure to use this is discussed next.

Dynamic Image

The **Dynamic Image** tool is used to examine and share result data. The dynamic images can be navigated and animated to examine the simulation.

- Click on **Dynamic Images** button from **Save** panel of **Decision Center** tab, the **Save Dynamic Image File** dialog box will be displayed.
- Specify the location, where you want to save file and click on **Save** button. The file will be saved at preferred location.

Static Image

The **Static Image** tool is used to save an image of current view. The procedure to use this tool is discussed next.

- Click on the **Static Image** button from **Save** panel of **Decision Center** tab, the **Save Image** dialog box will be displayed.
- Specify the location and file format where you want to save the image file, and click on **Save** button. The file will be saved at preferred location.
- Click on the **Set Resolution** button from **Static Image** drop-down of **Save** panel to set the resolution for saved static images and animation files; refer to Figure-6. The **Set Resolution** dialog box will be displayed; refer to Figure-7.

Figure-6. Set Resolution button

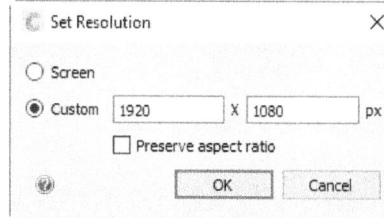

Figure-7. Set Resolution dialog box

- Select the **Screen** radio button from **Set Resolution** dialog box to use default screen resolution for image.
- Click on the **Custom** radio button from **Set Resolution** dialog box to manually set default resolution.
- Select the **Preserve aspect ratio** radio button to set the resolution of image in a balanced aspect ratio, which was defined by computer.
- After specifying the parameters, click on the **OK** button from **Set Resolution** dialog box. You will be returned to **Decision Center** tab.

VIEW TAB

The **View** tab is used to customize model appearance and its user interface; refer to Figure-8. The tools of this tab are discussed below.

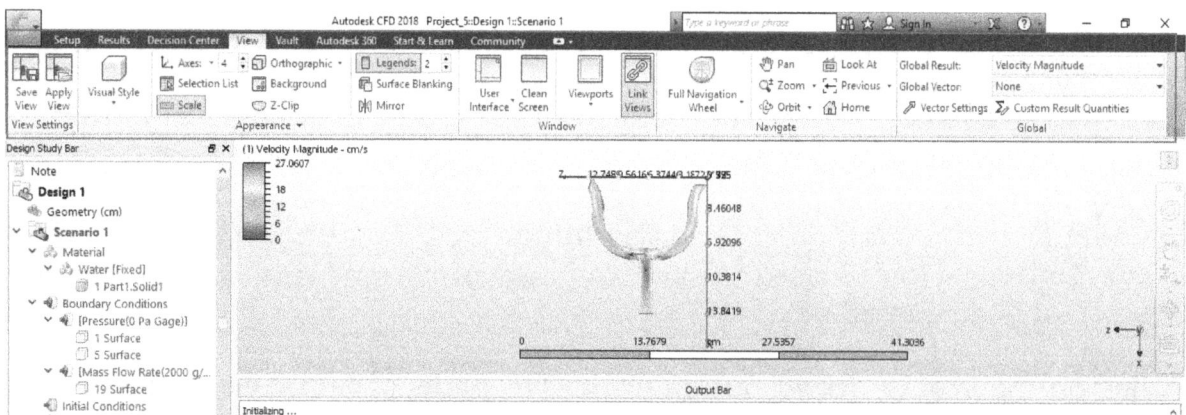

Figure-8. View tab

Appearance panel

The tools of **Appearance** panel are used to define model display. Most of the options of this panel are only available when results are displayed and the remaining are available for both setup and result views. The tools in this panel are discussed next.

Visual Style

- Click on the **Visual Style** drop-down form **Appearance** panel and select the desired visual style for model; refer to Figure-9.

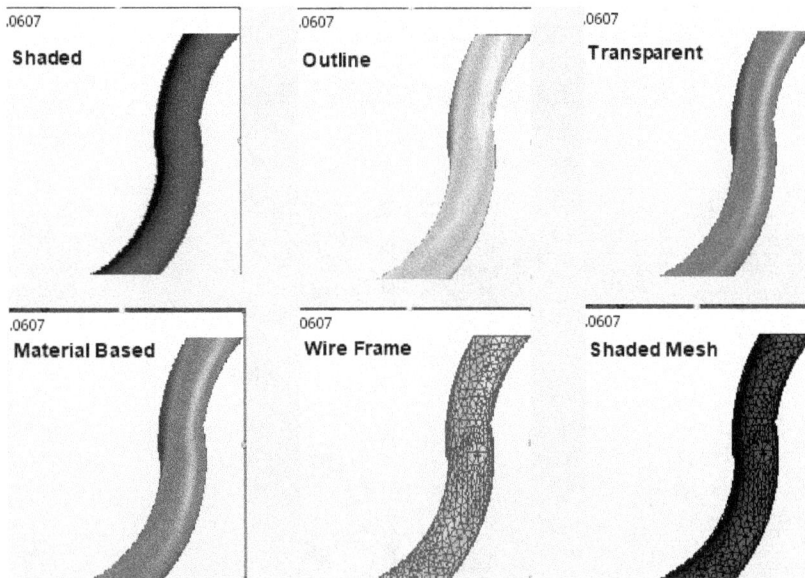

Figure-9. Visual Style

Axes

*   Click on the **Axes** drop-down from **Appearance** panel of **View** tab and select the required check box; refer to Figure-10. Clear the desired check box to hide the respective interface element; refer to Figure-11.

Figure-10. Axes drop-down

Figure-11. Axes option

- Click in the **Axis Gradient** edit box from **Appearance** panel and enter the value to specify the gradient lying on axis; refer to Figure-12.

Figure-12. Axis Gradient

Scale

- Click on the **Scales** button from **Appearance** panel of **View** tab to view model scale. Again, click on this button to hide the scale; refer to Figure-13.

Figure-13. Scale

Orthographic and Perspective view

- Click on the **Orthographic** or **Perspective** button from **Appearance** panel of **View** tab to control the depth view of the model; refer to Figure-14.
- The **Orthographic** button display model entities in their actual sizes. This button is useful for making selection when the model is aligned to Cartesian axis.
- The **Perspective** button provides depth to the model by reducing the size of objects that are far away from viewer. It provides more realistic view.

Figure-14. Orthographic and perspective

Background

The **Background** button is used to change the change the background color of graphics window. The procedure is discussed next.

- Click on the **Background** button from **Appearance** section of **View** tab, the **Background Color** dialog box will be displayed; refer to Figure-15.

Figure-15. Background tool

- Click on the **Color** drop-down and select the desired color, which you want to apply on background.
- Click on the **Type** drop-down from **Background Color** dialog box and select the desired type.
- After specifying the desired color, click on the **OK** button form **Background Color** dialog box. The background color of graphics window will be changed.

Z-Clip

The **Z-Clip** button is used to view interior of the model. The procedure to use this tool is discussed next.

- Click on the **Z-Clip** button from **Appearance** panel of **View** tab, the **Z-Clip Control and Crinkle Cut** dialog box will be displayed; refer to Figure-16.

Figure-16. Z – Clip button

- Move the **Front Plane** slider and **Back Plane** slider to adjust the visibility of model interior.
- The **Z Clip** plane remains static relative to the global coordinate system. As the model orientation changes, the interior view updates as the relative location of the **Z Clip** plane changes.
- Select the **Crinkle Cut** check box to view the mesh on the interior of the model. This tool is used to examine internal mesh distribution; refer to Figure-17.

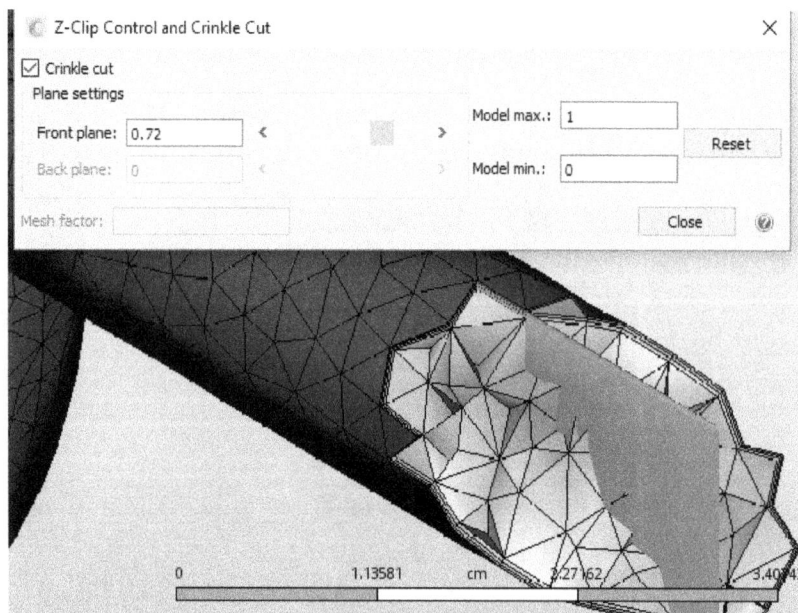

Figure-17. Crinkle cut

- Click on the **Reset** button to reset the entered parameters.
- After specifying the parameters, click on the **Close** button. You will be returned to **View** tab.

Legends

The **Legends** toggle is used to specify the number of legends on the screen. By default, the result legends will displayed when results are displayed.

- Click on the **Legends** edit box and enter the number of legends you wants to view in the graphics window; software will automatically adjust the size of current legend. You can view a maximum of 5 legends in graphics window; refer to

Figure-18. You can also toggle between increase and decrease buttons to specify the number of legends.

Figure-18. Legends

- Increase the legend value to reduce the legend size, and decrease the value to increase legend size. The legends will be displayed vertically.

Surface Blanking

The **Surface Blanking** tool is used to hide surfaces instead of volumes. This tool is used when viewing results.

- Click on the **Surface Blanking** button from **Appearance** panel of **View** tab, the tool will be activated; refer to Figure-19.

Figure-19. Surface Blanking button

Mirror

The **Mirror** tool is used to reflect the model and visualizations about selected plane. This tool is used when results are displayed. The procedure to use this tool is discussed next.

- Click on the **Mirror** button from **Appearance** panel of **View** tab, the **Mirror** dialog box will be displayed; refer to Figure-20.

Figure-20. Mirror dialog box

- Select the **Mirror enabled** check box from **Mirror** dialog box to enable the mirror for current project. All tools of **Mirror** dialog box will be activated.
- Select the desired plane from **Mirror** dialog box to define the reflection; refer to Figure-21.

Figure-21. Selecting requried plane

- After specifying the reflection plane, click on the **Close** button from **Mirror** dialog box. The result of mirror will be displayed.
- The model can be reflected about only one plane at a time.
- To disable mirror, clear the **Mirror enabled** check box from **Mirror** dialog box.

Mesh Seeds

The **Mesh Seeds** tool is used to define the mesh. Mesh Seeds indicate the location of nodes when the mesh is generated. These seeds help us to identify the areas which need mesh adjustment before its generation. On complex model, mesh seeds can slow your computer performance.

Model Shadow

The **Model Shadow** tool is used to display the model shadow just below the model geometry. The procedure to use this is discussed next.

- Click on the **Model Shadow** button from **Appearance** panel drop-down of **View** tab; the shadow will displayed just below the model geometry; refer to Figure-22.

Figure-22. Model shadow

- Click again on the **Model Shadow** button to hide shadow of model.

View Settings panel

The **View Settings** panel is used to save the current view of model for future references. You can also save the current view of model for comparison with other model. Tools of this panel are discussed below.

Save View

- Click on the **Save View** button from **View Settings** panel to save view setting file. The **Save View Settings** dialog box will be displayed; refer to Figure-23.

Figure-23. Save View Settings dialog box

- The **View Settings** file can save and apply visualization elements like planes, iso-surfaces, and traces as well as model orientation to the saving file.
- Specify the file location where you want to save the file and click on the **Save** button. The file will be saved at specified location. Now, you can use this **View Settings** file for future use.

Apply View

- Click on the **Apply View** button from **View Settings** panel to apply view setting file within a scenario or another scenario; the **Apply View Settings** dialog box will be displayed; refer to Figure-24.
- Select the desired view settings file and click on the **Open** button. The **View Settings** file will be applied.

Figure-24. Applying View Settings dialog Box

Window panel

The tools of **Window** panel are used to configure the graphics window. These tools are discussed next.

User Interface

The **User Interface** tool is used to hide or display the various options from graphics window.

- Click on the **User Interface** drop-down from **Window** panel of **View** tab and select the required check box option which you want to display on graphics window; refer to Figure-25.

Figure-25. User Interface drop-down

- Clear the desired check box from **User Interface** drop-down to hide the respective option from graphics window.

Clean Screen

The **Clean Screen** tool is used to maximise the graphics window.

- Click on the **Clean Screen** button from **Window** panel of **View** tab to hide **Design Study Bar**, **Status bar**, **Ribbon**, and **Output bar**. It will hide everything from graphic window other than model; refer to Figure-26.

Figure-26. Clean Screen

- To display the interface components, click again on **Clean Screen** button from **View** tab.

Viewports

The **Viewports** tool is used to increase or decrease the number of viewports in which model can be displayed. The procedure is discussed next.

- Click on the **Viewports** drop-down from **Window** panel of **View** tab and select the desired option from the list; refer to Figure-27.

Figure-27. Viewports drop-down

- Multiple viewports are useful for assessing results from individual scenarios as well as multi-scenario design studies.

Link Views

The **Link Views** tool is used to navigate all viewports together. The procedure to use this tool is discussed next.

- Click on the **Link Views** button from **Window** panel of **View** tab, the tool will be activated.
- Now, if you rotate/move model in one viewport then model will be rotated/moved accordingly in other viewports.
- Click again to disable this tool.

Other tools of **View** tab were discussed earlier in this book.

Till now, we have discussed all the tools and components of Autodesk CFD 2018 in the past chapters. Now it's time to do some real work; i.e it's time for some practical as per real conditions, which are given in next chapter.

End of Chapter

FOR STUDENTS NOTES

FOR STUDENTS NOTES

Practical

Chapter 7

Topics Covered

The major topics covered in this chapter are:

- *Practical 1*
- *Practical 2*
- *Practical 3*

INTRODUCTION

In past chapters, we have learned the tools used to create a simulation study. We had also learned the procedure of tools which are used after running simulation study. In this chapter, we will create analyses on different scenario conditions.

PRACTICAL 1

In this practical, we will simulate the air flow distribution through a manifold with two inlet and two outlet ports. The geometry consists of two inlet tube, two outlet tube and a distribution chamber; refer to Figure-1.

Figure-1. Practical 1

In this practical, our goal is to understand the effects of removing one of the inlet port. After running the initial scenario, we will clone the design , remove the 1st inlet tube from model, and compare the resultant flow distribution with the original design. We use the **Design Review Center** to visualize the effects of removing the inlet.

Opening the model

We are using SOLIDWORKS 2018 software for creating model here, but you can use other CAD software which supports Autodesk CFD 2018. We have created the model and saved in respective folder of Autodesk CFD folder.

We are using .IGS format to save part files because it is universally supported by all CAD software. You can use other formats to save your CAD model.

*   Double-click on the **Autodesk CFD 2018** icon from Desktop, the welcome window of **Autodesk CFD 2018** will be displayed. You can also open **Autodesk CFD 2018** from **Start Menu**; refer to Figure-2.

Figure-2. Opening Autodesk CFD from start menu

- Click on the **New** button from **Ribbon**; the **New Design Study** dialog box will be displayed; refer to Figure-3.

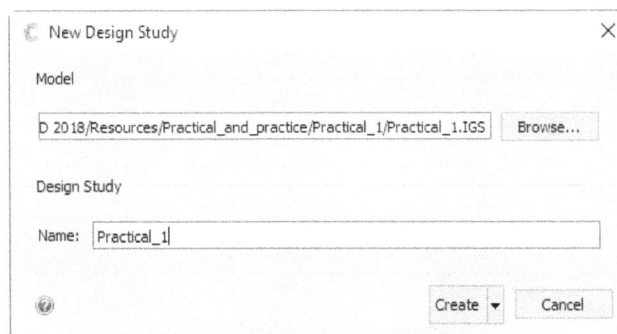

Figure-3. New Design Study dialog box practical 1

- Click on the **Browse** button from **New Design Study** dialog box and select **Practical 1.IGS** file from respective folder of resource kit for this book.
- Click in the **Name** edit box and enter the name as **Practical 1.** Click on the **Create** button. Software starts to read file.
- The **Geometry Tools** dialog box will be displayed which asks you to merge some of the edges below the specified angle. Click on the **Merge** button to merge edges. Close the **Geometry Tools** dialog box. The model will be displayed; refer to Figure-4.

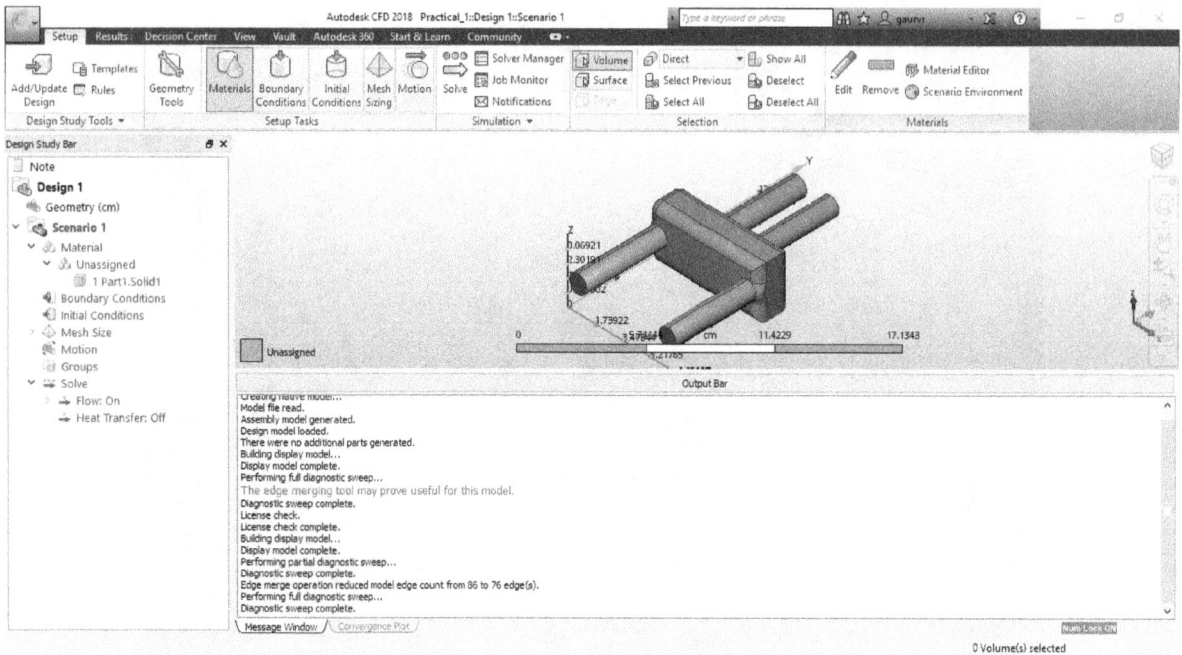

Figure-4. Practical 1 starting window

Changing Units

If the unit of your model is not selected to mm then you need to change the units to mm and the procedure is discussed below.

- Right-click on the **Geometry** from **Design Study Bar** and select **mm** from **Change length units to** cascading menu; refer to Figure-5. The units will be changed to **mm**.

Figure-5. Changing units

Assigning Material

Now, its time to assign **Air** as fluid for the final model, and the procedure is discussed next.

- Right-click on the **Unassigned** branch from **Design Study Bar** and click on **Edit** button; the **Materials** dialog box will be displayed; refer to Figure-6.

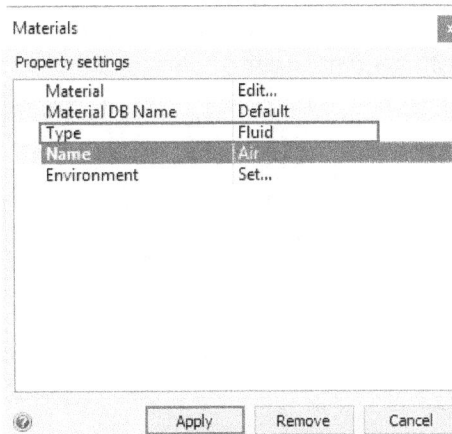

Figure-6. Specifying Air to model

- Select the **Type** as **Fluid** and **Name** as **Air** from list of **Materials** dialog box, and click on **Apply** button. The **Air** will be applied on model and mentioned in **Design Study Bar**. The color of model will be changed as per selected material.

Assigning Boundary Condition

Now, we will apply inlet boundary condition at two inlet and outlet boundary conditions at two outlet. The procedure is discussed next.

- Click on the **Boundary Condition** tool from **Setup** tab to enable this tool. Select the **Surface** button from **Selection** panel to activate surface selection and click on **Edit** button from **Boundary Conditions** panel; the **Boundary Conditions** dialog box will be displayed; refer to Figure-7.

Figure-7. Applying boundary condition to Practical 1

- Select the inlet surface of model and also specify the parameters of boundary condition as displayed in above figure. Click on **Apply** button. The boundary conditions will applied.

- Now, rotate the model to select the surface of two outlet pipe. Right-click on any one of the surface and click on **Edit** button; refer to Figure-8. The **Boundary Conditions** dialog box will be displayed.

Figure-8. Selecting outlet surface of practical 1

- Select the **Type** as **Pressure**, **Unit** as **atm**, and **Pressure** value as **1** from **Boundary Condition** dialog box; refer to Figure-9.

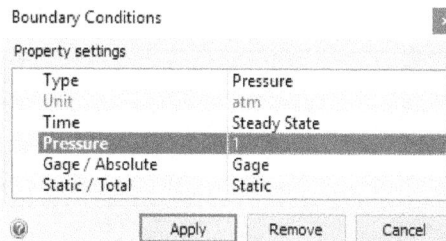

Figure-9. Outlet boundary condition Practical 1

- After specifying parameters, click on the **Apply** button to apply the boundary condition. The boundary conditions will be applied and displayed on graphic window; refer to Figure-10.

Figure-10. Displayed boundary conditions

Creating Mesh

For this model, we will create automatic mesh and the procedure is discussed next.

- Click on the **Mesh Sizing** tool from **Setup Tasks** panel of **Setup** tab to activate this tool.
- Click on **Autosize** button from **Automatic Sizing** panel of **Setup** tab. The mesh will be generated; refer to Figure-11.

Figure-11. Generating mesh of practical 1

Solving Analysis

- Click on the **Solve** button from **Setup** tab, the **Solve** dialog box will be displayed; refer to Figure-12.

Figure-12. Solve dialog box

- Click in the **Iterations to Run** edit box and enter the value of iteration as 100.
- Select the **Flow** check box from **Physics** tab of **Solve** dialog box and click on the **Solve** button. The data starts displaying in **Output** tab and on completion of calculations; **Convergence Plot** will be displayed; refer to Figure-13.

Figure-13. Convergence plot of Practical 1

Results of Design 1

Activate Plane tool for adding a plane to view the effects of air inside model.

- Click on the **Planes** tool from **Results Tasks** panel of **Results** tab; the related tools will be displayed.
- Click on the **Add** button from **Planes** panel; the plane will be added and displayed.
- Left-click on the plane and click on **Z axis** button from displayed context menu; refer to Figure-14. The plane will be align to z axis.

Figure-14. Aligning plane to z axis

- Click on the **Summary Image** button from **Image** panel of **Results** tab; the current image of plane will be saved and displayed in **Decision Center**; refer to Figure-15. If image is not displayed by default then click on the **Update All** tool from **Update** panel of **Decision Center** tab in the **Ribbon**.

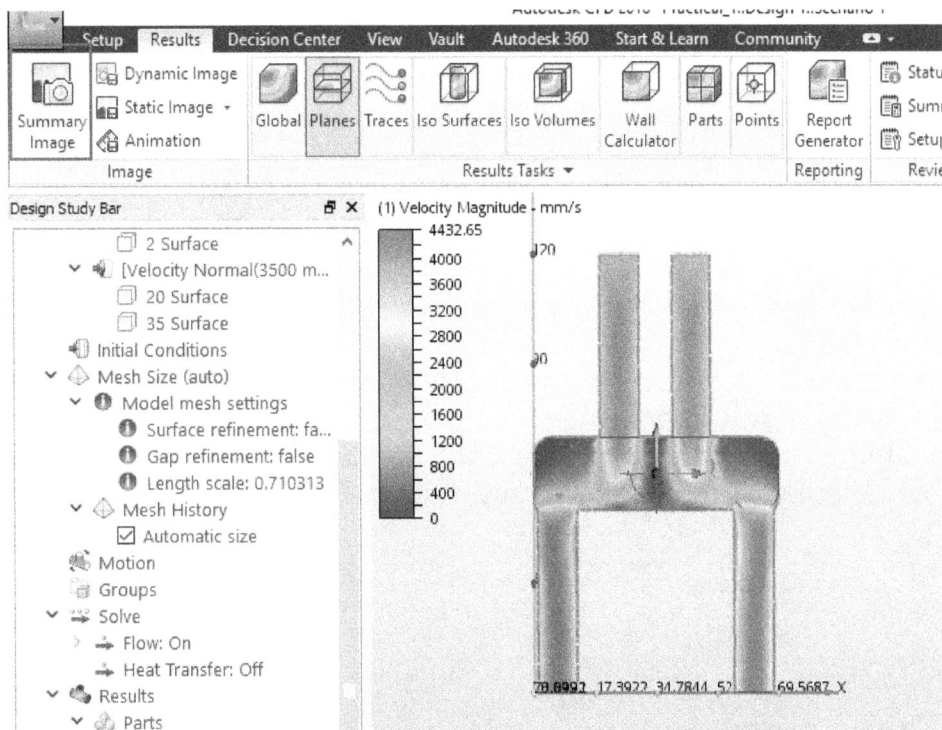

Figure-15. Creating summary image of Design 1

Cloning Model

Till now, we had solved the **Design 1** analysis. Before proceeding to view the results, we need to clone the current model to copy all the settings and current geometry to the other model. So that, we can compare the results of initial model and last model. The procedure to do so is discussed next.

- Right-click on the **Design 1** option from **Design Study Bar** and click on **Clone** button; refer to Figure-16. The **Clone Design** dialog box will be displayed; refer to Figure-17.

Figure-16. Cloning design of practical 1

Figure-17. Clone Design dialog box of practical 1

- Click in the **Design name** edit box from **Clone Design** dialog box and enter the name as **Design 2**.
- Select the **Scenario 1** and clear the **Include mesh and results** check box to not copy the results of initial design.
- After specifying the parameters, click on the **OK** button. The **Design 2** will be created and displayed in **Design Study Bar**; refer to Figure-18.

Figure-18. Cloned Design 2

Suppressing one of the inlet tube

In this step, we will modify the CAD geometry which is to remove one inlet from manifold. The following steps are created on the basis of SOLIDWORKS 2018. You can use other software too. To understand SOLIDWORKS 2018, you can buy this book from our website; i.e. WWW.CADCAMCAEWORKS.COM.

*   Open the **Practical 1** model in SOLIDWORKS. The file was given in respective folder.
*   Suppress the inlet of model as displayed in figure and save the file; refer to Figure-19.

Figure-19. Suppressing inlet

*   Now, click on the **Add/Update** button from **Design Study Panel** of **Setup** tab; the **Add Geometry File** dialog box will be displayed; refer to Figure-20.

Figure-20. Updating Practical 1

- Click on the **Browse** button from **Add Geometry File** dialog box and select the updated part file.
- Select the **Design 2** from **Design study** section to update the model in design 2 scenario and click on **Update selected design** button. The **Design 2** will be updated and displayed; refer to Figure-21.

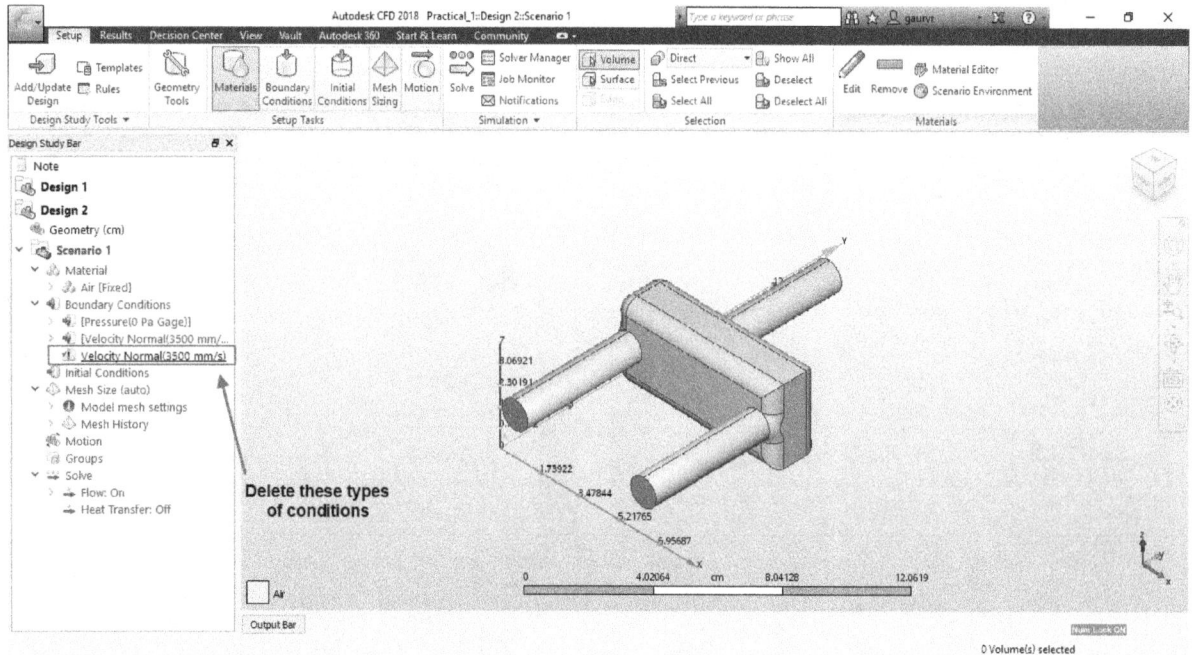

Figure-21. Updated Design 2

- Check the applied boundary conditions. If there is some kind of error in boundary conditions, remove the existing one and create again. These **Pressure** and **Velocity** boundary conditions are as same as we had applied in **Design 1** study. Remove the unnecessary boundary conditions.
- Till now, we had created both the design scenario and its time to solve the **Design 2**.

Solving Design 2

- Click on the **Solve** button from **Design 2** scenario; the **Solve** dialog box will be displayed.
- The default settings of **Solve** dialog box are appropriate for this scenario, like **Continue From** as **0** and **Iterations to Run** as **100**, etc. Click on the **Solve** button from **Solve** dialog box. The analysis will started and model will be displayed after completion of iterations; refer to Figure-22.

Figure-22. Model Design 2

- Click on the **Plane** tool from **Results Tasks** panel of **Results** tab; the tools related to plane will be activated and displayed.
- Add a plane along **Z axis** as described in **Design 1**; refer to Figure-23

Figure-23. Added plane of Design 2

- Click on **Summary Image** from **Image** panel of **Results** tab to snap the picture of current plane.

Comparing Results

Now, we will compare graphical results of **Design 1** and **Design 2** using **Design Center**, the procedure of which is discussed below.

- Click on the **Decision Center** tab, the tools will be displayed.
- Right-click on the **Summary Images** option from **Design Study Bar** and click on **Update all images** button from displayed menu; refer to Figure-24. The images will be updated and displayed; refer to Figure-25.

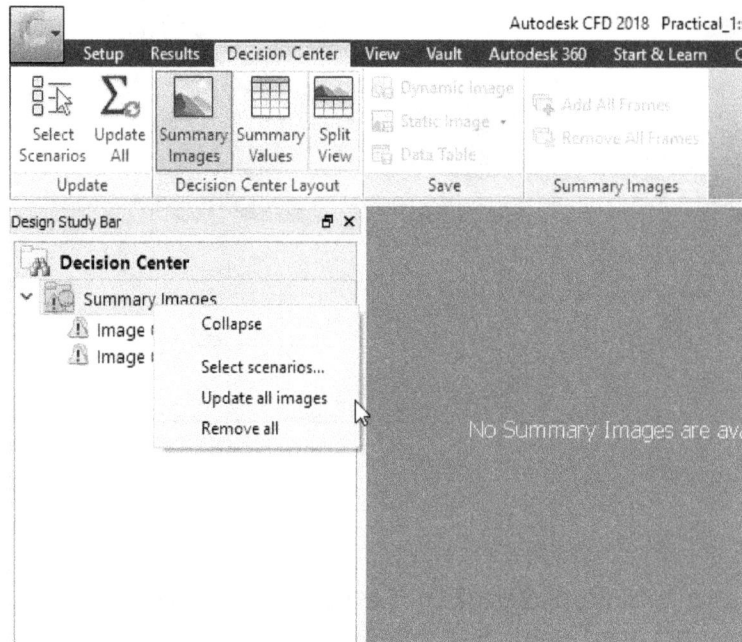

Figure-24. Updating images of Practical 1

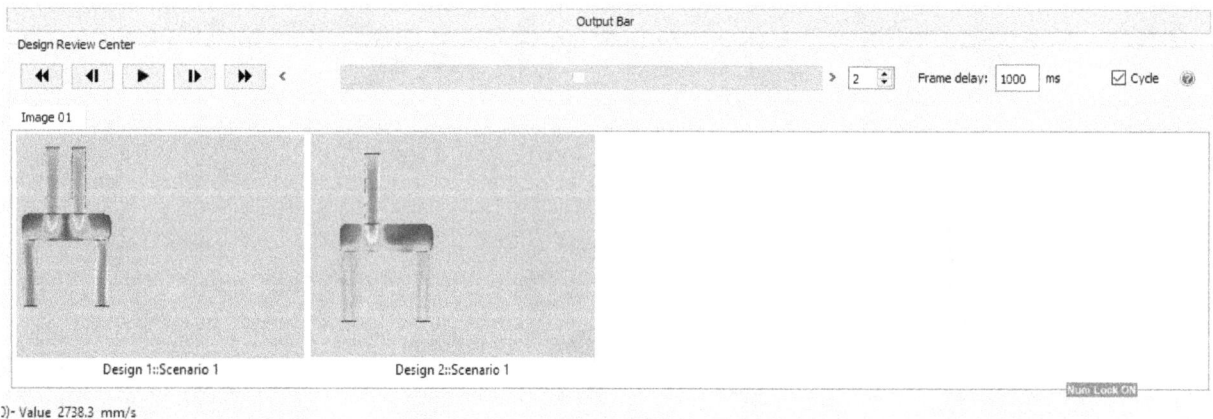

Figure-25. Design Review Center of Practical 1

- A thumbnail view from each design will be displayed in **Output** bar. To compare, use slider and VCR controls, which are placed just above the **Image 01** tab.
- You can check the graphical representation of Design 1 and Design 2, and compare the air flow.

PRACTICAL 2

In this practical, we will simulate the flow and heat transfer within an electronics enclosure. The electronics model contain several components and we model them with Autodesk CFD such as internal fan, capacitor, and so on; refer to Figure-26.

Figure-26. Practical 2

This CAD model is created in Autodesk Inventor.

Opening Model

The procedure to open Practical 2 is discussed next.

- Double-click on the **Autodesk CFD 2018** icon from **Desktop**. The welcome screen of **Autodesk CFD 2018** will be displayed.
- Click on the **New** button from **Ribbon**; the **New Design Study** dialog box will be displayed.
- Click on the **Browse** button and select the file **Practical 2 ASM.IAM** from Practical 2 folder (Download the files from our website i.e. WWW.CADCAMCAEWORKS. COM).
- Click in the **Name** edit box and enter the name as **Practical 2**; refer to Figure-27

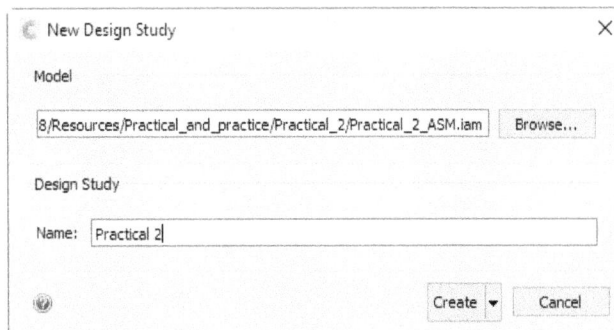

Figure-27. New Design Study Practical 2

- After specifying the parameters, click on the **Create** button from **New Design Study** dialog box. The assembly file will be displayed in **Autodesk CFD 2018**; refer to Figure-28. Click on the **Merge** button from the **Geometry Tools** dialog box and close the dialog box.

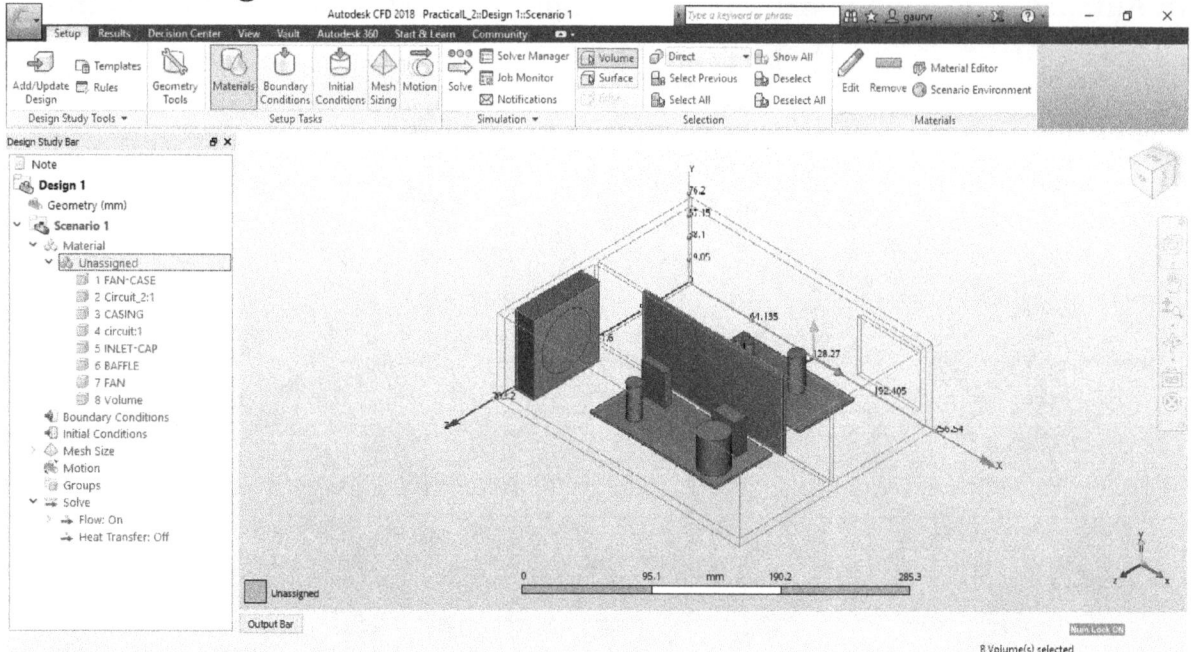

Figure-28. Displayed Practical 2

- The **Volume** and **Casing** option of **Design Study Bar** are set as outline for better visual appearance of other components.

Note: If **Geometry Tools** dialog box will appear, merge the necessary edges and proceed to the next step.

Changing Units

If the unit of current model is not in mm, then change it. The procedure is discussed next.

- Right-click on the **Geometry** feature from **Design Study Bar** and select the **mm** option from **Change length units to** cascading menu; refer to Figure-29.

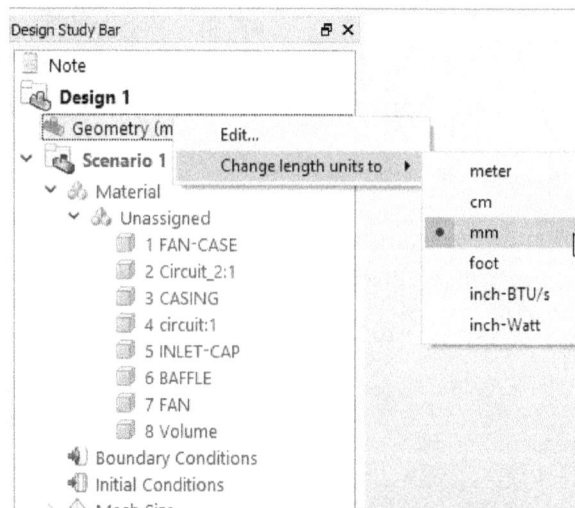

Figure-29. Changing units of practical 2

- The unit of current model will be changed.

Creating Flow Volume

There are two fluid regions in the model. One is created automatically when the model is added in Autodesk CFD because it is fully enclosed in casing. The other is not fully bounded, so we have to use **Void Fill Geometry** tool to create the other fluid volume, and the procedure is discussed next.

- Right-click on the **Casing** and click on the **Outline** option from the displayed menu to select the outlet edges easily; refer to Figure-30.

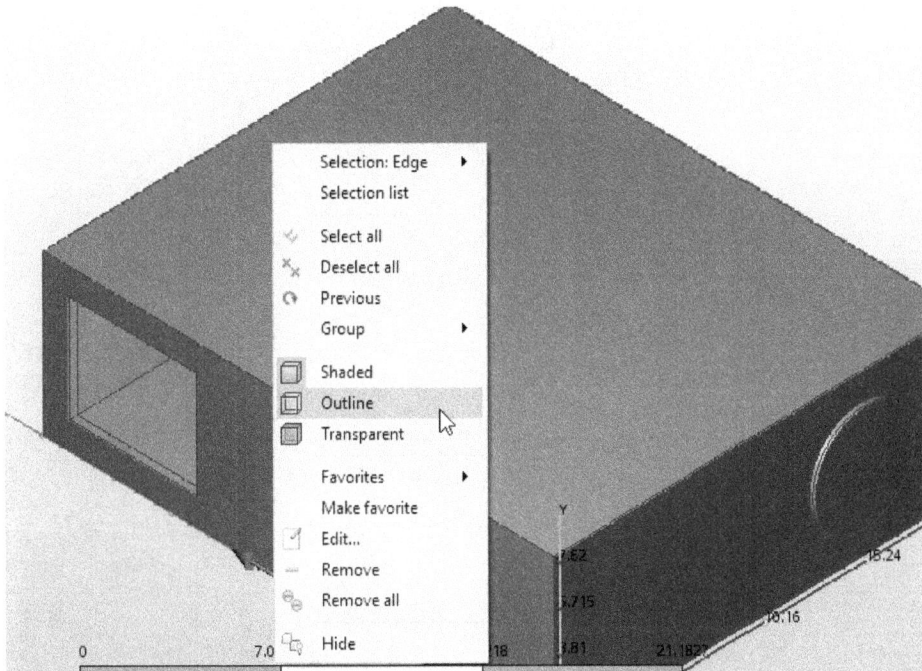

Figure-30. Selecting Outline visual stuyle of Casing

- Click on the **Geometry Tools** button from **Setup Tasks** panel of **Setup** tab; the **Geometry Tools** dialog box will be displayed.
- Click on **Void Fill** tab of **Geometry Tools** dialog box and select the two edges of outlet which are sharing the common vertex; refer to Figure-31. The other edges will be selected automatically, and displayed in **Model entity selection** section.

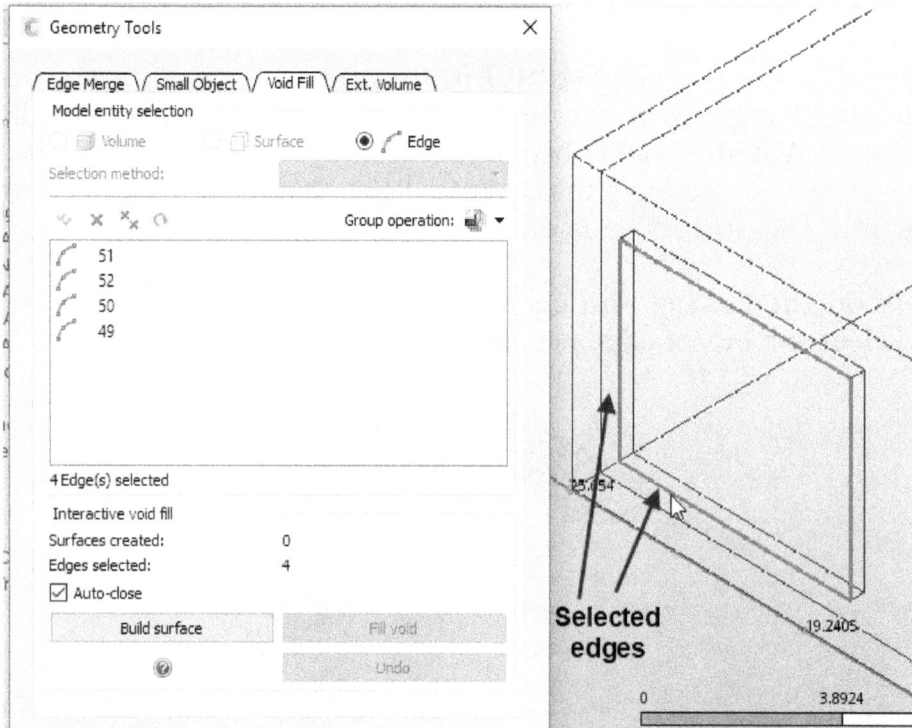

Figure-31. selecting edges of outlet

- After selecting the edges, click on the **Build Surface** button of **Geometry Tools** dialog box; the surface will be created on selected edges; refer to Figure-32.

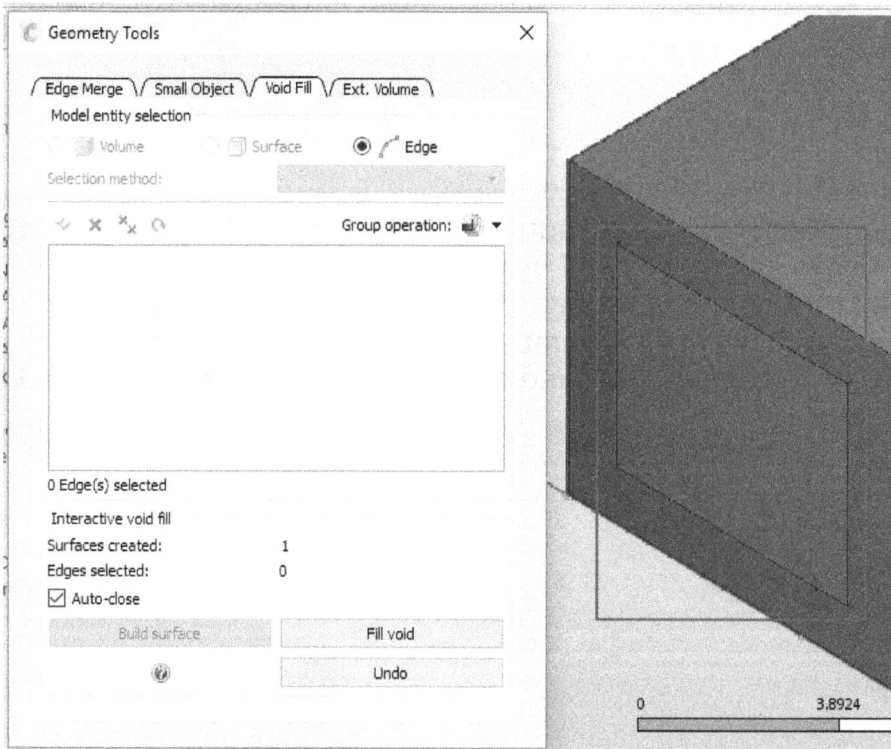

Figure-32. Created surface on outlet

- Click on the **Fill Void** button to complete the process of volume formation and close the **Geometry Tools** dialog box.

Creating groups of circuit boards

In this step, we will create a groups of similar component to assigning materials, boundary conditions, and mesh sizes at once. The procedure to create groups is discussed next.

- Click on the **Materials** tool from **Setup Tasks** panel of **Setup** tab to activate the material task.
- Right-click on casing and click on **Hide** button from the displayed menu to hide casing; refer to Figure-33.

Figure-33. Hiding Casing

- Similarly, hide the **CFDCreatedvolume** and **Volume** by pressing **CTRL** key and middle mouse button. You can also hide the same with the help of previous method; refer to Figure-34.

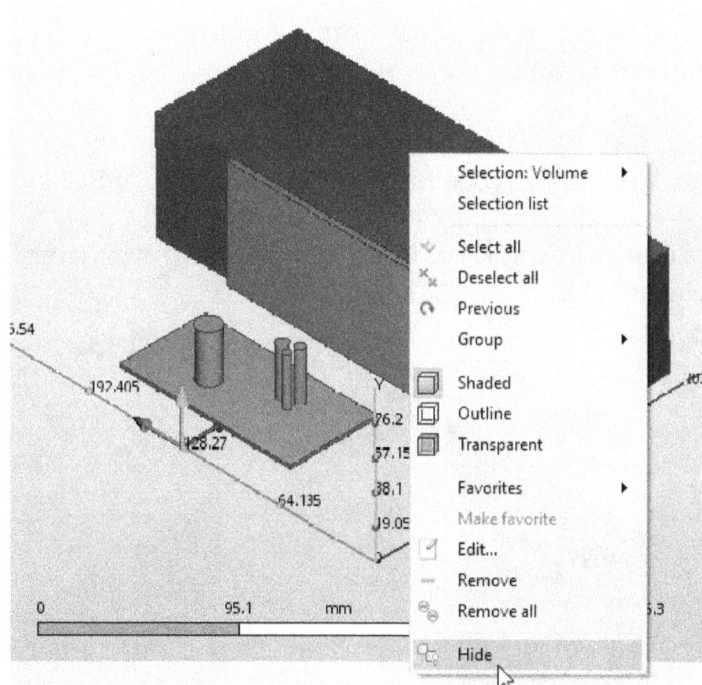

Figure-34. Hiding Volume

- Select the **Circuit 1** and **Circuit 2** objects from **Design Study Bar** and click on **Create Group** button from **Group** cascading menu of right-click menu; refer to Figure-35. The **Add to Group** dialog box will be displayed; refer to Figure-36.

Figure-35. Creating Group of Circuit board

Figure-36. Creating group

- Specify the name as **Circuit** in the **Group Name** edit box. Click on the **OK** button from **Add to Group** dialog box; the **Circuit** group will be created and displayed as **Circuit -(Volume)**; refer to Figure-37.

Figure-37. Circuit Volume

Assigning Material

Now, its time to assign material to all parts of model.

- Click on the **Materials** tool from **Setup Tasks** panel of **Setup** tab; the **Materials** task will be activated.
- Select the **Volume, Inlet-Cap,** and **CFDCreatedVolume** option from **Design Study Bar** and click on **Edit** button from **Materials** panel. The **Material** dialog box will be displayed.
- Select the **Material** as **Air** and click on **Apply** button; refer to Figure-38. The material will be applied and displayed on model.

Figure-38. Applying Materials to Practical 2

- Now, select the **FAN-CASE**, **Casing,Circuit 1**, and **Circuit 2** from **Design Study Bar** and right-click on it. The right-click menu will be displayed. Click on the **Edit** button; the **Material** dialog box will be displayed.
- Select the **Aluminum** as **Material** and click on **Apply** button; refer to Figure-39. The selected material will be applied.

Figure-39. Applying Aluminum as material

Creating and applying Baffle material

- Select the **Baffle** component from **Design Study Bar** and click on **Edit** button from **Materials** panel of **Setup** tab; the **Materials** dialog box will be displayed. Select **Resistance** option from the **Type** drop-down in the dialog box.
- Click on **Edit** button from **Material** option; the **Material Editor** dialog box will be displayed; refer to Figure-40.

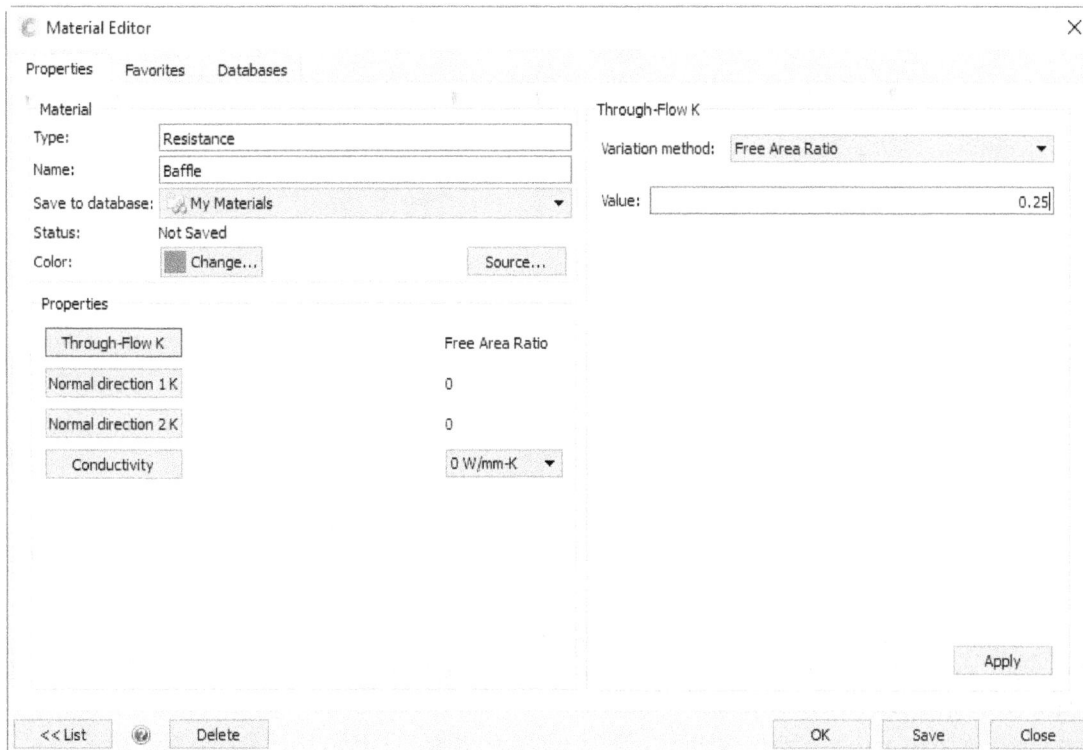

Figure-40. Creating material for baffle

- Click in the **Name** edit box from **Material Editor** dialog box and enter the name as **Baffle**.
- Select the **My Materials** option from **Save to database** drop-down to save the **Baffle** material in your selected list.
- Click on the **Through-Flow K** button; the parameters will be displayed at right of **Material Editor** dialog box.
- Click on the **Variation** method drop down and select the **Free Area Ratio** option.
- Click in the **Value** edit box and enter the value as **0.25** and click on the **Apply** button.
- Similarly, click on the **Normal direction 1K** button and specify the parameter of **Variation method** as **Free Area Ratio** and **Value** as **0**. After specifying, click on **Apply** button to save the parameters.
- The parameters of **Normal direction 2K** are same as **Normal direction 1K** option.
- Click on the **Conductivity** button from **Material Editor** dialog box and specify the value of **Variation** method as **Constant** and **Value** as **0.2 W/mm-K**, and don't forget to click on **Apply** button.
- After specifying the parameters for **Baffle**, click on the **Save** button and then **OK** button from **Material Editor** dialog box. You will be returned to **Materials** dialog box and the **Baffle** material will be displayed in **Name** option.
- Click on the **Global X** button for the **Flow Direction** field from **Materials** dialog box; the **Flow Direction** dialog box will be displayed; refer to Figure-41.

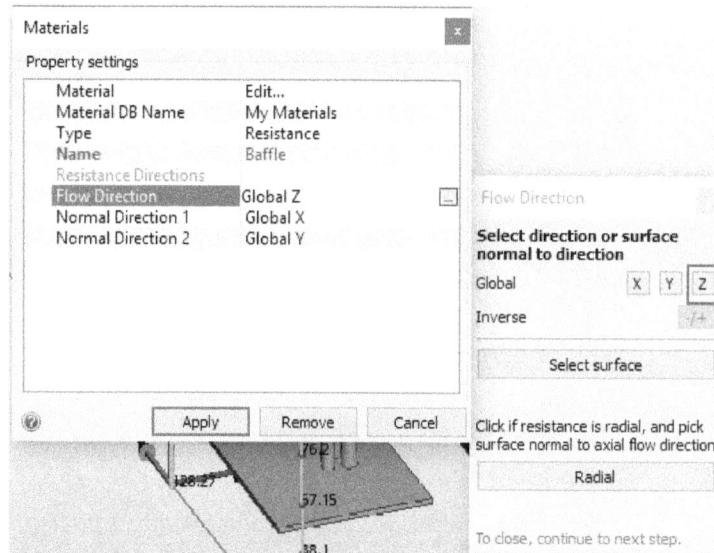

Figure-41. Flow Direction option

- Select the **Z axis** from **Flow Direction** dialog box and close it.
- Similarly, select the **Global X** in **Normal Direction 1** and **Global Y** in **Normal Direction 2** drop-downs.
- After specifying the parameters, click on the **Apply** button from **Materials** dialog box to apply **Baffle** resistance to model.

Creating Fan Material

- Select the **Fan** from **Design Study Bar** and click on **Edit** button from **Materials** panel of **Setup** tab; the **Materials** dialog box will be displayed.
- Click on the **Type** drop-down from **Materials** dialog box and select **Internal Fan/ Pump** button to specify the material type.
- Click on the **Edit** button from **Material** option of **Materials** dialog box; the **Material Editor** dialog box will be displayed.
- Click in the **Name** edit box of **Material Editor** dialog box and enter the name as **Fan**.
- Click on the **Save to database** drop-down from **Material Editor** dialog box and select the **My Materials** option.
- Click on **Flow** button to specify the flow parameters. The parameters will be displayed at right.
- Click on the **Variation method** drop-down and select the **Constant** button.
- Click in the **Value** edit box and enter the value as **0.50.** Change the units to **m3/ min**, and click on **Apply** button to apply these parameters.
- Now, click on **Rotational Speed** button from **Material Editor** dialog box; the **Rotational Speed** section will be displayed at right.
- Click in the **Value** edit box of **Rotational Speed** section and enter the value as **0** and rest of the parameters will be same. Click on **Apply** button to apply these parameters.
- Click on the **Slip factor** button from **Material Editor** dialog box; the **Slip factor** section will be displayed at right.
- Click in the **Value** edit box of **Slip factor** and enter the value as **1.** Rest of the parameters will be same as default. Click on the **Apply** button to apply the parameters.

- After specifying the parameters for **Fan**, click on the **Save** button and then on the **OK** button from **Material Editor** dialog box; refer to Figure-42. You will be returned to **Materials** dialog box.

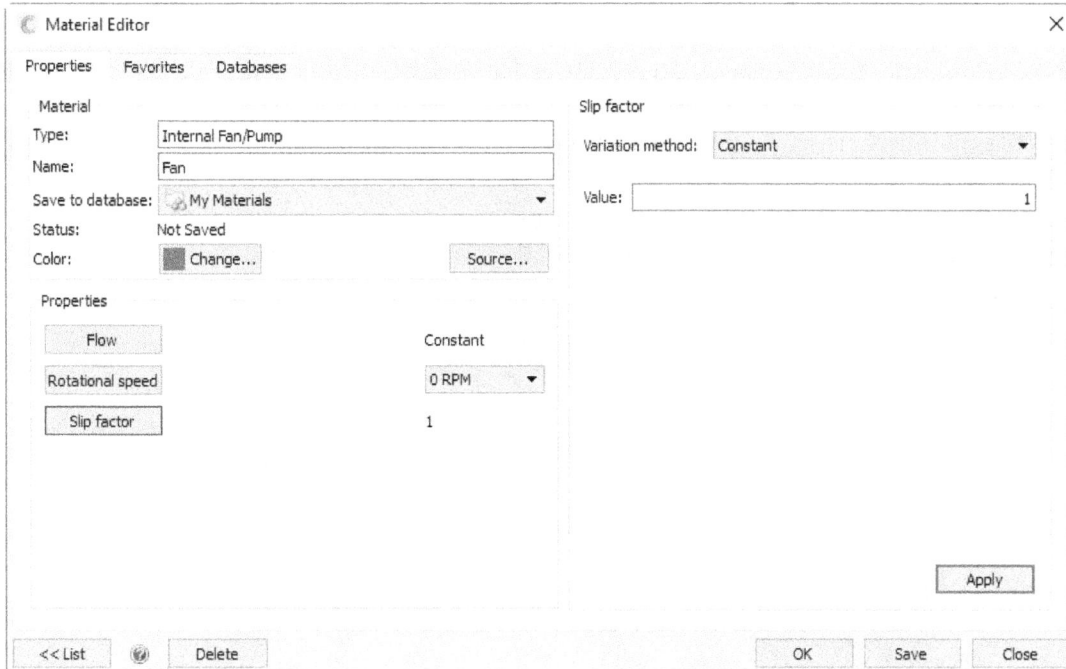

Figure-42. Fan material

- In **Materials** dialog box, select the **Name** as **Fan** and click on **Flow direction** button; the **Flow Direction** dialog box will be displayed; refer to Figure-43. Select the **X** as direction from **Flow Direction** dialog box and click on **Apply** button from **Materials** dialog box.

Figure-43. Specifying flow direction for Fan

Till now, we had applied materials to all component of model. Now, it's time to assign some boundary conditions.

Applying Boundary Conditions

In this section, we are going to apply boundary conditions to inlet and outlet of model.

- Click on the **Boundary Conditions** tool from **Setup** tab to activate boundary condition task.
- Click on the **Surface** selection button form **Selection** panel to select surface from model.
- Select the inlet surface and click on **Edit** button; the **Boundary Conditions** dialog box will be displayed.
- Enter the parameter of **Type** as **Pressure** and pressure value as **1 atm**, and click on the **Apply** button; refer to Figure-44. The pressure boundary condition will be applied.

Figure-44. Applying inlet presure boundary condition

- Select the inlet surface again and click on **Edit** button. Specify the parameter **Type** as **Temperature**, **Unit** as **Celsius**, and **Temperature** as **25**, and click on **Apply** button; refer to Figure-45. The **Temperature** boundary condition will be applied at the inlet.

Figure-45. Applying inlet temperature boundary condition

Outlet Boundary condition

- Select the outlet surface of model and click on **Edit** button from **Boundary Conditions** panel; the **Boundary Conditions** dialog box will be displayed.
- Specify the parameter of **Type** as **Pressure**, **Unit** as **atm**, and **Pressure** as **1** in **Boundary Conditions** dialog box; refer to Figure-46. The outlet boundary condition will applied.

Figure-46. Oulet Boundary Conditions of Practical 2

Heat Generation of Circuit Board

When electronic components work in circuit, they produce heat. We will now apply heat generation to the components.

- **Boundary Conditions** task is activated already, but you need to select the **Volume** selection button from **Selection** panel of **Setup** tab to select volume at once.
- Hide the Casing, CFDCreatedVolume, and Volume by pressing CTRL key plus middle mouse button.
- Now, select **Circuit 1** and **Circuit 2**, and click on **Edit** button; the **Boundary Conditions** dialog box will be displayed.
- Specify the **Type** as **Total Heat Generation**, **Unit** as **W**, **Total Heat Generation** as **2** in **Boundary Conditions** dialog box; refer to Figure-47. Click on the **Apply** button from the dialog box. The **Total Heat Generation** boundary condition will be applied.

Figure-47. Applying Heat Generation Boundary Condition

- You can also do the same by selecting the previously created group i.e. **Circuit -(Volume)** and click on **Edit** button from **Boundary Conditions** panel. The **Boundary Conditions** dialog box will be displayed. Rest of the process to apply heat generation boundary condition was discussed earlier.

Mesh Generating

Till now, we have applied materials to all parts of model and boundary conditions to inlet and outlet surfaces. Now, we are ready to generate mesh and the procedure is discussed next.

- Click on the **Mesh Sizing** tool from **Setup Tasks** panel to activate the **Mesh Sizing** task.
- Click on **Autosize** button from **Automatic Sizing** panel of **Setup** tab; the mesh will be generated and displayed on model; refer to Figure-48.

Figure-48. Mesh on Practical 2

- Click on **Edit** button to edit the parameters of mesh. The **Mesh Sizes** dialog box will be displayed. The need of changing the parameters of mesh, is because of some components on circuit board which are too small for analysis. If, we opt for automatic mesh, then the automatically generated mesh will not be so fine as our need. So, we will now refine those parts to make them more convenient for analysis.
- Now, select all surfaces of available component on circuit board and move the slider of **Size adjustment** towards **Fine** and set yy value; refer to Figure-49.

Figure-49. Adjusting mesh

- After adjusting the mesh, click on **Apply changes** and then **Spread changes** button Size adjustment section of dialog box.
- After setting mesh, click on **Apply** button from **Mesh Sizes** dialog box. You will be returned to **Setup** tab.

Solving Analysis

It's time to solve the analysis and the process is discussed below.

- Click on **Solve** button from **Simulation** panel of **Setup** tab; the **Solve** dialog box will be displayed.
- Click on the **Physics** tab from **Solve** dialog box and select the check box of **Flow**, **Heat Transfer**, and **Auto Forced Convection** options; refer to Figure-50.

Figure-50. Physics tab of Practical 2

- Click on the **Control** tab and specify the value of **Iterations to Run** as **100**, and click **Solve** button to solve the current analysis. The analysis will starts to solve and progress will be displayed in **Convergence** tab; refer to Figure-51.

Figure-51. Convergence tab of Practical 2

- The **Auto Forced Convection** causes the analysis to automatically run in two stages. The first stage is flow-only and the other stage solves the heat transfer only, and runs to an additional 100 iterations. We had set the numbers of iterations to 100 in **Solve** dialog box to reduce the overall time of exercise. Increase the number of iterations to 300 to run the analysis to convergence automatically.

Results

After the analysis is completed, it will be displayed in **Output Bar** and the **Results** tab will be displayed. It's time to check the result of analysis.

Planes

- Click on the **Planes** button from **Results** tab and click on **Add** button from **Planes** panel. The plane will be created along X axis.

- Click on the added plane and select **Y** axis from context menu; refer to Figure-52.

Figure-52. Plane along Y axis

- Move the plane downward by dragging the triad axis normal to plane; refer to Figure-53.

Figure-53. Plane draged to normal

Velocity Vector

- To display vectors, click on the **Vector** drop-down from **Planes** panel and select **Velocity Vector** option. The vectors will be displayed on added plane.
- Click on the **Edit** button from **Planes** panel to edit the vector spacing; the **Plane Control** dialog box will be displayed.
- Move the **Grid Spacing** slider to **Fine** from **Plane Control** dialog box to increase the number of vector on plane, and to decrease the spacing between vectors; refer to Figure-54.

Figure-54. Grid Spacing

- Click on the **Vector settings** tab of **Plane Control** dialog box and specify the parameters as displayed in Figure-55.

Figure-55. Vector Settings tab of Practical 2

- To clearly view the vectors, change the visual style of plane from **Shaded** to **Outline** by clicking on **Outline** button of **Plane** right-click menu; refer to Figure-56.

Figure-56. Changing Appearance of plane

Iso Surfaces

- Click on the **Iso Surfaces** tool of **Results Tasks** panel of **Results** tab and click on **Add** button to add an iso surface plane. Some type of presentations will be displayed inside model.
- Right-click on added Iso-surface and click on **Edit** button from displayed right-click menu to edit the parameters; the **Iso Surface Control** dialog box will be displayed.
- Move the slider in **Controls** tab to change the Iso Quantity value; refer to Figure-57.

Figure-57. Specifying parameters of iso surfaces

- The **Iso Surface** is generally used to understand how the flow influence the heat transfer. Regions, where movement of air is low leads to poor heat transfer and high component temperatures.
- After checking the result, remove the iso-surface by clicking **Remove** button from right-click menu of **IsoSurface** of **Design Study Bar**; refer to Figure-58.

Figure-58. Removing iso surface

- Similarly, remove the previously created plane. We are removing these for better appearance in next step.

Temperature Results

- Click on the **Planes** tool from **Results Tasks** panel of **Results** tab and click on Add button to add a plane.
- Click on the recently created plane and click on Y axis to align the plane towards y-axis.
- Click on **Results** drop-down from **Planes** panel and select **Temperature** from the list. The changes as per temperature will be displayed on plane.

- Move the triad axis of plane towards normal and the plane will somewhat look like Figure-59. This process was discussed earlier of moving the plane downward.

Figure-59. Temperature plane

- Similarly, you can view the regions where temperature are highest and lowest with the help of Iso Surface tool. This process is discussed earlier.
- To view **Iso Surface** properly, you may need to change the visual style of created plane from **Shaded** to **Outline**. After applying **Iso Surface**, the model will look like Figure-60.

Figure-60. Added Iso Surface for temperature

Summary Parts

The **Summary Parts** tool is used for quick comparing of two parts, like temperature. To compare results of several parts, make them summary parts. In the below procedure, we compare the temperature of two circuit board.

- Click on **Parts** tool from **Results Tasks** panel of **Results** tab; the **Parts** dialog box will be displayed at left of graphic window.
- Click on the **Group** operation button from **Parts** dialog box and select **Circuit** group. The **Circuit 1** and **Circuit 2** will be displayed in **Parts** dialog box; refer to Figure-61.

Figure-61. Selecting Circuit group

- Select the **Circuit 1** and **Circuit 2** check box to designate these parts as summary parts.
- Click on **Decision Center** tab to compare result. The added summary values will be displayed in **Design Study Bar**.
- To update all these values, click on **Update All** button from **Update** panel; the values will be updated and displayed; refer to Figure-62.

Figure-62. Comparing Values of Practical 2

- The discussed procedure provides the result in simple data. It is now easier to plot and compare results between to components.

PRACTICAL 3

In this practical, we simulate air flow and temperature distribution due to natural convection in a telecommunication model. The Practical 3 contain many heat generating components. The flow around the model is done naturally (with the use of gravity) and density variations caused by gradients in air temperature, also known as buoyancy. In this practical, we are going to create the analysis of natural convection inside telecommunication module.

We will study the effects of natural convection inside the model; refer to Figure-63.

Figure-63. Practical 3

Opening the model

- Double-click on the Autodesk CFD icon from Desktop or click from the Start menu; the welcome screen of Autodesk CFD 2018 will be displayed.
- Click on **New** button from **Ribbon** and open the file **Telecommunication Module Assembly.iam** with the name design study as **Practical 3**; refer to Figure-64.

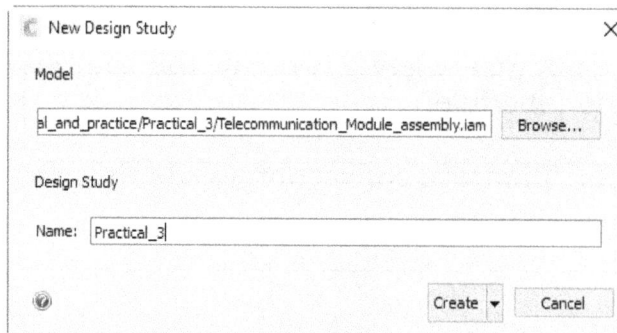

Figure-64. Opening Practical 3

- Click on **Create** button from **New Design Study** dialog box; the **Geometry Tools** dialog box will be displayed; refer to Figure-65.

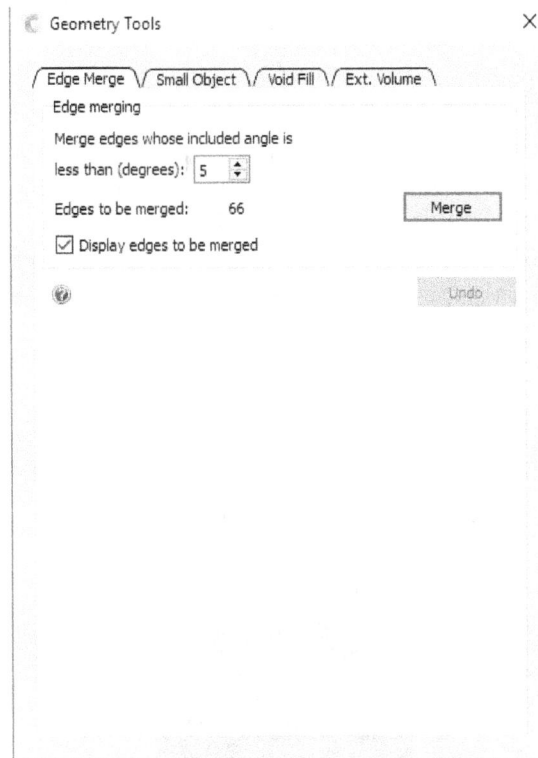

Figure-65. Geometry Tools dialog box of Practical 3

- Click on the **Merge** button to merge some small edges and close the dialog box.
- Change the units of model from **CM** to **MM**, from **Design Study Bar**.

Applying Materials

- Click on the **Materials** tool from **Setup Tasks** panel of **Setup** tab to activate the **Materials** task.
- Select the **Outer case**, and click on **Edit** button from **Materials** panel. The **Materials** dialog box will be displayed.
- Select the **Type** as **Solid** and **Material** as **Aluminium**, and click on **Apply** button; refer to Figure-66. The material will be applied to selected components.

Figure-66. Applying Aluminium on outer case

- Hide the **Outer** case to assign the material to inner area with the help of **CTRL** key and middle mouse button.
- Select the internal area and click on **Edit** button; the **Materials** dialog box will be displayed.
- Select the **Type** as **Fluid** and **Material** as **Air**, and click on **Set** button from **Materials** dialog box to specify the properties to vary with temperature. The **Material Environment** dialog box will be displayed.
- Select the **Variable** radio button from **Material Environment** dialog box and click on **OK** button; refer to Figure-67. You will be returned to **Materials** dialog box.

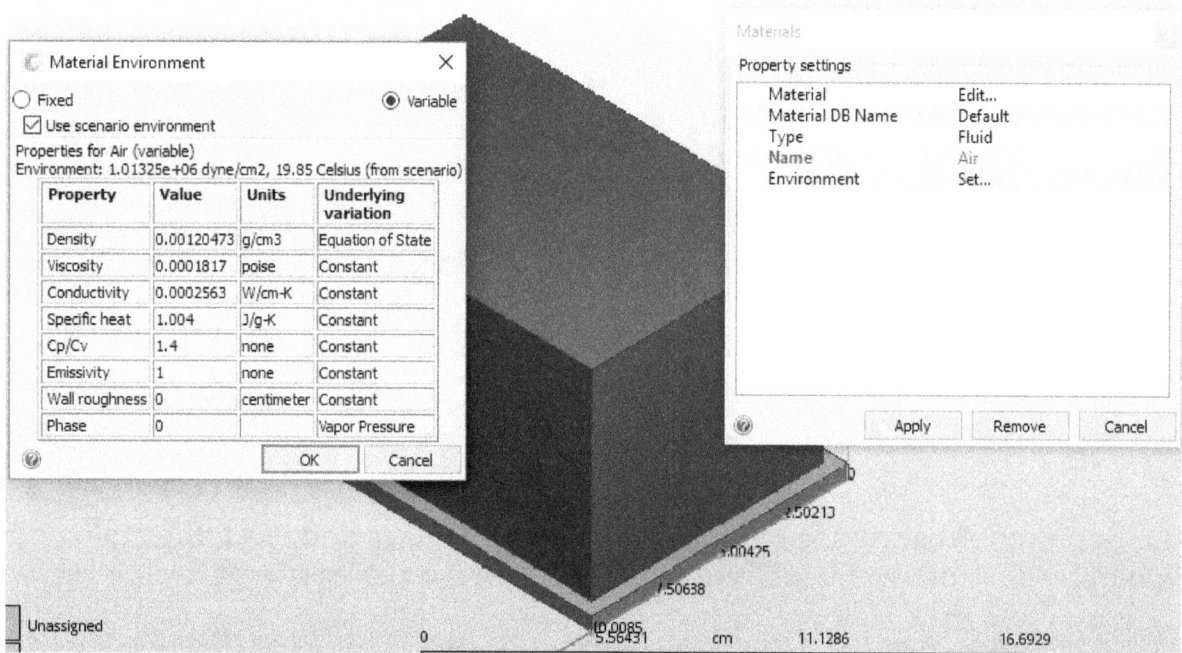

Figure-67. Specifying variable condition

- Click on **Apply** button from **Materials** dialog box to apply the boundary condition.

- Now, we will apply materials to other parts like **Receiver** and **Transceiver**.
- First of all, hide the case and air volume from the model and select all three receiver and transceiver from **Design Study Bar;** refer to Figure-68.

Figure-68. Selecting other components

- Right-click on any of the selected components and click on **Edit** button from menu; the **Materials** dialog box will be displayed.
- Select the **Type** as **Solid** and **Name** as **Silicon** from **Materials** dialog box, and click on **Apply** button to apply. The selected material will be applied.
- Select the **Base** component and click on **Edit** button; the material dialog box will be displayed.
- Select the **Type** as **Solid** and **Name** as **PCB 12-Layer(X),** and click on **Apply** button. The selected material will be applied. The material we applied is a solid with conductivity equivalent to a 12-layer PCB.
- Till now, we had applied materials to all component of model and it's time to apply some boundary condition.

Boundary Conditions

- Click on **Boundary Conditions** tool from **Results Tasks** panel of **Setup** tab; the **Boundary Conditions** task will be activated.
- Select the **Volume** button from **Selection** panel of **Setup** tab to select volume from model.
- Hide the **Outer** case and air volume from model and select **Receiver 1, Receiver 2**, and **Receiver 3**.
- Click on **Edit** button from desired procedure; the **Boundary Conditions** dialog box will be displayed.
- Click in the **Total Heat Generation** edit box from **Boundary Conditions** dialog box and enter the value as **6**; click on the **Apply** button specifying value. The boundary condition will be applied and displayed in Graphic window and Design Study Bar.
- Select the **Transceiver** from model and click on **Edit** button. The Boundary **Conditions** dialog box will be displayed.
- Click in the **Total Heat Generation** edit box and enter the value as **10**, and click on **Apply** button to apply the boundary condition.

Assigning Film Coefficient boundary condition

A Film Coefficient Boundary Condition simulates exposure to external flow, without modeling the air that surrounds it. A higher value of Film Coefficient is used to simulate forced convection situation. Applying this boundary condition is little bit tricky because we need to select all the external surface of model, even the surfaces of heat sink.

- Show the outer case of model using Navigation Cube. Align the model such that you can easily count the number of heat fins, i.e Left or Right; refer to Figure-69.

Figure-69. Align model to Right

- Make sure, your model is enabled with **Orthographic** view so that it is easy to select surfaces of the fins. If not enabled then enable it from **Appearance** panel of **View** tab.
- Select the **Surface** selection mode from **Selection** panel of **Setup** tab to select surfaces of model.
- With the help of boundary selection, select the surfaces of fins by making a rectangle covering all fins; refer to Figure-70.

Figure-70. Selection of heat fins surfaces

- Select the remaining external surfaces of model; refer to Figure-71.

Figure-71. Selecting remaining surfaces

- After selecting all the external surfaces, click on **Edit** button from **Boundary Conditions** panel and specify the parameters as displayed in Figure-72.

Figure-72. Parameters of Film Coefficient

- After specifying the parameters, click on **Apply** button from **Boundary Conditions** dialog box. The boundary condition will be applied.

Generating Mesh

Till now, we have applied material and boundary conditions to all components of model, and the next step to proceed is generating mesh.

- Click on the **Mesh Sizing** tool from **Setup Tasks** panel of **Setup** tab; the meshing tool will be activated.
- Click on the **Autosize** tool from **Automatic Sizing** panel of **Setup** tab; the mesh will be displayed on model; refer to Figure-73.

Figure-73. Mesh of Practical 2

Solving Analysis

- Click on the **Solve** button from **Simulation** panel of **Setup** tab; the **Solve** dialog box will be displayed.
- Enter the value of **Iterations to Run** as 200 in **Control** tab.
- Click on the **Physics** tab and select the **Flow** & **Heat Transfer** check boxes.
- Select the **Gravity Method** as **Earth**. Click in the **Gravity Direction** edit box and specify the parameters as 0,-1,0. Here -1 refers to reverse direction of Y axis.
- After specifying the parameters, click on **Solve** button from **Solve** dialog box. The software starts to generate mesh.

Note: If you want to generate mesh other than the process of **Solve** dialog box, then right-click on **Mesh Size** option from **Design Study Bar**. The right-click menu will displayed. Click on **Generate Mesh** button; refer to Figure-74. The mesh will be generated. Now, you can directly solve the analysis and the procedure is same i.e. by **Solve** dialog box.

Figure-74. Generate Mesh button

- After generating mesh, iterations will start; refer to Figure-75.

Figure-75. Analyaia Practical 3

Results

After completion of iterations, the **Results** tab will be displayed. Now, we will examine the velocity results using a cutting plane and an iso surface.

- Click on **Planes** tool from **Results Tasks** panel of **Results** tab and click on **Add** button from **Planes** panel. The plane along X axis will be created on model; refer to Figure-76.

Figure-76. Added velocity plane

- Click on **Vector** drop-down from **Planes** panel and select the **Velocity Vector** option to view vectors on plane.
- Click on **Edit** button from **Planes** panel; the **Plane Control** dialog box will be displayed.
- Move the **Grid spacing** slider of **Plane Control** dialog box towards **Fine,** or directly enter the value as **2.5** in edit box (located in middle of **Grid Spacing** option).
- Change the visual style of added plane from **Shaded** to **Outline** to clearly view the vectors.
- Now, click on **Vector settings** tab of **Plane Control** dialog box and select the **Length Range** radio button.
- Move the **Min** slider towards right, or enter the value as **0.04**. Press enter to apply results.
- Move the **Max** slider towards right, or enter the value as **0.15** and press enter to apply.
- After specifying the parameters for vectors, close the dialog box. The vectors of this model should look like Figure-77.

Figure-77. Vectors Practical 3

Iso Surface

- Click on **Iso Surfaces** tool from **Results Tasks** panel of **Results** tab and click on **Add** button from **Iso Surfaces** panel. The iso surface will be displayed on model.
- In this model, the **Iso Surface** tool is used to understand how the flow influences the heat transfer. The regions with little air movement leads to poor heat transfer and high temperature of components.
- Click on **Edit** button from **Iso Surfaces** panel to edit the iso quantity value; the **Iso Surface Control** dialog box will be displayed.
- Move the slider to view the effects of heat transfer; refer to Figure-78

Figure-78. Iso Surface of Practical 3

- Remove the iso surface to see the results in next step.

Results based on Temperature

- Activate the **Planes** task and select **None** from **Vector** drop-down to remove the added vectors.
- Change the visual style of previously added plane to **Shaded** and select **Temperature** from **Result** drop-down of **Planes** panel. The temperature will be displayed on plane; refer to Figure-79.

Figure-79. Added Temperature plane

- In the above image, you can see two legends are available, i.e. **Velocity Magnitude** and **Temperature.** If you want to remove the **Velocity Magnitude** legend, select the **Temperature** option from **Global Result** drop-down of **Global** tab; refer to Figure-80.

Figure-80. Removed legend

- Again come back to **Planes** tool and select the visual style of plane to **Outline**.
- Click on **Iso Surfaces** tool from **Result Tasks** panel of **Results** tab and click on **Add** button. The iso surface will be displayed.
- Click on **Quantity** drop-down from **Iso Surface** panel and select **Temperature** option. Similarly, select the **Temperature** in **Color By** drop-down to view temperature in iso surface. This iso surface is used to determine the lowest and highest temperature in model. Now, remove the iso surface as desired.

Result Parts

The result **Parts** is generally used to determine the temperature of selected parts. In this step, we will determine the temperature values on three receiver and a transceiver.

- Click on **Parts** tool from **Result Tasks** panel of **Results** tab; the **Parts** dialog box will be displayed.
- Hide the Outer Case and Air volume from model and select the three receiver and transceiver. The selected parts will be listed in **Parts** dialog box.
- Click on **Calculate** button from **Parts** dialog box. The temperature values on parts will be displayed in **Output** tab of **Parts** dialog box; refer to Figure-81.

Figure-81. Temperature values in Parts dialog box

FOR STUDENTS NOTES

Practical and Practice

Chapter 8

Topics Covered

The major topics covered in this chapter are:

- *Practical 4*
- *Practical 5*
- *Practice 1*
- *Practice 2*
- *Practice 3*

INTRODUCTION

In past chapters, we have learned the tools used to create a simulation studies. We have also learned the procedure of tools which were used during simulation study. In this chapter, we will create analyses on different scenario conditions.

PRACTICAL 4

In this practical, we will simulate the flow is centrifugal pump with back - swept blades. The model consists of the volute, inlet pipe, the impeller, and rotating region. The rotating region is a volume that is completely surrounded by the impeller. The working fluid is water and impeller spins at 600 RPM. The pump is operated at the zero head state (maximum flow rate). A head loss can be imposed on the pump by assigning a positive gage pressure boundary condition to the outlet or a negative gage pressure to the inlet. During the analysis, the impeller rotates within the stationary volute. Approximately four complete revolutions are needed for a steady state result. At the beginning of the analysis, we will slowly ramp up the rotational speed to ensure stability and solution accuracy. Once the impeller is rotating at the desired speed, we will use a time step that causes the impeller to rotate through one blade passage per time step.

Opening Model

- Double-click on Autodesk CFD 2018 icon from Desktop; the welcome screen of Autodesk CFD will be displayed.
- Click on **New** button from **Ribbon** and **Browse** the file **Centrifugal Pump Practical 4** in the resource folder available on www.cadcamcaeworks.com.
- Click in the **Name** edit box of **New Design Study** dialog box and enter the name as **Practical 4**, and click on **Create** button; refer to Figure-1. The model will be displayed. Along with **Geometry Tools** dialog box. Click on the **Merge** button from the dialog box and click on the **Close** button; refer to Figure-2.

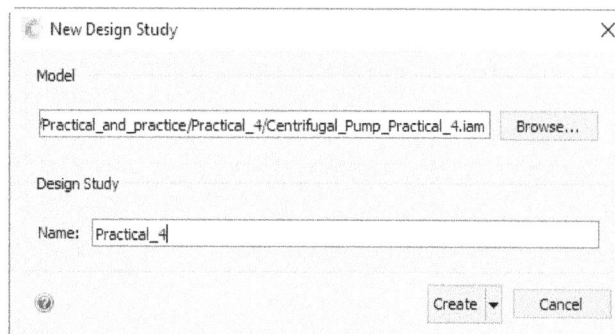

Figure-1. New Desgn Study dialog box of Practical

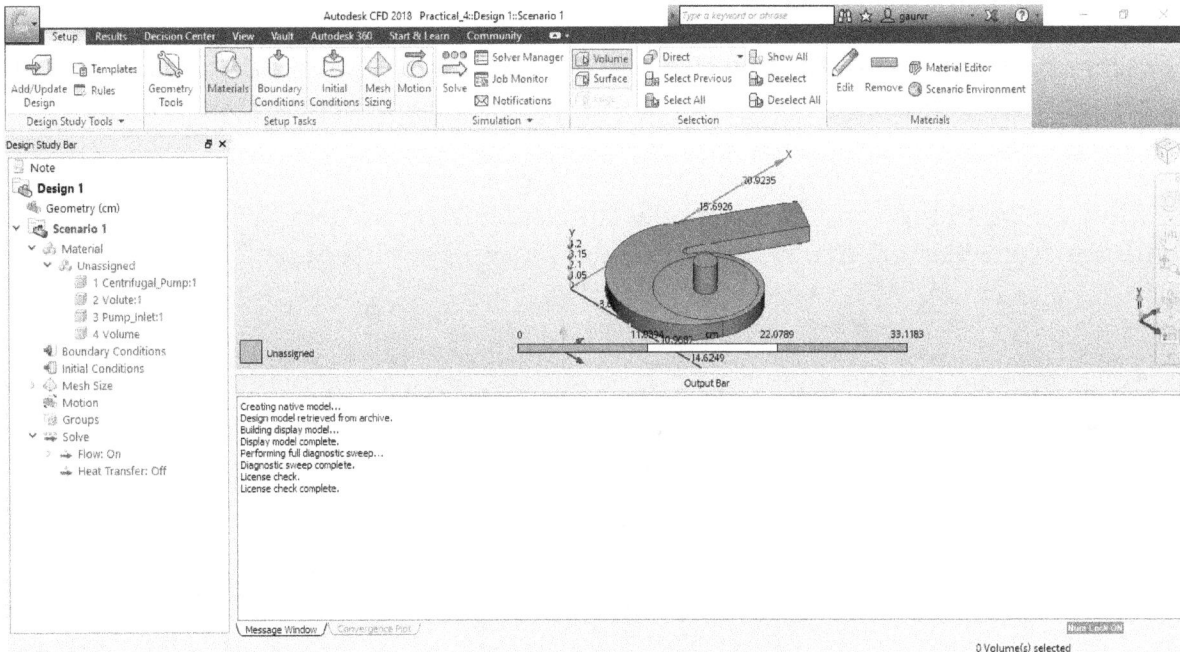

Figure-2. Practical 4

- Change the units of current model from **CM** to **MM**, and the procedure to do so was discussed earlier.

Assigning Materials

In this step, we are going to assign material to all parts of model.

- Activate the **Materials** tool from **Setup** tab and click on **Edit** button. The **Materials** dialog box will be displayed.
- Select the **Volute**, and **Pump Inlet** from **Design Study Bar**. These components will be highlighted in Graphics Window.
- Select the **Type** as **Fluid** and **Name** as **Water** in **Materials** dialog box, and click on **Apply** button; refer to Figure-3.

Figure-3. Specifying material to components

- Click on the **Impeller** from Graphics Window or **Design Study Bar**, and click on **Edit** button. The **Materials** dialog box will be displayed.
- Select the **Type** as **Solid** and **Name** as **Aluminium** in **Materials** dialog box, and click on **Apply** button. The material will be applied to selected parts.

Applying Rotating Region Material

- Hide the **Impeller** part from model and select the **Volume**. You can also select **Volume** from **Design Study Bar**, without hiding **Impeller;** refer to Figure-4.

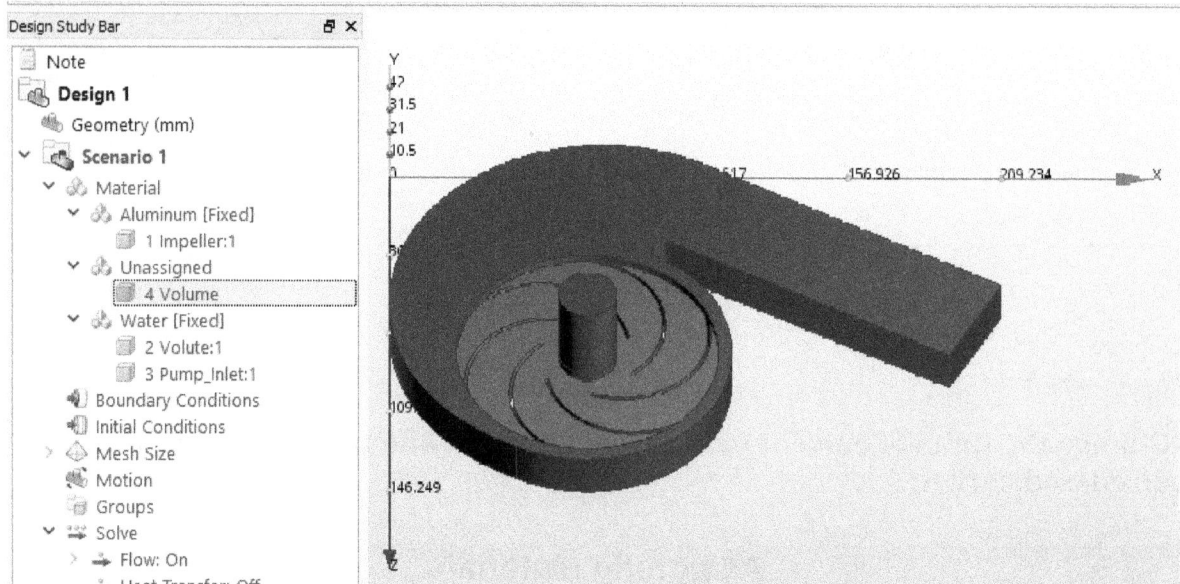

Figure-4. Selecting Volume part

- Click on **Edit** button from **Materials** panel and click on **Type** drop-down from **Materials** dialog box and select **Rotating Region** option to create a rotating region material.
- Click on **Edit** button from **Material** dialog box; the **Material Editor** dialog box will be displayed.
- Specify the parameters of **Name** as **Rotor, Save to database** as **My Materials, Scenario Type** as **Known Rotational Speed** option in **Material Editor** dialog box and enter the parameters of **Rotational speed** section (displayed at right of **Material Editor**) as displayed in below figure; refer to Figure-5.

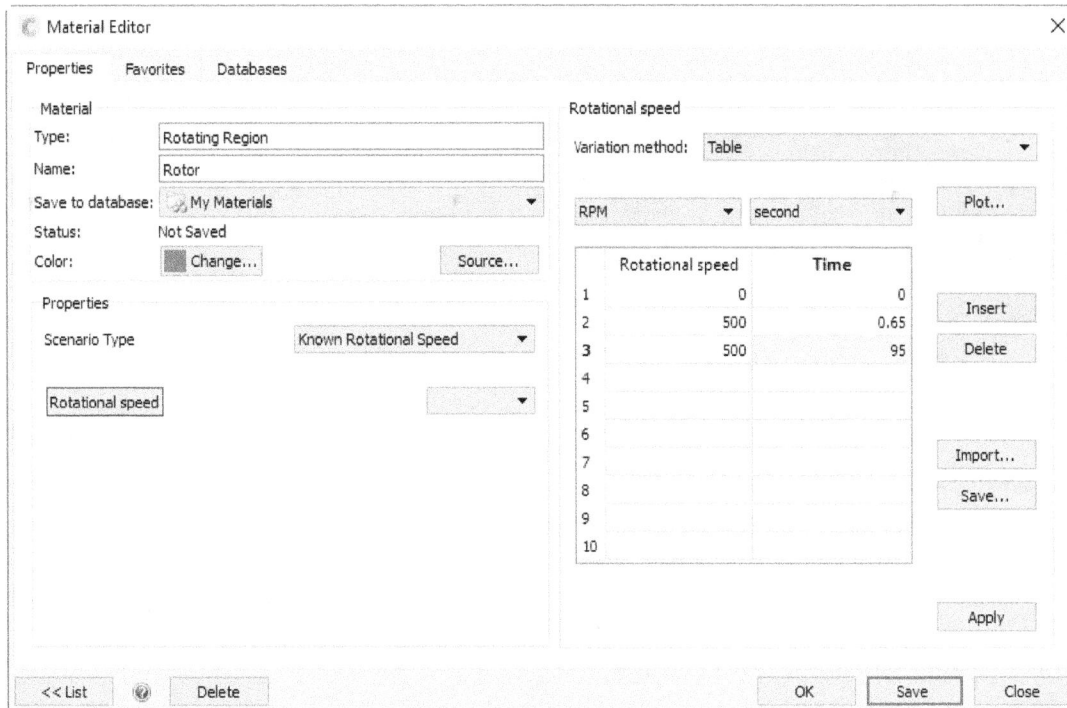

Figure-5. Specifying parameters of Rotational speed

- The values in the table are specified to ramp up the rotational speed of the impeller gradually to avoid impulsive start. This technique often reduces analysis instability, and improves overall accuracy of the solution.
- After specifying the parameters, click on **Apply** button, then **Save** button, and then **OK** button to save and apply this data. You will be returned to **Materials** dialog box and recently created material will be mentioned there as **Rotor** in **Name** option.
- Click on **Axis of Rotation** button and select the **Y** axis from **Axis of Rotation** dialog box. Here, Y axis refers to rotation axis along which impeller rotates.
- After specifying the parameters from **Materials** dialog box, click on **Apply** button. The material will be applied.

Assign Boundary Conditions

Till now, we have created and applied necessary materials to all components of model, and in this step, we are going to assign boundary conditions to model.

- Activate the **Boundary Conditions** tool and click on **Edit** button from **Boundary Conditions** panel. The **Boundary Conditions** dialog box will be displayed.
- Select the **Inlet** surface and Outlet surface from the model; refer to Figure-6.

Figure-6. Selecting inlet and outlet surface

- Specify the parameters of **Type** as **Pressure**, **Unit** as **Pa**, and **Pressure** as **0** in the **Boundary conditions** dialog box. We are assigning the zero pressure to both inlet and outlet because fluid is flowing naturally without use of any external force.
- After specifying the parameters, click on **Apply** button. The boundary conditions will be applied on selected surface.

Generating Mesh

Generating mesh is kind of a easy task, but we have to refine the mesh of impeller for creating uniform mesh of whole model.

- Activate the **Mesh Sizing** tool and click on **Autosize** button from **Automatic sizing** panel; the results will be displayed on model.
- To make the mesh of rotating region uniform for rotating analyses, hide the impeller and right-click on volume. The right-click menu will be displayed.
- Click on **Edit** button from right-click menu; the **Mesh Sizes** dialog box will be displayed.
- Click in the **Size adjustment** edit box and enter the value as **2**, or move the slider to **2**.
- Click on the **Use Uniform** button for uniform mesh, click on **Apply changes** button and then **Spread Changes** button to apply and spread this setting to whole model.
- Click on **Apply** button to apply the mesh changes; refer to Figure-7.

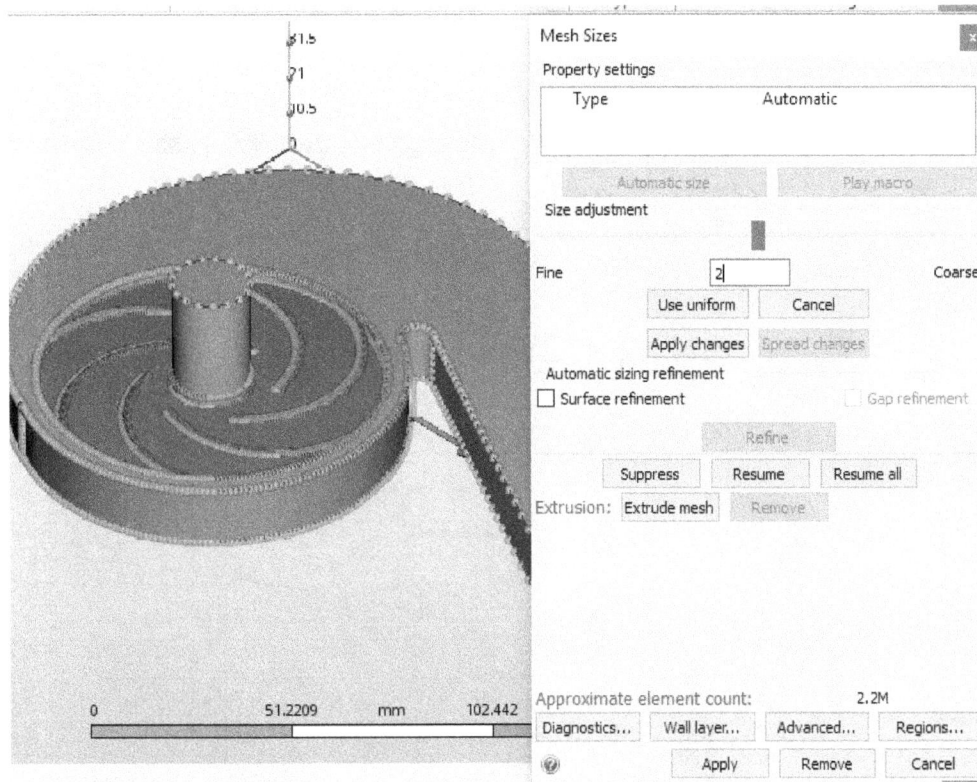

Figure-7. Refining mesh

Solving Analysis

- Click on **Solve** button to solve the analysis, the **Solve** dialog box will be displayed.
- Set the **Solution Mode** to **Transient** option and click on **Time Step Size** button, the **Time Step Size** dialog box will be displayed. The **Time Step Size** option is used to run several complete rotations quickly. We will use **Time Step Size** such that the impeller rotates a complete blade passage with every time step.
- Select the **Number of blades** radio button from **Time Step Size** dialog box and enter the value as **6** in respected edit box.
- After this, click on **Calculate** button. This sets the time step value as 0.02; refer to Figure-8. Close the **Time Step Size** dialog box.

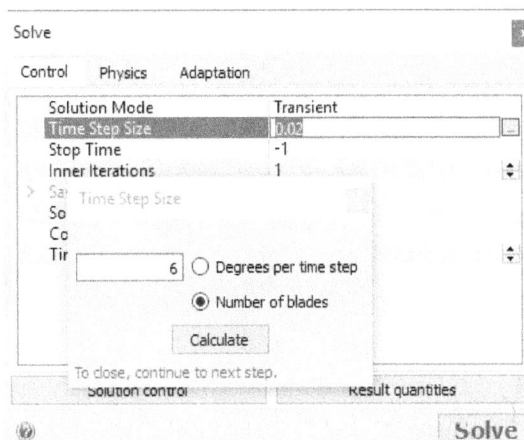

Figure-8. Time Step Size

- Click on the **Save Intervals** node and enter the value of **Results** as 5 and **Time Steps to Run** as **70**. This allows impeller to complete 10 revolutions at full speed.

- After specifying the parameters, click on **Solve** button from **Solve** dialog box. The software starts the analysis and results will be displayed on completion; refer to Figure-9.

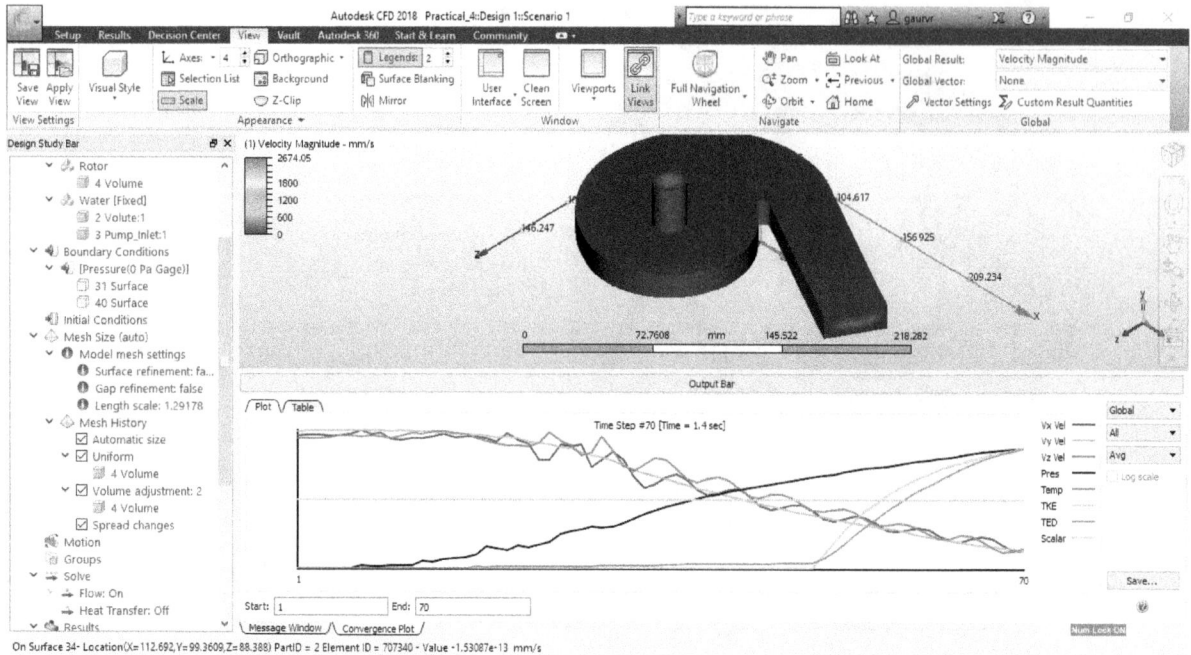

Figure-9. Practical 2 completed analysis

Results

Now, we will examine the velocity results using a cutting plane and vectors.

- Click on the **Planes** tool and click on **Add** button from **Planes** panel. The plane will be added along X axis.
- Left-click on plane and click on Y axis from displayed menu. Hold the Y triad axis and move the plane downward normal to the model; refer to Figure-10.

Figure-10. Moving triad axis normal to plane

Animating Velocity Results

Animating the results provides the time history of results. In this model, it is very helpful to understand the flow inside the pump. The animation process helps us to understand how the flow evolves and how long it takes the pump to achieve steady state. The process to view animation is discussed next.

*   Right-click on **Results** node in **Design Study Bar** and click on **Animation** button; the **Animation** dialog box will be displayed; refer to Figure-11.

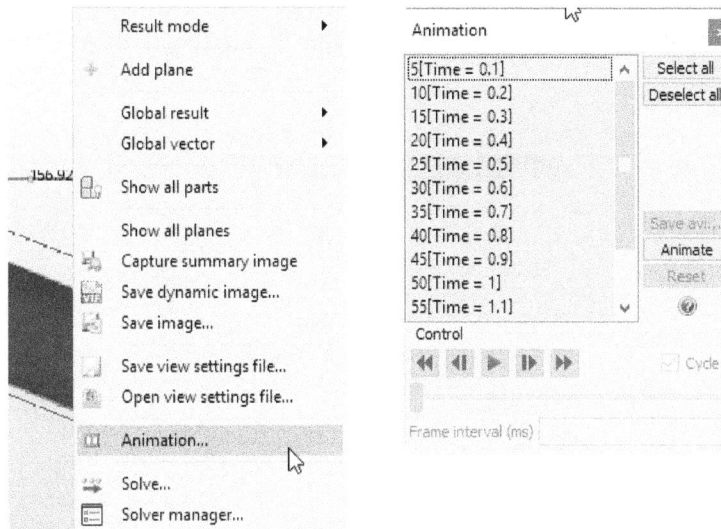

Figure-11. Animation button and Animation dialog box

*   Click on **Animate** button from **Animation** dialog box to activate the animation controls.
*   Use the animation control buttons to view the animation.

Note- Due to the animated results, you might not able to see the animation of rotating impeller because the time step was equal to amount of time for single passage to rotate. However, you may see the velocity develop through the impeller, and move into volute.

Volume Flow Rate

In this step, we will use Summary Planes and the Critical Values section to access volume flow rate at the current operating point.

*   Change the visual style of model to **Outline** and the process to do so was discussed many times in this book.
*   Left-click on plane and click on **Align Surface** button from displayed context menu.
*   Click on **Make Summary** tool from **Planes** panel to make the plane a summary plane.
*   Activate the **Decision Center** tab and update the summary values; refer to Figure-12.

Figure-12. Updating-Summary Values

- The **Summary Plane data** will be displayed at right after updating data; refer to Figure-13.

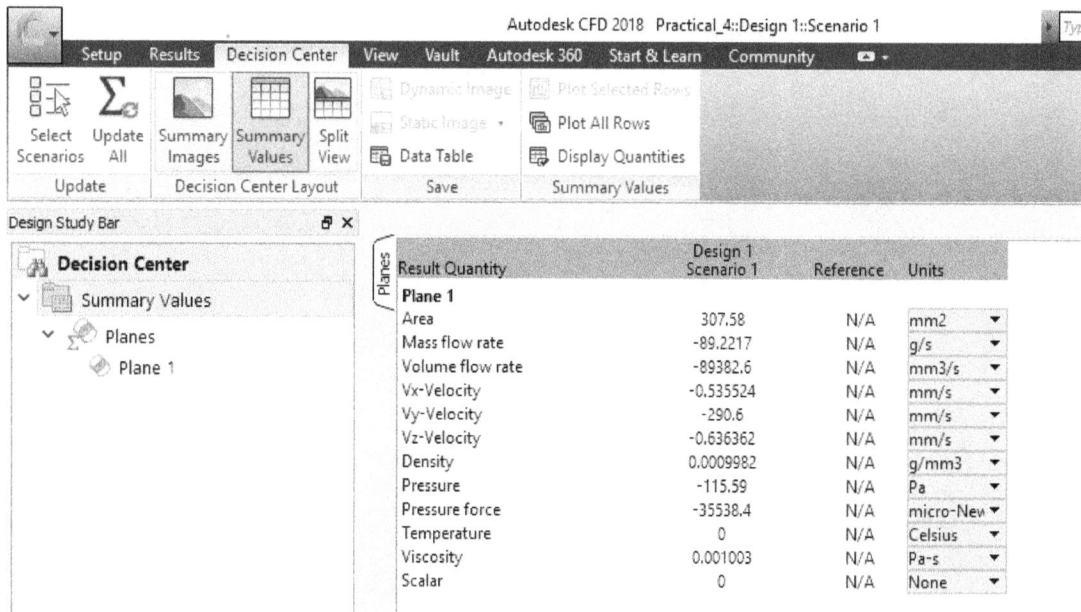

Figure-13. Summary Values data

PRACTICAL 5

In this practical, we will study the external flow aerodynamics around a car. In this model, we need to create an external volume around the model. The air flows around the car at a speed of 90 mph.

Opening the Model

- Double-click on Autodesk CFD 2018 icon from Desktop; the welcome screen will be displayed.
- Click on **New** button from **Ribbon**; the **New Design Study** dialog box will be displayed.
- Browse the **Aerodynamic Model.ipt** file from **Practical 5** folder and enter the **Name** as **Practical 5** in **New Design Study** dialog box. Click on **Create** button. The model will be displayed; refer to Figure-14. Also, the **Geometry Tools** dialog box will be displayed. Click on **Merge** button in the dialog box and close it.

Figure-14. Practical 5

- Change the units from **CM** to **MM** from **Design Study Bar**.

Creating External Volume

- Click on **Geometry Tools** button from **Setup Tasks** tab. The **Geometry Tools** dialog box will be displayed.
- Click on **Ext. Volume** tab; the external volume will displayed on model.
- Change the parameters of external volume as displayed in Figure-15, and click on **Create** button from **Geometry Tools** dialog box. The volume will be created. Close the **Geometry Tools** dialog box.

Figure-15. Parameters of external volume

- A new volume named as **CFDCreatedVolume** will be displayed in **Design Study Bar**.

Assigning Material

In this step, we are going to assign materials to all part before starting the analysis.

- Select the Part 1, Part 2, and Part 3 solid from **Design Study Bar** and right-click on it. Select the **Edit** button from right-click menu. The **Materials** dialog box will be displayed.
- Select the **Type** as **Solid** and **Material** as **Aluminium** from **Materials** dialog box, and click on **Apply** button. The **Aluminium** material will be applied to whole car. We are considering this model for learning basis only.
- Similarly, right-click on **Unassigned** option from **Design Study Bar** and click on **Edit** button; the **Materials** dialog box will be displayed.
- Select the **Type** as **Fluid** and **Material** as **Air** from **Materials** dialog box and click on **Apply** button. The **Air** material will be applied to CFDCreatedVolume; refer to Figure-16.

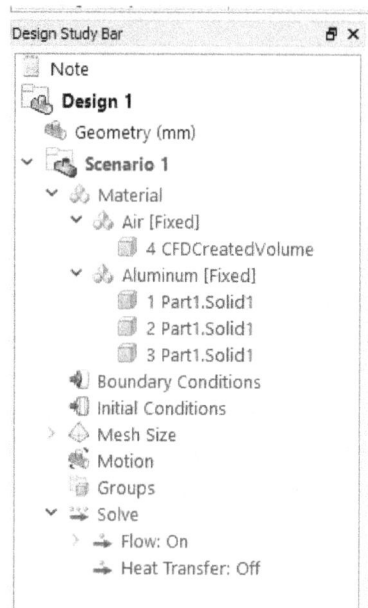

Figure-16. Applied material

Assigning Boundary Condition

In this step, we are going to apply a free stream velocity to inlet face and pressure to outlet face.

Assigning Inlet Boundary Condition

- Activate the **Boundary Conditions** tool from **Setup** tab and click on **Edit** button; the **Boundary Conditions** dialog box will be displayed
- Click on the Inlet face and specify the parameters of **Type** as **Velocity**, **Unit** as **mph**, and **Velocity Magnitude** as **100** in **Boundary Conditions** dialog box; refer to Figure-17.

Figure-17. Assigning Inlet boundary condition

- After specifying the parameters, click on **Apply** button. The inlet boundary condition will be applied.

Assigning Outlet Boundary Condition

- Similarly, select the outlet face and click on **Edit** button from displayed context menu; the **Boundary Conditions** dialog box will displayed.
- Specify the parameters of **Type** as **Pressure**, **Unit** as **atm**, and **Pressure** as **1** in **Boundary Conditions** dialog box; refer to Figure-18.

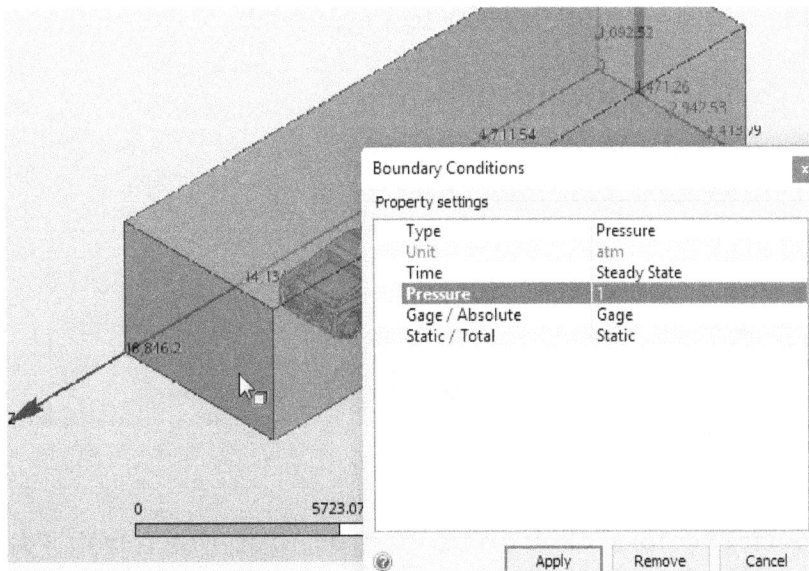

Figure-18. Outlet boundary condition of Practical 5

- After specifying the parameters, click on **Apply** button. The outlet boundary condition will applied.
- Till now, we have had applied materials to all components and boundary condition to inlet and outlet faces. Now, it's time to generate the mesh and solve the analysis.

Mesh Generating and Solving analysis

- Activate the **Mesh Sizing** tool and click on **Autosize** button from **Automatic Sizing** panel; the mesh will be generated and displayed on model.
- For mesh refinement of car, you need to hide the outer solid. So, hide the **CFDCreatedVolume** from graphic window.
- Click on **Edit** button from **Automatic Sizing** panel; the **Mesh Sizes** dialog box will be displayed.
- Select the car to activate the **Size adjustment** and move the **Size adjustment** slider to make it **0.9**, and click on **Apply Changes** button from **Mesh Sizes** dialog box.
- After specifying the parameters, click on **Apply** button from **Mesh Sizes** dialog box. The mesh of selected area will be refined.
- After generating the mesh, click on **Solve** button. The **Solve** dialog box will be displayed.
- Enter the **Iterations to Run** as **100**, and other setting of **Solve** dialog box should remain default.
- After specifying the parameters of **Solve** dialog box, click on **Solve** button. The software starts to solve the analysis and results will be displayed on completion of analysis.

Results

In results, we are going to examine the velocity results using plane and vectors.

- Activate the **Planes** tool and click on **Add** button; the plane will be added along X axis and displayed on model; refer to Figure-19.

Figure-19. Added plane

- To display velocity vectors, click on the **Vector** drop-down from **Planes** panel and select **Velocity Vector**; the vectors will displayed on model.
- Now, we need to adjust the spacing of the vectors to understand the analysis. Click on **Edit** button; the **Plane Control** dialog box will be displayed.
- Set the **Visual Style** of plane to **Outline** for clear view of vectors.
- Click on **Vector settings** tab of **Plane Control** dialog box.
- Select the **Length range** radio button and move the **Max** slider towards right to adjust the length range of vectors; refer to Figure-20.

Figure-20. Vector Setting

- After adjusting the vectors, close the **Plane Control** dialog box.
- After analyzing results, remove the plane for particle traces analysis.

Particle Traces

In this step, we examine the velocity results using particle traces. Particle traces show the path of the fluid as it passes around the solid obstructions. We will use these particles to understand the flow path, circulation, and regions of swirl.

- Set the view of model towards inlet because we have to create a particle study and the origin of the particles is inlet of model.
- Activate the **Traces** panel and click on **Add** button. The seeds will be attached with the cursor. The default parameters of traces are good for this study.
- Click on the inlet face to start seed distribution and click again to finalize it. You need to make a rectangular like shape on the half of inlet face; refer to Figure-21. You would know the reason behind the seed distribution on only half face, after few steps.

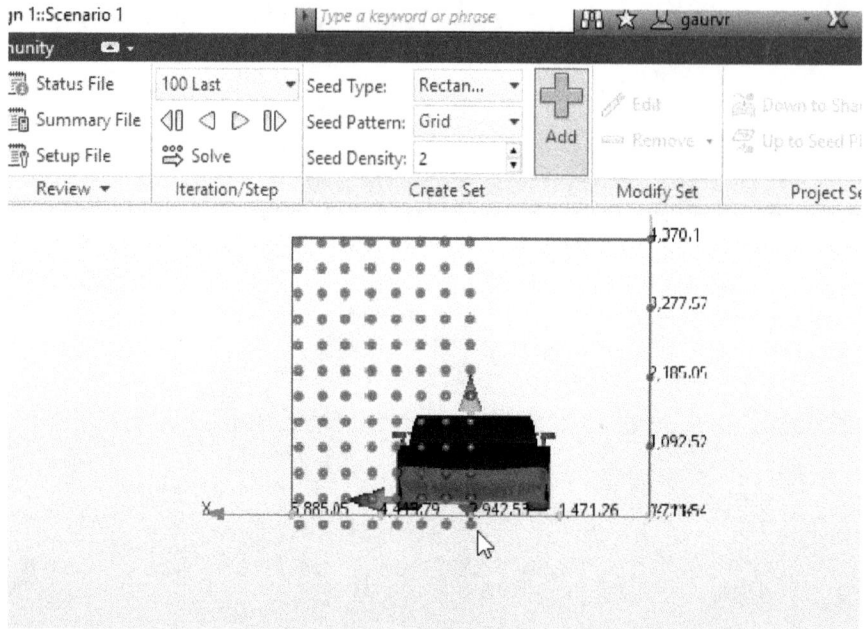

Figure-21. Creating seed distribution for Practical 5

- On second click, the particles will be traces along the path from inlet to outlet of model.
- To clearly view the traces, change **Air** material visual style to **Outline** and **Aluminium** material visual style to **Shaded** in **Results** node. The model will be displayed as Figure-22.

Figure-22. Traces

- With the help of yellow arrow, move the traces on the car to view the effects of traces; refer to Figure-23.

Figure-23. Moving seeds

Animation

- To animate the seeds from inlet to outlet of model, click on **Animate** button from **Process Traces** panel of **Results** tab; the **Animate Traces** dialog box will be displayed.
- Use the animation control button to control the flow of traces; refer to Figure-24.

Figure-24. Animating traces

- To save this animation as a video file, click on **Save avi.** button from **Animate Traces** dialog box. The **Save AVI File** dialog box will be displayed.
- Specify the destination folder and save the animation file.
- Similarly, you can save any type of result in animation mode from **Animate** button.
- Remove the traces for further analysis.

Aerodynamic Force

In this step, we compute the flow induced forces on the car using the **Wall Calculator** tool from **Results** tab.

- Click on **Wall Calculator** button from **Result Tasks** panel of **Results** tab; the **Wall Results** dialog box will be displayed at left of graphics window.
- Change the visual style of model from **Outline** to **Shaded** from **View** tab.
- Click on **Select All** button from **Wall Results** dialog box, the walls will be selected for analysis but we don't need outer walls, So, deselect them using left mouse key; refer to Figure-25.

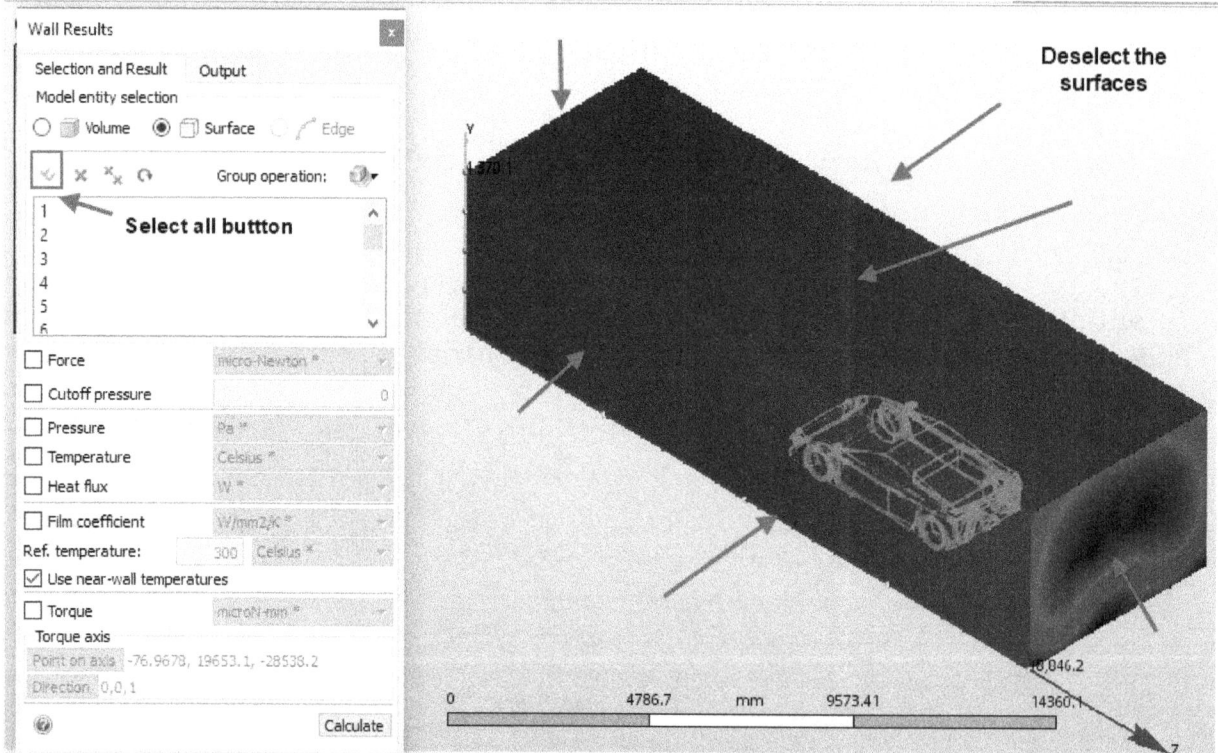

Figure-25. Deselect outer surface

- Select the **Force** radio button and change its unit to **Newton**, and click on **Calculate** button. The **Output** tab is displayed with calculated results.
- Scroll this list towards the end because the total force on the car is mentioned in summary section of this **Output** tab which is placed at last of **Output** tab; refer to Figure-26.

Figure-26. Total force on Car

PRACTICE 1

Below is a centrifugal pump used to mix two types of fluid. The model consists of two fluid inlet and a outlet. Oxygen and Hydrogen are the working fluid, and the centrifugal pump runs at 3000 RPM. The model is available in Practice 1 folder. The model as shown in Figure-27.

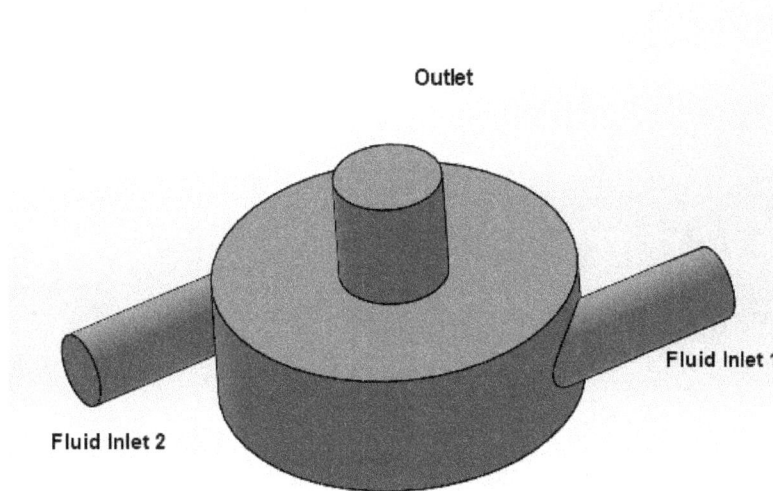

Figure-27. Practice 1

What you need to find is:
- Identify the flow distribution inside the pump due to mixing of two fluid.
- Animate development of flow through the pumps
- Determine the flow rate at outlet.

PRACTICE 2

In this model, there are two trees and two house. We need to access just how hot the houses are going to get and how much shade they and the tree provide each other. While creating analysis remember the below points:
- Create an external volume of height 20,000 MM like a square box above the ground level.
- Apply Air material to external volume, Brick material to House, Hardwood material to Tree.
- Assign temperature boundary condition to Environment, and Ground.
- Refine the mesh size of 2 houses and trees.
- Create and assign a Grass material for ground; refer to Figure-28.

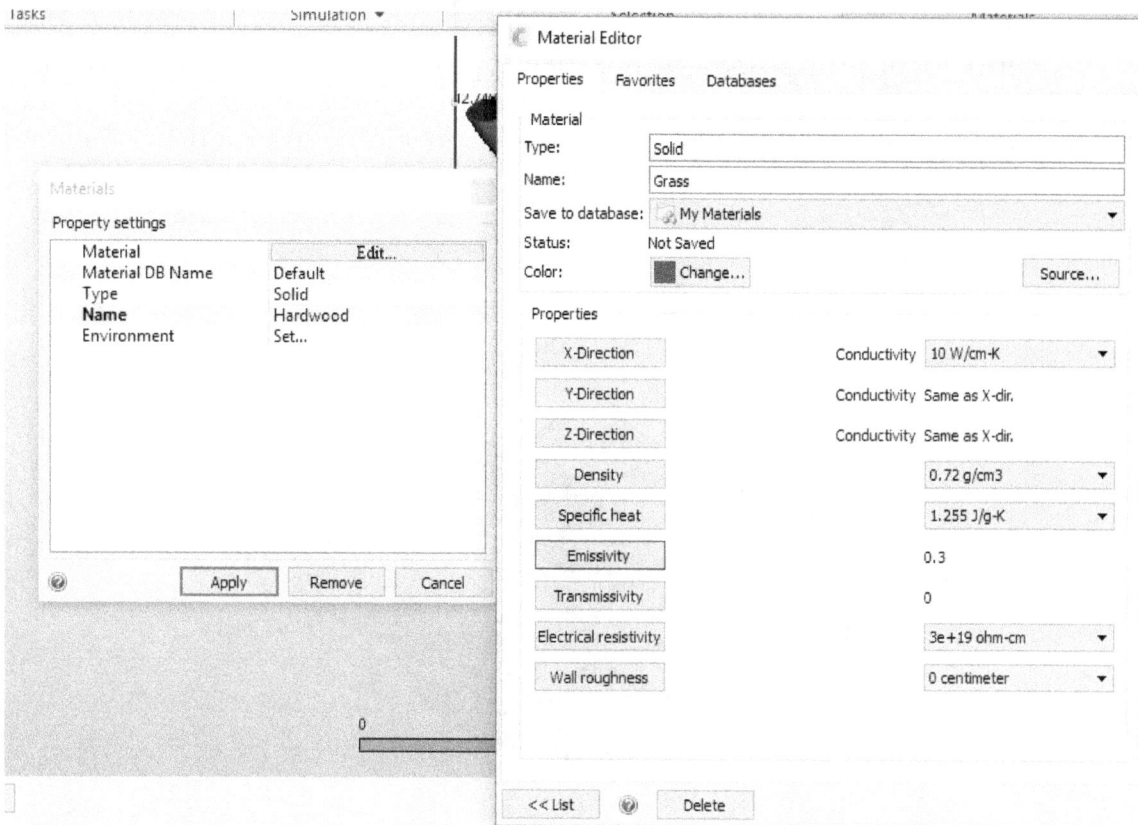

Figure-28. Grass Material

- The model of Practice 2 is looks like Figure-29. This is an inventor file and air material should be created in Autodesk CFD 2018.

Figure-29. Model Practice 2

What you need to find is:
- Determine the temperature on two houses

PRACTICE 3

In this Practice, we will study the compressible flow in a converting diverging nozzle. The geometry of this model is pretty simple; refer to Figure-30.

Figure-30. Practice 3

The converging-diverging nozzle has an exit area of 0.014 m² ,and a throat area of 0.008 m² resulting in an area ratio of 2. The inlet stagnation temperature is 600 K, and the mass flow rate is known to be 4.2 kg/s. Use this information to determine the Mach number and pressure at inlet & outlet. In this Practice, you need to :

- Visualize the flow within the nozzle, and determine the outlet Mach number.
- Determine the pressure drop inside the model.

***End of Chapter ***

FOR STUDENTS NOTES

Index

www.ingramcontent.com/pod-product-compliance
Lightning Source LLC
Chambersburg PA
CBHW081805200326
41597CB00023B/4159